Directing
Plays

Don Taylor

D0300732

A & C Black · London
Routledge/Theatre Arts · New York

Published in 1996
A & C Black (Publishers) Limited
35 Bedford Row, London WC1R 4JH

© 1996 Don Taylor

The right of Don Taylor to be identified as author of this Work
has been asserted by him in accordance with the Copyright,
Designs and Patents Act 1988.

ISBN 0-7136-4326-9

Published in the USA in 1997 by
Routledge/Theatre Arts Books
29 West 35 Street, New York, NY 10001

ISBN 0-87830-065-1

CIP catalogue records for this book are available from the
British Library and the Library of Congress.

Cover illustration by Dennis Tinkler.

Typeset in 10 on 11¾pt Garamond Light
Printed in Great Britain by Redwood Books,
Trowbridge, Wilts

Contents

*Interpretation is the revenge of the intellect upon art...
Real art has the capacity to make us nervous. By
reducing the work of art to its content, and then inter-
preting that, one tames the work of art. Interpretation
makes art manageable, comfortable.*

Susan Sontag

Against Interpretation (Vintage)

Foreword

It is no longer possible to write a book about directing plays which concentrates solely on the practicalities of the craft. Theatre directors today have moved into the centre of the creative world, and are often considered as artists in their own right, independent of the playwrights of their age. So a director must know something of the history of the craft, if only to define his or her place in the tradition, and must also understand something of the philosophical and aesthetic arguments which underpin the day to day business of directing. Directors in the contemporary theatre work at the very centre of a series of intellectual disagreements which have split the creative and critical world, and questions of judgement and evaluation are crucial to the creative decisions they must take ten or twenty times every day. The practicalities, grouping, rehearsal technique, handling actors, talking to playwrights, are as important as they have always been, but directors now have to answer a question which would not have been asked in earlier centuries of people doing the work they do: why are you doing it, and why are you doing it that particular way?

No one today can become a good director without making some kind of answer to these subversive questions. So this book, while giving full value to the practicalities of direction technique, must seek to find some answer to these deeper questions, or at least, set out clearly what the questions are, so that each director can construct his or her own answer. There is no right answer. Directors are as various as people, and all directors will find solutions to suit the particular work they want to do. But the questions must be addressed. Only when they are satisfactorily answered for each individual, does it become possible to do decent work.

Author's Note

English lacks a third person personal pronoun without gender associations at a time when it is beginning to need one. *S/he* is unpronounceable, and the endless repetition of *he or she* is stylistically disastrous.

The theatre, on the other hand, is one of the few professions in which talent really does matter more than gender. Real talent is always in such short supply, that when it appears, no one cares whether *x* or *y* chromosomes are dominant. The Euro-American theatre is full of brilliant women writers and directors, and actresses have been at the very centre of theatre culture since 1660.

Being male, I have used the masculine form when referring to directors, writers and actors. If I had been female, I would as naturally have used the female form. So if any of my readers, of whatever gender, find all those *hes* oppressive, let me invite them to change them, in their mind – or in their copy too, if they wish.

1

What is a Director?

Plays have been performed in public, within European culture at least, for about two-and-a-half thousand years. The first actor whose name we know, Thespis, was active in Athens in the mid sixth century BC, and the first surviving play, Aeschylus's *The Persians*, dates from 472.

Who the first director was is a matter open to some argument. If we assume that we are talking about a stage organiser and interpreter of plays who is a specialist in that field and earns his living from it, not principally an actor or playwright, then we must certainly look just before or just after World War I to find him. The masculine pronoun is precise. I know of no specialist female director recorded as working regularly before 1930. The first, in England at least, was probably Joan Littlewood, in the earliest days of Theatre Workshop during the 1940s.

So if we assume that the theatre is two-and-a-half thousand years old, and directors have been around for about seventy-five, the theatre has managed quite well without them for about two thousand four hundred and twenty-five years.

Like the appearance of human beings on the planet Earth, directors arrived very late in the day. They are a new-born child in the lifetime of the theatre, barely out of the womb. There are people still living who were born before there was any such profession.

So how did the theatre survive during the 97% of its existence when directors were not around?

The answer is that most of the tasks performed today by a director were performed by the playwright or the leading actor or the stage manager, and what we think of as the director's principal task, interpretation, was simply not an issue before the beginning of the twentieth century. There was little doubt about how plays should be done while the playwrights and actors were in charge. Early skirmishes of what was to become at times a large scale and bloody battle were heard as the nineteenth became the twentieth century, when Chekhov complained that his plays were meant to be comedies and were being played too seriously. The man who was in charge of the production of Chekhov's plays was a leading actor, not a specialist director, but he was certainly one of the principal candidates for the title of father of the craft: Konstantin Stanislavski, of the Moscow Arts Theatre.

So how were plays staged before the craft of directing as a specialised discipline emerged?

Directing without directors

Any play can be directed by a group of actors among themselves, with or without the assistance of the playwright. In a simple or limited space, that solution is often as good as any. There is a great deal about presenting plays which actors learn through daily experience which no one else, not even the most talented or experienced director quite knows, and that knowledge of the craft from the inside can create powerful productions. But in a large or complex space, or with an unconventional play, it quickly becomes clear that an overall controlling imagination needs to be at work, and whether the choices such a space presents are resolved by the playwright, an actor, or some other person, they must be resolved.

There are many times and places during the history of western theatre when something which we would recognise as directing must have taken place. Classical Greek plays, with their dancing and singing choruses, and their spectacular effects – chariots descending from machines, and doors opening to reveal bodies on moving trucks – must have required a controlling intelligence. Tradition tells us that the playwrights themselves performed this function, writing the text and the music and organising every aspect of the production except for the actual training – and financing – of the chorus, even at times playing the leading parts themselves. Similarly, Purcell's semi-operas, with their moving scenery, incredibly spectacular machines descending from the flies or rising from under the stage, their singing choruses and grotesque dancers, must have been very precisely directed by Betterton, the great actor-manager, who ought perhaps to be called the first great English Director too.

At every stage in theatre history plays must have been directed by *somebody*, in a more or less sophisticated manner, but the fact is that we know very little about these processes before the twentieth century. We don't know how playwrights and actor managers spoke to their actors, how they moved them, whether character motivations were discussed at all, nor do we know much about how the design and dressing of plays was undertaken. Perhaps the key element in modern directing is to have in the mind some overall vision of how the play will appear on the stage, but whether that happened, or whether the production of plays was a pragmatic business, built up in daily rehearsal, is also largely unknown. We guess that something like the imaginative directing process as we understand it must have taken place, but it is guesswork. For hard fact, we are almost completely in the dark.

There are some clues. There are a few scenes in plays from the past which show the process of play-direction taking place, there is the famous row between Ben Jonson and Inigo Jones about the purpose of dramatic representation, and there is the conscious recreation of the Restoration Theatre after the Civil War and Interregnum. All these moments give us some insight into the direction of plays as historical fact. It is no part of the purpose of this book to write a detailed history of directing or the emergence of the modern director. Students and interested readers will know where to consult books that will lead them to a deeper understanding of that process. But if we want to know where we are now, we have to have some idea where we have come from, and a brief examination of these primary sources from pre-twentieth century theatre is important to the understanding of a directors task at the present time.

Players and masquers

Paradoxically, we know even less about the staging of plays during the first great period of the English Theatre, from 1590-1640 than we know about the Greeks, whose theatres do at least survive physically. We know the names of the London theatres, the outdoor venues which attracted large popular audiences, The Globe, The Rose and The Red Bull, and the more sophisticated and refined first generation of indoor theatres, starting with the Blackfriars in 1608, and going on to include The Cockpit in Drury Lane, and Salisbury Court, between the eastern end of Fleet Street and the Thames. But we can't walk into one and have a look around.

It seems likely that plays during this golden age, were even less directed, in the modern sense, than the Greek plays had been, because the architecture of the theatre that had developed from the Inn-yard, and which still retained a good deal of the Inn-yard layout when the theatres moved indoors, was very much less capable of spectacular staging effects than the Greek amphitheatre was. Hamlet's scene with the players probably gives us as much insight as to how plays were directed in Shakespeare's company as we are likely to get. Hamlet himself, as the author of a speech to be inserted into a preexistent play, probably stands in the position of the playwright, and perhaps gives us some indication how Shakespeare himself spoke to the actors when one of his plays was in preparation. He is concerned with the realism of the actors' presentation, the need *to hold the mirror up to nature, to show virtue her own feature and scorn her own image, and the very age and body of the time his form and pressure...* He asks the players to avoid over stagey gestures, in an age when a formal language of gesture was very much part of an actor's equipment, and he requests, with a recognisable sharp edge to his tone of voice, that the comedians should not improvise their own lines or play too many unscripted gags. Otherwise, he treats the actors with great respect, as masters of their art. Having given them a clear indication of how they should act, he defers in practice to their experience. It is significant that he says nothing at all about how his speech should be staged. He assumes that is the actors' business. When we look at Shakespeare's comic version of the same process, we see much the same thing. Peter Quince, the playwright, is entirely in charge, though he has to cope with a pretty monstrous ego in his leading actor, Bottom. He duly butters him up and flatters him, as directors have doubtless done since the year dot, and then gives his players the very simplest instructions as to where to make their entrances. Anything at all complicated or sophisticated, the simple stage-effects of the moon and the wall, is discussed between the whole group, and the views of the most dominant personality, Bottom, are adopted.

It seems to me that a number of things can be inferred from these two famous rehearsal scenes. The first is that the play was staged by an interaction between the playwright and the leading actor, with the playwright providing the intellectual insight, and the actor the charisma. No change there then, you might say. Certainly Shakespeare and his fellow playwrights were dealing with the first generation of great actors, the first men in the modern world who became famous for their acting. They, far more than the playwrights, were the public's darlings, and it seems likely that when the chips were down, the great actors, who were the principal sharers and managers of the theatres, and therefore the dominant financial interest, got their way. It takes no great insight to infer that Shakespeare probably had a difficult time with the popular comedian Will Kempe, and it is perhaps not too much to suggest that the portrait of the overbearing Bottom and the harassed Peter Quince, might represent a comic picture of Shakespeare's irritation with Burbage on a bad day. Certainly the scene contains many moments which any working director will ruefully recognise, from the actor rewriting the script to suit himself, to meaningless tantrums that have to be soothed by outrageous flattery, and ill-timed questions about beards.

But the clearest indications of the limited nature of direction in Shakespeare's day are given by the layout of the theatre itself, that exposed platform, playing in daylight and the open air, to four galleries and a raked pit, that had developed from the architecture of the Inn-yards within which the players had first set up their portable stages.

When you work on such a stage – and I worked on one not unlike the traditional shape, at the St George's Theatre in the mid 1970s – you are very conscious that this is a space that naturally favours the actors, and through them, the playwright. It is a simple platform for acting upon, with no permanent scenery, simple entrances, a plain and practical balcony and a curtained alcove that is very flexible in use, but provides no stimulus for the eye. The Elizabethan/Jacobean stage is an amazingly flexible theatrical instrument, as the plays of that great age, in their infinite variety of strategies for staging everything from bedroom scenes to battles, amply prove, but its drama is all in the imagination: the vivid words, the rhetorical acting, the accompanying music of lutes and recorders, the simple props, flags, swords and drums brought on stage and taken off again by the actors. There is very little opportunity for spectacle in any sense that we, or the Restoration, or the Greeks would have understood it. Pageantry, shields and flags and banners, works well in such a space, and the History plays are full of opportunities for its exploitation, but there is little further opportunity to stun the imagination of the eye rather than the mind. It is a platform whose infinite possibilities the actors must have got to know intimately, and learned how to exploit, so that any sensible playwright working with them, particularly one like Shakespeare who had been an actor himself, would have deferred to their experience again and again. It was, quite simply, an actors' kingdom. What was there for a director to do? To tell the actors where to stand, or how to group themselves? Playing the same theatre every afternoon, the actors knew the answers to those questions far better than anyone else did.

A playwright had plenty of other considerations to occupy his time. He had to be sure that his text was fully understood, and that it told its story as well as it could in the theatre space for which it had been written. He had to ensure that what had fired his imagination, burst into flame in the imaginative space of the theatre, and this might involve his participation in movement, in what costuming there was – not much, as all actors had their own acting suits which they wore in every play – and in effects such as battles and storms. Otherwise it was up to the actors. The balance of power between the two, playwright and actor, doubtless varied, depending upon the relative fame

of each. Shakespeare, Jonson and Fletcher probably had a good deal
of say in what was done with their works within their own companies,
at least as much as Prince Hamlet does. But Burbage and Alleyn and
Will Kempe were out there in front of the public, and I suspect, as in
modern theatre, in the last analysis the man on stage got his own way.

However, the public theatres were not the only place where
theatrical entertainments were staged. From his accession in 1603,
James I, encouraged by his Queen, Anne of Denmark, who at her
brother's court had met the young architect Inigo Jones, had delighted
in the presentation of masques, courtly entertainments in which
royalty and nobility themselves participated, and which were staged
with incredible expense and splendour. Initially stimulated by the
Florentine Intermedii of 1589, these spectacular events united poetry
and action with music, singing and dancing, together with the most
sumptuous and imaginative staging. Painted scenery, lighting effects,
machines that raised whole mountains, with ridges big enough for
actors to stand upon, from beneath a stage that appeared to be too
small to contain them, chariots coming down from the heavens, sea-
battles enacted – nothing could have been further from the poetic
intensity and theatrical simplicity of what was being staged in the
public theatres than these intellectually flimsy and sycophantic spectacles, conspicuous theatrical consumption for a Court that did not
share the tastes of the majority of its subjects, and whose alienation
from them would lead, forty years later, to Civil War.

There was no doubt how the Court regarded these entertainments,
and the participation in them of the architectural and theatrical genius,
Inigo Jones. Samuel Daniel remarked of them, *the art and invention
of the Architect gives the greatest grace, and is of the most importance*.
But Ben Jonson, brought in to work with Jones as the poet for the
venture, had other ideas. For him the *show* furnished by the architect,
however elaborate, was only *the bodily part*, which the poet's invention had to animate.

The two men were powerful personalities, both supreme artists in
their fields, Jonson, fiercely proud of the depth of his hard-earned
Classical learning (as working-class boys usually are), Jones fresh from
Italy, and fired by his studies of Palladio. They were chalk and cheese,
and wanted to achieve quite different things in their masques. Jonson
aspired to give moral and poetic depth to what was essentially a
flimsy and unserious form. Jones wished to create ever more stunning
and imaginative spectacles to amaze the eye. Jonson was at a disadvantage from the start, not only because the Masque form was probably too flimsy to bear the structure of ideas and poetry he wished to
build upon it, but also because the Queen and the Court much

preferred looking at Jones's pictures to hearing, and thinking about, Jonson's verses.

The row between them was of titanic proportions, and went on for the best part of twenty years. Finally, in 1631, when Jonson insisted his name came before Jones's in the publication of the current masque, it became an irreparable breach. Jonson, old and ill, was cast out from the Court, and younger and more amenable poets, Aurelian Townshend and William Davenant, who would do what Jones told them, were brought in in his place.

The story represents a crucial moment in the history of the emergence of the director. The poet, who up to that time had expected to be the one who principally directed how the performance should go, found himself in competition with, and eventually defeated by, the designer. It is the first evidence we have of a fundamental disagreement among working professionals about what their production should be.

The sumptuous masques, performed to an invited aristocratic audience only, had little lasting effect upon the public theatres. As news of what was going on at Whitehall gradually filtered out, playwrights quickly borrowed those aspects of the masque they could use in their own plays, the mythological formality and some of the music, singing and dancing, but little of the conspicuous expense. The playwrights and actors made sure they stayed in control. There was little, anyway, that could be done to follow up Jones's experiments on the open platform stage. His new forms of staging depended upon degrees of illusion, not on the simplicity allied to imagination of the traditional Elizabethan Theatre. They needed a new kind of theatre, and were eventually to find one. In the long run Jones was to have a far greater influence on the history of the theatre than Jonson, but not until after the Civil War, when both men were dead.

From our perspective, this row between two powerful geniuses, is full of pregnant implications for the gradual birth of the specialist theatre director. The masque was a collaboration between many aspects of theatre art, words, actions, music, dancing and visual spectacle, in a way the plays in the public theatre were not. All those different disciplines follow different agendas and have different priorities, and if a form of theatre were to arise which was as collaborative as masques were, then the question of who had overall control was bound to become significant. The idea of a director hadn't been conceived yet, and it would be centuries before the conception would be brought to birth. But the necessity for his eventual existence was, in a shadowy way, implied by the twenty-year quarrel between Ben Jonson and Inigo Jones.

Sir William Davenant

The extraordinary figure of Sir William Davenant is an even louder
pre-echo and sharper foreshadowing of the modern director, occu-
pying, as he did in the 1660s, very much the position the Director of
the Royal National Theatre or the RSC holds today.

As plain William Davenant, son of an Oxford vintner – and even,
according to local gossip, the bastard son of Shakespeare, who stayed
regularly at his father's Inn on his journeys to and from Stratford – he
had made his mark very early in London as a young playwright and
poet. His first play was staged when he was only twenty-one, and
though it wasn't enormously successful, it was to the taste of the
Court, and he soon found himself in that circle of poets, musicians
and painters clustered round Charles I and his French wife. The fashionable young poet and playwright soon became the principal
provider of texts for the Court masques, by then being staged in a
specially constructed masquing house, just to the south of Inigo
Jones's Banqueting house at Whitehall, which was no longer in use
because it was thought the smoke from the candles required for
Jones's lighting effects was damaging the Reubens paintings on the
ceiling.

Davenant worked for about five years with Jones, his principal
works being the two propaganda pieces, *Britannia Triumphans* (1638)
and *Salmacida Spolia* (1640). These are worthless as theatre poetry,
and rare examples in English literary culture of a poet slavishly serving
the political needs of a Royal patron. *Britannia Triumphans* is principally a justification of the King's ship-money policy, one of the main
causes of the Civil War, and contains crude caricatures of wicked
Puritans, which must have pleased the Court as much as they alienated
the London populace, who already loathed the King's masques for
their conspicuous expense, and the fact that they played on Sundays.

The Civil War brought an end to masques and masquing. The
poets, musicians and artists of Charles's court scattered, and survived
as best they could, or died, as William Lawes did at the battle of Ches-
ter. Davenant himself fought for three years as a gunnery officer, was
knighted in the field for his services, acted as a diplomat, was impris-
oned by the Commonwealth, and narrowly escaped execution, and
finally married a French widow with money, and settled in London.
There he made his peace with the Cromwellian regime, became one
of a group of unofficial court poets that included Marvell, Dryden and
Waller, and almost certainly engaged in a little elegant spying on
behalf of Oliver's Government. There is an extant note, in which he
offers his services – unspecified – to Thurloe, Cromwell's spy-master,

and people only offered their services to that ominous figure for one reason. He managed to set up a theatre in his own house in 1656, staged the first English Opera, *The Siege of Rhodes*, in his dining room, and survived from hand to mouth, as all theatre artists did, during the Protectorate.

But with the Restoration of Charles II in 1660 everything changed. The theatres were reopened, the King was known to love plays and dislike operas, and it was clear that English theatrical culture would be very swiftly reborn. The crucial question was how.

Davenant himself was in a difficult position. In order to make theatrical entertainments of any kind, he had been required to make himself *persona grata* in Cromwell's circle at Hampton Court. That fact alone made him to some degree *persona **non** grata* among the newly returned Cavaliers. He was also fifty-four, and too old for the society of dissolute young sparks gathered about the pleasure-loving King. He had only two things in his favour. He was still, though unpaid for years, and destined never to be paid again, the Poet Laureate, appointed by the new King's martyred father. He also held, granted by the Royal Martyr's sacred hand in 1639 but never used, a patent to open, even to build, a new theatre.

With the insight of genius, he saw two crucial things, which were to have a permanent effect on the future of the theatre. The first was that the audience had changed during the war years, and that London would no longer sustain the six or seven theatres that had co-existed simultaneously during the great years of the Elizabethan and Jacobean theatre. The second, was that if he were to offer the public theatre what he had learned from Jones in the King's masquing house, he would need to build a completely different kind of theatre building. These two insights, political and artistic, were to change the English theatre for ever, and they still cast shadows right down to our present time.

His first task was to make the production of plays financially viable. Even before the King had set foot back in England, three ad-hoc companies had formed from those actors who had survived the lean years of the Republic. Mohun and Hart, stalwarts of the pre-war Blackfriars troupe, set up a company at the Red Bull, the bookseller Rhodes set up a new company of young actors at The Cockpit, and William Beeston's men began to play at Salisbury Court.

Davenant set up nothing at once, but went into negotiations with Sir Thomas Killigrew, a minor playwright and universal fixer close to the centre of the Court, to acquire monopoly rights in theatre performance. Davenant's old patent and Killigrew's political clout had the desired effect, and by August 1660, the two men had been granted the sole rights to present plays in London. There followed a three month struggle with the actors' companies, which was overwhelmingly won by Davenant and Killigrew, who, by October 1660, had set up a united company, employing all the best actors from the three pre-existing companies. Any actors who were not working for them, were forbidden to act at all, on pain of jail. This totalitarian coup by Davenant and Killigrew at least ensured that one theatre kept open and solvent, and was based on the clear-eyed view that the audience for the new theatre was no more than two or three thousand people at the most, largely the Court and its hangers on. The old unified audience, which had ranged from the nobility to the groundlings, and covered all classes in between, and which had kept the Globe, the Blackfriars, The Red Bull, The Cockpit and Salisbury Court, prosperous for thirty years, was gone for ever, destroyed by the war, and the political ideologies that had arisen from it.

Within six weeks of their coup, Killigrew and Davenant had split into two separate companies, Killigrew having all the best-known actors working for him, and most of the money and court favour on his side, Davenant having a new idea of what theatre might become and a twenty-five year old novice called Thomas Betterton leading his company. Killigrew set up his company at Gibbons's Tennis Court in Drury Lane, calling it the Theatre Royal, but the theatre structure he erected in the old Tennis court was very much the same that had served since the first indoor theatre opened at Blackfriars in 1608, a thrust stage, curtained alcove and balcony, and no scenic effects.

Davenant had bought Lisle's Tennis Court in Lincoln's Inn fields several months earlier, and here Jones's ideas were to be brought to the public theatre. Davenant planned to built an Italianate proscenium arch, and to have a deep inner stage behind it as well as a twenty-foot platform stage in front. There were to be doors either side of the proscenium, and flats either side of the inner stage, which moved in slots so that they could be instantaneously reversed, thus changing the scene in full view of the audience in a matter of seconds. The back of the stage operated an ingenious system of shutters, so that the back-cloth, itself a new invention, could be changed as quickly as the flats, and there were large trapdoors and flying-systems, so that whole islands, mountains or grottoes could arise from under the stage, or chariots, gods in clouds, or airborne countries could descend from the heavens. The art of the scene painter, and the costume designer were to enter the theatre for the first time in England, and there was to be a theatre orchestra on a more or less permanent basis. In effect, at Lisle's Tennis Court Davenant created every feature of the Restoration theatre as we know it, and that theatre has been, with modifications, the basis of theatre down to the present time. The only feature in which Killigrew out-thought him was in the positioning of the theatre orchestra. In the Lincoln's Inn Fields theatre it was on stage, though we don't know precisely where; at the Theatre Royal a few years later, Killigrew introduced the orchestra pit, across the front of the stage, and beneath stage height.

Davenant's crucial position in the history of the theatre is fully documented, but the sense in which he is the first director-figure has not been so widely noted. He was, of course, a playwright-director, as many were before and after him, but he was also the proprietor and principal shareholder, so that he had complete power in the running of the whole enterprise. Shakespeare had had no such power, and, while other actors wrote plays and ran companies, none had quite such a degree of control over all aspects of the production as Davenant had. Most of his time, in a theatre culture where a play rarely ran longer than four days, must have been spent in keeping the theatre afloat and seeing his own and other people's plays, old and new, onto the stage. From 1660 till his death in 1668 he ran his company, The Duke's Theatre, very much as a modern artistic director runs a large company today, except that he had no subsidy.

Of course, Davenant has taken a great deal of stick for his rewriting of Shakespeare, particularly for what he did to *Measure For Measure* and *Much Ado about Nothing* – he used the plot of the latter as a sub plot for the former – and in his substantial rewrite of *The Tempest*. In absolute terms these are disastrous works, unerringly substituting bad writing for good, and imposing formal structures on the plotting that remove them from any sort of reality. Miranda, for instance, the woman who has never seen a man, has to be balanced in Davenant's version by Hippolito, the man who has never seen a woman. But that grotesque invention gives us the clue. Davenant knew his clientèle, far better than we do. He knew that the semi-literate Cavaliers and Court butterflies, and their brawling, drunken sons, who made up his audience, would hardly understand genuine Shakespeare, in a language that was already seeming archaic and removed from common speech. He also sensed crucial and deep-seated cultural changes, the classical age of rationality and balance which had already dawned in educated men's consciousness, and which he had recognised and incorporated into his own work very early. Like modern concept directors, he re-interpreted theatre works to suit the preconceptions of his own age. Being created to please a particular audience, those works do not survive into our age, and now seem as grotesque as the products of some of today's concept directors will doubtless seem in the future. Davenant loved Shakespeare's works deeply, and lived in an age which by no means considered Shake-

speare an undisputed master. What he did seemed to him the best
way to keep Shakespeare's plays alive in his own culture, and that
attitude, among his many gifts to the modern theatre, is vividly current
in our own day. Consideration of some of its implications will be one
of the prime concerns of this book, as they are close to the very centre
of what a modern director is and does.

Without doubt, the balance of power between playwrights and
leading actors continued to shift, according to the relative status of
each. By the end of the seventeenth century, Betterton, as actor-
manager, was clearly in charge of what went on in the companies he
led, and Garrick, in an age of minor playwrights and great actors –
himself, Peg Woffington, Charles Kemble and Sarah Siddons – was the
creative force in all his companies. Nor can one imagine the nineteenth-century giants, Kean or Macready, taking much notice of
anything mere playwrights said – Shaw's experience with Irving at the
end of the century confirms the point. So the overall situation
remained the same, fixed and largely unquestioned, for two hundred
years. There was no need for directors in the modern sense of the
word. Playwrights explained what they wanted, and actors decided
whether it suited them to take any notice or not.

Sheridan and Pinero

During the last two decades of the nineteenth century ideas began to
ferment within the theatre, reflecting disturbances in the wider artistic
and intellectual world, that would eventually create a need for specialist directors to come into existence. But before we go on to consider
that period of extraordinary turmoil, whose volcanic eruptions have
not yet ceased, and whose tremors have shaken the whole world of
twentieth-century art, it is worth while considering two further rehearsal scenes, which reveal a great deal more about the manner of directing in their respective ages than any amount of anecdotage or riffling
through old theatre archives. These two primary sources are Sheridan's
The Critic and Pinero's *Trelawney of the Wells*.

Both are plays which purport to give a picture of the normal conditions of theatre rehearsal, the former satirical in intention, the latter
attempting to express in a mildly sentimental way the great love most
theatre people feel for their profession.

In both plays the playwright is clearly in charge of rehearsals, and
his second in command is the stage manager – but there the similarity
ceases. In *The Critic*, the officious Puff interferes at every level of the
rehearsal, but the joke is that he is always overridden or ignored by
the actors, who do what they have always done, whether he likes it

or not. To begin with, they have cut his play to pieces, quite without his knowledge or permission, so that the play no longer makes sense as a story.

Puff: What the plague! What a cut is here! What has become of the description of her first meeting with Don Whiskerandos, his gallant behaviour in the sea fight, and the simile of the canary bird?

Tilburina: Indeed sir, you will find they will not be missed...

Puff: Here has been such a cutting and slashing, I don't know where they've got to myself!

Tilburina: Indeed sir, you will find it will connect very well.

Mr Puff is, of course, a terrible playwright, and a hopeless director, but for satire to have its point, it must have some connection with reality. Sheridan, the long-time theatre manager, must have met some incompetent playwright-directors in his time, and he doubtless remembered them all when he began to write.

The Critic is principally a critique of bad playwriting. Crude, ill-motivated expositions, ludicrous plots, dreary passages of rhetoric and overdone metaphors are defined with wicked accuracy, but there are in addition some interesting passages which throw a similarly satirical light on what direction the actors of the time were likely to receive, or tolerate. *Pray sir, don't interrupt us here, you'll ruin our feelings*, says the leading actress, playing Tilburina, when Puff makes a comment at the height of her sentimental farewell to her lover. Throughout the rehearsal, the actors do exactly what they like, and barely tolerate Puff's interjections. When they do ask him for some help, he is less than useful. At the end of his first scene, he has five noble lords kneeling in prayer, presumably downstage centre, as the scene ends. The actor playing Leicester makes a reasonable enough request:

Leicester: But sir, you haven't settled how we are to get off here?

Puff: You couldn't go off kneeling, could you?

Raleigh: No sir, quite impossible!

Puff: It would have a good effect, i'faith, if you could. Exeunt praying! And would vary the established mode of springing off with a glance at the pit.... Very well, repeat the last line standing, and go off the old way.

The exchange is very funny, both to read and in performance, and a rapier thrust into the vitals of playwright-directors who don't have the first grasp of stage technique, but it also shows how formal a style of acting the eighteenth century employed. Actors knew what they were doing and how they customarily did things, and it probably took a very experienced and widely-respected playwright to have any real effect on them at all. The whole business of staging seems to have been a question of established formalities with the actors sorting out for them-selves what they would do. When, at the end of their sentimental parting, Tilburina and Whiskerandos go off, Puff cries out in despair:

Puff: Sir, Madam, if you go out without the parting look,
               you might as well dance out!

How we would love to know what that parting look was like, and, come to that, the established mode of springing off with a glance at the pit! But Sheridan's joke isn't quite finished. Tilburina has been accompanied throughout by a Confidante, who has said nothing, but imitated her mistress's every move. *Pray sir*, she asks, as Tilburina prepares to exit, *how am I to get off here? What the devil signifies how you get off*, Mr Puff replies, somewhat ungallantly *Edge away at the top, or how you will!*

Perhaps the richest irony of a play which makes a wry comment in almost every line, is that when Mr Puff does give positive direction to his actors, telling Tilburina to use her handkerchief to dab her eye on a certain line, and to start more dramatically when she hears her lover's voice offstage, it is to insert two thunderous acting clichés.

Of course, *The Critic* is an outrageous, over-the-top joke at the expense of a whole variety of bad theatre practices, the modern equivalents of which are still to be criticised in our own age. But reading between the funny lines, it does give us a remarkable insight into the theatre of Sheridan's day. The playwrights were expected to do a great deal of production, from setting the scenes to arranging the spectacular effects – Mr Puff is wholly responsible for the spectacular (and disastrous) sea-fight on stage which, accompanied by Handel and Purcell, ends his play – but they seem to have had no real power. The playwrights' theatre of the seventeenth century, had become an actors' theatre in the late eighteenth and that process intensified in the nineteenth. Nowhere in any material concerning playwrights staging their plays is there anything to suggest that there were playwrights who had sufficient understanding of the techniques of staging and acting plays to compete with and criticise their actors on equal terms. Most actors surely felt they knew a great deal more about such things than any playwright did, and they were probably right. They were doing the job every day, and the playwright was lucky if he had a play on in the theatre once every two or three years. In those circumstances, direction, as we understand it, would not be possible. Indeed, it is not possible now, if the actors have no respect for the director they are working with.

In *Trelawney of the Wells,* premiered in 1898, and described by Pinero, in his note significantly addressed to the stage manager, as being set in the 1860s, we see the first rehearsal of the first play by a young actor, Tom Wrench. This is usually supposed to be a portrait of the playwright Tom Robertson, one of the first to attempt to rouse English playwriting from the long sleep into which it had fallen since Sheridan's day.

On the first morning, the actors are handed their scrolls – still, even at that late date, being given their own part, not the whole play – and the blocking rehearsal begins. This is conducted initially by the stage manager, a noisy stage Irishman called O'Dwyer, who is mainly characterised as shouting all the time, losing his temper, and calling all the actresses *darlin',* much to the disgust of Tom, who insists on a formal Miss and surname. The stage manager starts the blocking rehearsal, but gets it all wrong, swearing the script is the worst written he has ever seen and that he can't read the stage directions at all.

> *'Peggy is engaged in – in –' I can't decipher it...*(to Imogen) *I don't know what you're doin' 'Dora is... is...'* (to Rose) *You are also doin' something or another. Now then. When the curtain rises, you are discovered, both of ye, employed in the way described...*

When Tom returns to the stage, O'Dwyer announces *I've got it smooth as far as there,* a startling assertion, as he has given the actresses no direction at all!

Tom soon puts the scene right, seating the two women at a central table and chair, one reading a book, the other knitting, while they chat. Tom then gives both the actresses the simplest acting instructions: to yawn before uttering the opening line, and to do it realistically, not in a stagey way, to close the book with a bang, and to Rose, to get up and walk about disconsolately. There is no more detailed instruction, where she should walk, on what part of the stage, what she is feeling. The generalisation is deemed to be enough, and presumably the actress will work out the rest for herself. Tom then walks down some preset steps into the stalls, and according to Pinero's stage direction, *moves from one side of the stalls to the other, gesticulating in the manner of a conductor of an orchestra,* a director's mannerism which many actors will recognise, and which I recognise in myself. The rehearsal doesn't go on much further – the plot of the play intervenes in the shape of Arthur Gower, who has run away from home to become an actor – but these few moments are evocative, as they show the playwright still giving much the same kind of direction as Sir William Davenant would have given in 1660. Nowhere does Tom give any specific direction, as any modern director would fifty times a day. And nowhere in any of the scenes depicting actors in rehearsal that I have read, is that kind of detailed work shown. It is unlikely that all the playwrights who have written rehearsal scenes should have conspired to leave out the real work that was done. It is much more likely that the main function playwright-directors performed was to make sure all the implications of their text were understood, a job which even now the playwright can usually do much better than the director. Whatever subtleties and originalities appeared in the performances – and we can be quite sure that when Garrick, Siddons and Kean were on stage, there were many – were the product of the artistic insight and long experience of the actors.

But by the time *Trelawney of the Wells* was staged, the storm that was to blow away that long lived mode of theatre for ever was already beginning, and the theatre run by actors and actor-managers and playwrights who might or might not know what they were doing, had almost come to an end.

I caught one late glimpse of it at the very beginning of my own career when, in 1960, at the age of twenty-four, I worked with an old actor of eighty-one called Frank Royde. Frank was reminiscing to me about what it was like to be a young actor at the turn of the century, before the agent system had been established. In those days, he told me, actors called into The Salisbury in St Martin's Lane, to see what was going in the way of work. Each actor had his *line*, the kind of parts he customarily played, light hero, heavy hero, villain, comedian, and within that line particular parts which were his speciality. *At The Salisbury*, he told me, *you would perhaps hear that, say, they wanted an Orsino down in Plymouth. So, you would get on the phone and say, 'I do an Orsino old boy, and I am free,' a fee would be discussed, and if everyone was in agreement, you would be on the evening train.* There was no real problem fitting in. An actor always did his Orsino the same way, and could walk into any production at a few hours' notice. No one needed directors in that world of the theatre. They would just get in the way.

Frank died soon after our meeting, and I should think it is unlikely that there are many actors now who have any recollection of that lost world of the theatre. But let us not get too sentimental about it. By 1900 that kind of theatre was already living on borrowed time.

Changes were taking place in the world of the arts that made it quite certain that the theatre would have to change radically, if it were to continue its historic task of trying to reflect the age it lived in.

Modernism, and the birth of the director

Between 1880 and 1920 the world changed faster and more completely than in any previous period of recorded history, and the pace of change throughout the twentieth century has, if anything, increased. The most immediately influential of these changes were technological: mass production, the creation of the popular press, flying, the motor-car revolution, industrialised warfare, the invention and development of film making, music-recording, and radio communication. But even in the face of these transforming technologies, it is probably true to say that the revolution in ideas was even more overwhelming, destined to have as great an influence on the intellectual world as technological revolutions had done and were doing. Indeed, the one created the other. Without intellectual ferment, technologies would not have developed as they did, and without the technologies intellectual development would certainly have been different.

The revolution in thinking in those forty years was greater than anything like it in the world's history. Not even the Renaissance, or the birth of Classical Athens had such a cataclysmic effect. The Renaissance was a slow process, taking several hundred years, and based fundamentally on a single idea, the re-discovery of antiquity. Classical Athens was the glorious climax of several hundred years of Greek cultural development, a steady growth and wonderful flowering. What happened between 1880 and 1920 took a very firmly set and long-lived structure of ideas, completely overturned it, and put a new structure in its place. The old ideas, some would say, were destroyed for ever, and at the very least, they were radically transformed.

It happened in every aspect of human thinking. Max Planck and Einstein made discoveries in particle physics that led in the not very long run to the dethroning of Newtonian physics, the rationality of cause and effect, at least in the sub-atomic world, and opened up an alarming indeterminate universe where all the answers were no longer scientifically predictable. The full subversive theories of two earlier nineteenth-century thinkers, Marx and Darwin, were just beginning to be widely understood, and were overturning previously accepted ideas of political progress and human biological history, and Freud in Vienna was putting forward theories which, though many of them, and his own bona fides, have been challenged since, changed forever the way we look at the human personality. Philosophy began to look at the way we think and the language we think with, rather than the old simple questions of life, death and society, and organised Christian religion, that pattern of social order, which had structured and partly civilised the European world since the end of the Roman Empire, and had spread by means of European colonisation across the rest of the world, began a catastrophic decline which, after World War II accelerated into almost complete collapse. Sexual morality came into question, and new ways of social and political living, Utopian and Reactionary, became a part of every intelligent person's intellectual agenda. As a programme for forty years of human thought, it was startling, and even more startling in what it actually achieved. No one in 1880 could possibly have imagined the sort of things that were being thought and said in 1920.

All the arts, being the spiritual, intellectual and imaginative expression of the deepest thoughts and feelings of humankind, were at the very heart of this overturning of all the old ideas. The initial impulse was destructive: the whole vast, respectable, hypocritical edifice of nineteenth-century thought, practice and art had to be pulled down, before anything new could be created to take its place.

In music, the idea of key, which had been under pressure since Wagner had taken chromaticism to the edges of the possible, finally broke down. Memorable tunes, based on simple key progressions and returns, went out of the window, as did simple rhythms based on walking, running and dancing. The new music was difficult to listen to and impossible to remember, but it seemed to express the violent overturnings of the age that created it. The world of visual art threw out figurative painting and naturalistic sculpture, and created a whole new aesthetic which could include violent distortions of ocular experience, to express on canvas or in plastic forms inner feelings, as well as pure abstractions, patterns whose meaning was purely visual, and the subversive realisation that art need not be a carefully made and crafted object at all, but could be anything an artist decided was relevant. Both these arts, eighty years later, are still coping with the full implications of this cataclysmic overturning of accepted ways of doing things. Conservative forms have survived alongside the most radical innovations, and both musicians and painters now inhabit a kind of wilderness through which each must find his or her own way.

The verbal arts of poetry and fiction experienced similar revolutionary changes. Cause and effect story-telling, plain speaking or logically argued poetry, gave way to imagist and expressionist techniques, stream of consciousness narration, and every kind of experiment with form and content, to the extremes of pure abstraction and noise-making. Accepted forms went out of the window, strict metre and rhyme-schemes in verse, third person narrative in the novel. Writers tried to express perceptions that were only half-understood, flashes of imaginative lightning, feelings that could be expressed only through clusters of related images rather than by connected thought, through quotation and cross-reference rather than by plain statement.

But the odd thing about this revolution in the arts, and what made it quite unlike any other period in artistic history, was that it was by no means total. In the past, when art of any kind was nearly always the province of a tiny minority of educated people or religious patrons, changes in European art had tended to be wholesale. They took time, but they influenced every kind of art. No artists in Europe, neither poets, painters nor musicians, simply contracted out of the Renaissance and decided to go another way. Southern Europe was about a hundred years ahead of Northern Europe, but the same slow processes affected both in due time. Similarly, the Enlightenment and the Romantic movement spread over the whole of Europe, from St Petersburg to Dublin, from Stockholm to Palermo. In each of the great ages of European art there was at some point an artistic Lingua Franca, spoken across the whole cultural zone. The music being played by Paisello in St Petersburg and Haydn in London sounded the same, but for the relative genius of the two composers.

Modernism wasn't like that. Throughout the whole period and up to the present time, traditional forms continued to flourish and to be popular, influenced and modified by what the modern movement was doing, but not fundamentally changed by it. There were still serious figurative painters, important poets who wrote in rhyming stanzas, literary novelists who told stories, major composers who wrote symphonies and concertos and grand operas. In addition, there was a whole area of popular art, particularly in music, and later in the new art-forms of cinema and television, serving a vast new emancipated mass audience who had never participated in the world of the arts before, where the revolutions of the avant-garde had no real effect at all. Jazz and popular musical theatre developed at their own speed and in their own way, largely unaffected by what the most advanced artists were doing. The popular cinema told its stories simply and dramatically, as the great nineteenth-century serialised novels had done, or borrowed light comedy and melodramatic strategies from the popular nineteenth-century stage. A considerable number of artists, and some of the greatest – Mahler, Richard Strauss, Shostakovich, Auden, George Orwell, Philip Larkin are obvious examples among very many – continued to express the complex realities of the new century through modifications of the old conservative forms. There was no Lingua Franca in any of the arts any more, no sound everyone made. The first thing any serious artist had to do after 1920, was to decide what kind of an artist he or she wanted to be, and what particular originality or modified conservatism would best express what was in them to be expressed.

The theatre was not immune to these revolutions, but the changes that occurred there were not as obvious as they were in the other arts. Pictures and music looked and sounded quite different in 1920, but an 1880 theatregoer in 1920, in nine theatres out of ten, would have seen much the same kind of spectacle as he or she had witnessed forty years earlier. Small avant garde theatres in Paris and Berlin and Vienna (but not yet in London) would have offered radically different fare though there were very few of them, and the vast majority of normal theatre-goers never visited them. The significant changes in the theatre were less visible than they were in painting or music, but they were there, and slowly at work. One of the most significant in the 20s would have been that, though there were as yet few specialist directors earning their living in the theatre, the concept existed, there were a few people who fitted the description, and there was a growing need for their existence.

Whether it was principally the revolution in thinking or technology that caused the specialist director to come into existence is an arguable point. Both factors were important, and without one or the other we might still be in the age of the playwright director or the actor manager.

Theatre technology during the period between 1880 and 1920 changed radically, with the introduction of electric lighting, the building of massive stages in huge auditoriums, and a much greater sophistication of scenery construction and manipulation. Huge fly towers with dozens of flying bars, deep wing spaces with large numbers of poorly paid stage hands to work them, made it possible to create a degree of theatrical illusion far beyond anything previous ages could have produced. All these technological advances enlarged the range of choices open to people who presented plays, and whether an actor or a playwright was in charge of the direction, there began to be several ways any play could be physically staged. With so much that was possible, particularly with the exciting combination of scenery and directional focused light, it was no longer necessary to work within the old unquestioned tradition. And when anything becomes possible, someone has to make a choice.

The revolution in ideas was an equally powerful contribution to the circumstances that made it necessary for specialist directors to emerge. Modern painting was certain to affect theatre design, just as much as imagism and expressionism in poetry bred a generation of playwrights who wished to use some of those techniques in the theatre. There might be some argument over the precise tone of Chekhov's plays, but confronted with the dream plays of Strindberg, decisions of a quite different order have to be taken, what it should look like, how it should be acted, what function music should play, in fact a whole artistic statement to be made when the play takes the stage. As the playwrights of the first thirty years of the century assimilated Marx and Freud, Picasso and T S Eliot, the Surrealists and the Futurists, the theatre had to think about the direction it was taking, or be left behind. Plays could no longer be done just as they had always been done, or staged simply to suit the star. Gradually the director emerged from the shell of the playwright and actor. Both playwrights and actors continued to direct plays. But by the late 1920s men had emerged who were neither, who devoted their whole time to thinking about how to express the modern realities for which the procedures of the traditional theatre now seemed inadequate. And since that first generation, of Granville Barker, Basil Dean, Meyerhold and Piscator, directors have become more and more specialist. Nowadays most directors have not been either playwrights or actors, and a good many have studied directing as an academic subject at university.

The other huge influence on the birth and growth of the specialist director, was the cinema, born as a technique at the high point of the modernist explosion, and developing into a commercial entertainment industry in not much more than ten years. In the beginning no one knew how to make films, and theatre people would have nothing to do with the new upstart. But someone had to decide where to stand the camera, even if it couldn't be moved, how to place the actors in front of it, and how to cut the shots together. No playwrights were required, as no audible words were spoken, and the actors were in front of the camera, not behind it, so some other kind of person had to do the job, a person who probably had no kind of theatrical background at all, and may well have been a half literate recent immigrant to the USA. The rapid development of the cinema meant that the man behind the camera soon became very important indeed, as the only one who really knew, either on paper, or, very often, within his head, what was going on at all. Great directors emerged within a very few years of the creation of the commercial industry, D. W. Griffiths before 1920, and in the 20s one of the very greatest of them all, Sergei Eisenstein. As sound was developed and film making became more and more complex, it was clear that in this most technological of media, the director, far more than the writer, actor, designer or composer, was the true creative force, and it was his creative personality that was stamped upon the final film. It was inevitable that the growing cult of the film director should affect the theatre, and encourage theatre directors to become similar masters of all they surveyed. They couldn't control their medium, in the ultimate way a film director can, by holding the uncut rushes in his hand, and joining them together in whatever way he pleases, but they could go a good way towards it, trying to organise all the other creative contributors to see the play in the light of their own personal vision. No director of theatre had ever thought in quite that way before the beginning of the twentieth century, except the megalomaniac Wagner, who even built a special theatre in which only his own works were to be performed. But everyone knew Wagner was *sui generis*, and his sprawling undisciplined works pay the price for his refusal to listen to anyone else at all. Theatre has always been at bottom a collaborative art, and there has never been a playwright of any stature who strove for, or I suspect even wanted, the total monomaniac control Wagner imposed on his own work. It is coincidental though, to put it no higher, that the first theatre directors to aspire to something like overall control of the expression of their own imaginations on the stage, began to emerge in the late 20s and early 30s, just at the same time as their counterparts in the film world were achieving international fame. To be an international film director now is the ultimate megalomaniac ambition, the one way an artist can hope to create the total Wagnerian control over every aspect of a dramatic work, and throughout the second half of the century, some theatre directors, in their much less controllable medium, have been trying to emulate them.

The first generation of theatre directors require, and have received, specialist studies of their own. Theatre studies courses take their students through the twentieth century succession, from Stanislavski, Granville Barker, Craig, Dean, Max Reinhardt, Meyerhold and Piscator, through Guthrie and Brecht, Peter Hall, Grotowski and Peter Brook down to Peter Stein, Peter Sellars, and Robert Lepage. One general point might be made, in the light of my brief comments on some of their predecessors, in the years before directors existed. Almost the first thing specialist directors did was to question the architecture of Sir William Davenant's Restoration theatre, which had lasted for more than two hundred years. Out went the proscenium arch, back in came the thrust stage, the platform stage, the Greek arena, and new concepts like theatre-in-the-round and traverse theatre were created. Partly influenced by ideas which were to lead to installations in the visual arts, theatre became any space within which theatre might be made, from an upstairs room in a pub, through an open air English country garden to an ancient ruin in the Middle East. Tramsheds, warehouses, engine roundhouses, shipyards, derelict churches, community centres, patches of floor in the middle of school halls, street corners, the back of lorries, gothic basements and deserted television and film studios, all became spaces within which drama could be created. Theatre became, in Peter Brook's memorable phrase, *an empty space*, to be filled by the theatrical imagination. That is the great gift the first generations of directors have presented to the modern theatre, the freedom to choose its own space, to rediscover past theatres, and to create in the most unlikely nooks and corners whatever kind of theatre that space can best contain.

Directors today

If we want to understand where we are now, we have to understand where we have come from, and what has made us the people we are. This brief survey of some aspects of directing in the past has made it possible to approach an answer to the initial question, *what is a director?*: except that the closer we look, the more clearly we see that there is not a single answer at all, but at least three, and probably many more.

A director is a theatre worker who is responsible for every aspect of the theatre experience as it appears on the stage, the man or woman who carries the can for failure, or if the project is successful, shares the plaudits with the playwright – if there is one. It sounds simple enough, but it isn't adequate. Modernism's destruction of the old ways without instituting a universally accepted new way, has led to an increasing bifurcation of methods and forms in all the arts as the century has progressed, like a great tree spreading into huge trunks, big boughs, decent sized branches, long withies, frail twigs and thousands upon thousands of leaves. The choices which confront theatre workers in the 1990s are bewilderingly vast, and the honest answer is to say that theatre can be made at the present moment in any way that the maker likes or can make effective. So what is a director, beyond someone who decides he or she is a director, hires a hall and phones up some actors?

However, we must try to cut some of the leaves and twigs away if we are get any idea at all of the inner shape of the tree. In the massive developments that have occurred in the craft of directing in the last fifty years, and even more in the last twenty, we can identify three broad and flourishing trunks, and most people who call themselves directors draw their sap from one or the other. Therefore, with due apologies to all the oddballs and mavericks who direct in quite

different ways, unique to themselves, it seems useful to try to charac-
terise those three great trunks, the ideas which nourish their work,
and the sort of theatre they produce – at least, as it appears at the
present moment. The theatre is developing very quickly, and even
five years from now crucial focuses might have changed. For the sake
of simplicity, we shall call these three kinds the text director, the transformational director, and the auteur director. All such labels are
simplifications, and all directors have at least some degree of all three
in their nature. But their practitioners do produce very different kinds
of work, and they are at least a way of starting the discussion.

As always, radical new ideas lie behind changes in practice. After
World War II, the destructive processes of tearing down old buildings
in order to build new ones didn't only happen in the centres of
English country towns. The forms of art had received the treatment at
the beginning of the century, in the great days of modernism. As the
50s turned into the 60s, the very processes of critical evaluation, how
to judge what was good and what was bad, found themselves facing
the bulldozers.

When I was reading English at Oxford in the 50s, the canon was
still intact, Leavis was king, and a way of making judgements about
art and the validity of art which was broadly that developed by the
Greeks and modified by the Renaissance and the Enlightenment, was
still generally accepted. We knew who were the best poets and why,
but we were probably the last intellectual generation of whom that
could confidently be said.

The attack on the Graeco-Renaissance standards of judgement was
a pincer movement, the two converging wings led by philosophers
and political theorists. Relativism had not been confined to physics,
but had entered both into questions of morality, and the whole business of making critical judgements about anything at all. If consciousness was subjective, then so must judgement be, in every sphere. One
man makes one perception, and one another, and who is to say which
is true? By what external measure can a judgement be made that isn't
the subjective expression of one or the other of the two men? But can
they not agree between them on some objective standards of judgement to which they will both give consent? Even if they do, what
words will they use to make their judgements that are not subjectively
perceived? Clarity? Economy? Vividness? Originality? One man's clarity
is another man's confusion, and relativity reigns.

Social theory brought powerful support to the relative idea. With
the breakdown of Universal Christianity as a serious intellectual structure, it was realised that other civilisations and cultures had quite
different ways of making their judgements, about behaviour and

about art. Europeans could no longer dismiss the rest of the wor,
savages and heathens, as they had done for fifteen centuries. Wer꜀
educated Europeans' cultural attitudes and judgements in any way
superior to the attitudes and judgements of educated Chinese; or infe-
rior, or the same? And on what conceivable bases could such comparisons be made? Political thought too added its own dimension. Who
was to say that the views of the educated minority were the correct
views? In the age of popular democracy, every man's views, like every
man's vote, have equal worth. If a man knows nothing at all about the
subject at issue, this doesn't disqualify him from having an opinion,
and by what criteria do we value one man's opinion over another? It
was an observable fact that the art preferred by the educated minority
was quite different from that preferred by the uneducated mass. Who
was to say, and by what criteria of judgement, that one form was
superior to the other? Wasn't there an argument for saying that what
the majority liked was by definition the best, and if that was so, then
international soap-operas were far superior to Shakespeare, and Abba,
Take That and Snoop Doggy-Dog wrote better music than Mozart and
Beethoven.

New reinforcements came up in the 1970s and joined the forces of
the cultural relativists, a crack battalion of French philosophers.
Language, they said, was a social construct, a system of signs and
symbols, with their own socially-validated meanings, which were far
more powerful than any meanings given to words by mere authors.
Everybody could recognise the signs and symbols, and read them in
their own personal ways. What the author thought he or she put in to
them was of no relevance at all to anyone, except the author. The
author, even the living author, was dead, the true creative artist was
the reader. So works of art, in themselves, had no meaning. Meaning
was created by the reader, the viewer, the member of the audience.
In the theatre, the implications for the production process were shattering. If no play had any meaning, meaning had to be created by the
actors, working under the supervision of the director: which in practice meant by the director.

On the whole, theatre directors do not spend a great deal of time,
certainly in rehearsal, discussing these ideas, which are controversial,
and by no means generally accepted. The vast majority of the popu-
lation is completely unaware of them, and so, probably are a good
many theatre directors. But these structures of argument have created
the intellectual spirit of the age, and theatre directors, who have to
make artistic judgements every time they make a decision, many times
a day, cannot help being affected by them. The stance directors take
in their direction methods, whether conscious or instinctive, either

the new ideas, makes them the kinds of directors they
why the general intellectual situation has to be made
ve can begin to consider the details of direction practice.
cause they are the ones, by and large, who decide how
s to be made, stand at the very centre of this cultural
connict, ... each production they do contributes, in however small a
way, to the developing cultural struggle.

Texts

Most of the directors who first began to emerge as professionals didn't
concern themselves with their position in the intellectual world, and
saw themselves very much as part of a continuing theatrical tradition.
They were doing exactly what the playwright-directors and actor-
directors had done in the past, but doing it in a much more wholesale and artistic manner, with an overall idea of the play in view, and
a degree of experience of the theatre and its workings as least as great
as the actors. Playwrights, almost certainly, and new playwrights for
sure, knew far less than specialist directors about how a theatre was
run or a play rehearsed, so that experienced directors became, in the
best cases, almost father-figures to new playwrights, nursing them into
maturity.

The main thing that such directors took from the past was a respect
for the author and his written word. Good actors and directors knew
that in the last analysis they were dependent on the playwright, that
all their experience and insight was likely to come to nothing if the
play didn't work as a theatrical structure. It didn't have to be deep or
meaningful. The theatre has never demanded that plays should be
literature, or of any lasting worth. That happens, or does not happen,
and it is incidental. The theatre has always demanded that plays
should *work*, by which they mean keep the interest of their audience,
entertain and move them, make them laugh or cry, and send them out
into the night satisfied with what they have seen and the way they
have spent three hours. It takes a particular kind of highly-developed
skill to do that, and good playwrights have it, whether they are good
writers, in the literary sense, or not. *Charley's Aunt* has it, and so does
When We are Married, and *Hobson's Choice*, and *Journey's End*,
though none of them can really be called dramatic literature, or
writing of the highest class. *Juno and the Paycock* has it too, and so
does *The Crucible*, both masterpieces of dramatic writing. They are all
works of professional theatre playwrights who knew what they were
doing, and for that quality, far more than for literary merit, theatre
directors and actors have always had the very greatest respect,

because it makes their own best work possible. They can all pick up the pieces for a bad playwright if they have to, and most of them have done it many times, but they would much rather *not* have to.

Directors who work in this tradition have come a long way since the beginning of the century, assimilating all the techniques and devices of theatre direction, both technical and artistic, that have developed right up to the present time. They may well be as much at home with lasers, projections, electronic scenery, rehearsal games and stunning visual effects as any other director of the age, but their reason for working in the theatre at all remains a deep love and abiding respect for playwrights as the true authors of theatre. Of course, they will be prepared to criticise, and argue with their playwrights, and even persuade them to rewrite their work, if experience tells them that a scene or an act has been misjudged and will not work. That is a part of respect for a good writer, just as it is a part of love. But the director's overall intention is always the same: to find a new or established play he likes, to exert his judgement, scholarship and understanding to penetrate every cranny of the author's meaning, including alternative meanings that have crept in in spite of the author, and to imagine the best possible way of presenting those meanings on the stage. Such a director, though he might have a great deal more experience than his playwright, is ultimately the playwright's servant. The playwright's vision of people and society excites him, and it is that vision that he wishes to embody in living actors and set out in concrete form on the stage.

It follows that such a director has no time for the deconstructionist ideas outlined above, nor even much interest in them. He knows from daily experience that good playwrights *do* know what they are trying to express in their plays, that plays *do* have meaning, a good deal of which the playwright has quite consciously put into his or her work, and the function of which can easily be described: *I put this particular bit here because I wanted to convey this that or the other, and this is how I intended to do it.* He knows, too, that in spite of the impenetrable thickets of language, most of his actors will have the gist of that meaning conveyed to them in their first reading of the text, and will not create in their minds an entirely new play of their own. Communication, even if it is initially at a rather crude level, does occur, and it is very rare that an actor completely misunderstands what the playwright is trying to tell him. The director knows that one of his principal functions will be to convey to the actors aspects of the play's meaning that they haven't grasped at once, and which he has teased out through long discussions with the author or in the case of a dead playwright, through scholarship and study. In this aspect of his work he is only doing what the playwright himself did in the past. Of course, the playwright knows that there are other ideas in his work that he didn't consciously put there, ideas that come from his own hidden areas, or which are a part of the spirit of the age, which manage to creep into the works of all good writers. Most writers enjoy this realisation, they like the feeling that they are channels for what their times have to say. But that doesn't mean they abdicate responsibility for their own meaning in the least degree, only that they know it is a little more subtle and complicated than they imagined. Theories about the meaninglessness of words, the symbolic nature of language, subjectivity of perception, may be philosophically valid, but like a lot of philosophical concepts, they have very little connection with observed reality, the world in which playwrights know jolly well what their meaning is, and can explain it to you, practically and in detail, for hours on end.

The play itself, the pattern of words on the author's page, is always the centre of the text-based director's work, and it is to the play that he always returns to solve whatever problems arise. This does not mean that he abdicates his own responsibility. He cannot be the playwright, or operate with the playwright's mind. His imaginative responses are his own, and they, in the long run, will dictate to him how the play is to be done. If he is an experienced director, and the playwright is a beginner, he may come to the conclusion that crucial changes must be made, if the playwright's vision is to be communicated. But the playwright's vision is always the touchstone, the base camp to which the expedition must always return.

Such a director's commitment to the text and intentions of the writer does not mean that he cannot have radical and startling thoughts about the best way of conveying the writer's meaning, that his imagination cannot be at full stretch. In the case of a play from the past, it may be that he feels he must do quite new things, which would have been unimaginable to the author, in order to get the author's meaning across in a society completely alien from the one he lived in. This is a problem that confronts every director of Greek tragedy, fifth century Athenian society being so unimaginably different from our own. But the definition of the task remains the same: to understand the author's meaning and intentions as profoundly as you can, and to make them as clear as possible, in whatever context you are working.

This makes considerable demands on the director. If he is directing a new play, he must spend many hours with the author, invite him to watch and participate in rehearsal, and share every problem of staging or interpretation with him. Working with a living playwright in this manner is like entering into a kind of short-lived artistic marriage. You must find out everything you can about your partner, and live as intensely in his or her imagination as possible – until the run ends, at least. Then you can both agree to a civilised, and perhaps temporary, divorce.

With a play from the past there is no substitute for hard study, and it is a study that must extend over a director's lifetime, not just the period of a particular production. You must immerse yourself completely in all your author's works, make sure you understand what they are saying, and be prepared to investigate areas of knowledge or structures of ideas that are no longer as available to you as they were to the author. You must find out all you can about the life of your playwright, and evaluate to what degree it colours his or her work, and you must study the theatre conditions, social background and historical circumstances, both political and moral, that accompanied the play's making. You must become both historian and literary critic, and be prepared to spend long hours in libraries or your private study, enriching your mind in the particular areas of theatre that are of interest to you. Ironically, however hard you work, all this scholarship is no substitute for theatrical imagination. Eventually, you will have to decide how you will make this carefully acquired understanding of the play's meaning and context live on the stage. However you do it, and however deep your understanding of the work in its own age, the old play must become living theatre, a performance that speaks to an audience about the problems of the present day, not an exercise in archaeology. If you didn't think the play had something to say to a modern audience, that theatre poetry, despite its having a local habitation and a name, speaks to all sorts and conditions of men and women across centuries, you wouldn't, presumably, have chosen to direct it at all. Historical reconstructions are interesting at times, but they are not the principal business of the theatre.

Let us take a text from the past, and consider how a text-based director might approach it, and to bring some of the problems into sharper focus, let us take a text which provokes some controversy in the modern theatre, *The Merchant of Venice*. The Director, we will assume, knows his Shakespeare, plays and poems, and all the generally available details about the Elizabethan theatre and the life and politics of Shakespeare's time. He will also have seen a good many of the plays in performance, some of them many times, and he will have read some critical books on Shakespeare, some of which he might agree with (*The Shakespearean Tempest*, *Political Shakespeare*) and some of which he might loathe (*Political Shakespeare*, *The Shakespearean Tempest*). If he has done none of these things, he ought perhaps to question whether he should be directing Shakespeare at all.

The first thing he would do would be to note that the play touches on a red-hot modern subject, racism. A little historical study would reveal to him that it was a much less hot subject in 1598. Racism was endemic, everybody knew the white Christian races were superior to blacks and Jews, and there was nothing to argue about. So the director would immediately sense a danger. A modern production of the play cannot and would not wish to avoid the importance of racial questions today. But the temptation to distort the play to suit a modern agenda which is quite alien to its nature would have to be identified, and tactics considered to avoid it. Any director who considered the play to be in itself a racist work would presumably not have chosen to direct it in the first place: one might be tempted to say that if that is how he read Shakespeare's morally radical and libertarian text, he was not fit to direct it.

A little closer reading would reveal that, though the play is full of racist characters – so is modern London, quite as much as Renaissance Venice – the play, through Shylock, who, in spite of his villainy, is a thoroughly rounded and humanised figure, makes a passionate plea for the rights of ethnic minorities. I know of no work in English literature written before Shylock made his great speech that raises the standard of the equality of human rights. In an age which took racism for granted, the speech is an extraordinary moral triumph, a flag waved for liberty that seems naturally to belong with the rhetoric of 1647 rather than 1598. The fact that the speech is uttered by the character who is clearly the play's villain, a man of narrow and perverted human sympathies, adds to the dramatic enigma.

But a still closer study, and particularly a study of the play's imagery, which is always the principal source of meaning for a poet, reveals a quite different play, a play which is concerned with the clash of two systems of value, the financial system based on money, which is a the life blood of trade and the engine of material progress, and the humanitarian system, based on love, which more than anything else is what makes us the creatures we are. He would note that there is something even more subversive going on, particularly in the trial scene, and in the contorted character of Antonio, the man who bears the play's title, and who utters its enigmatically gloomy first lines. What is at issue is nothing less than an examination of some of the fundamental tenets of Christian morality in action, the idea of mercy, crucial to the whole Christian philosophy, and the idea of usury, lending money at interest, equally crucial to the mercantile capitalism just developing in Europe, and destined to play such a great part in its history over the next three hundred years. He would see in the play a fundamental clash between the values of Christianity and the values of the new economics, a clash in which Shylock, and his persecuted race, and Antonio, the supposedly Christian, but by his actions very unchristian, financier both play pivotal parts. His reading of the plays of the middle period, would have led him to expect this examination of Christian principle in the light of real, lived experience, that being the underlying subject of a good many of Shakespeare's mature plays, as though, as a Christian himself, the poet was troubled by the way in which Christian ethical ideas so noticeably failed when forced to live in the harsh world of experience. He will also have made himself familiar with E. A. Honigman's essay '*A world elsewhere,*' which points out, with all the relevant documentation, that both Shakespeares, father and son, were well-known moneylenders, that the successful player-poet carried on his money lending and land speculation throughout his theatre career, and was known as a hard man from whom no financial favours could be expected.

None of this material will tell him how to direct the play, but it will tell him where his production should start from, the areas of meaning the playwright is exploring. Particular problems, like the precise nature of the unpleasant Antonio's character – whether he is, as some have suggested, a guilt-ridden portrait of an anguished homosexual, or in what particular way he is *a tainted wether of the flock* – a gelded ram, unable to reproduce himself, defined by an adjective most commonly used to describe rotting meat – will require solutions that suit not only the director's understanding, but also the particular qualities the actor he has cast can bring to the part. Every director will have his or her own solution.

That is, of course, if he or she is a text-based director, to whom the playwright's intentions are important. If you are not, there is no problem. You just twist the scene in whatever way you please, to fit in with what you have decided to use the play to say.

Shakespeare's plays always require the most careful and detailed textual examination. In addition to being the greatest playwright English culture has produced, with a richer mastery over every element of theatre practice than any other, he is also our greatest poet, which means that his language, and in particular his employment of the arts of language, metaphor, simile and rhetorical figure, contains the very heart of what he wants to say. When you look at a Shakespeare play you do not go first to the characters or situations. You go to the actual choice of words, how they are related rhythmi-cally, and in terms of sound, as well as associations and actual meaning. You look, from line to line, at what is being compared to what, in the most concrete terms, and why one word has been chosen rather than any other. When the image-patterns begin to speak to you, and the intensity of what is compressed into the poetry begins to move you, the characters will become clear, and what matters to them, expressed through their metaphors, will sharply define the sort of people they are. Then, as you perceive them interacting, the nature of the situations they inhabit will become clear. The poetry is always the key to Shakespeare, and because it is bottomless in its ambiguity and in its changing relevance to the world around us, it changes for each person, as his own life changes. I have known Shakespeare's works now for something over forty years, and every time I reread a play, or see a new production, there is always at least one line that strikes me afresh and reveals new meanings, as though it were new-minted on that day, and I am sure that experience is commonplace to all readers and theatregoers who have more than a passing acquaintance with the poet. It isn't that each reader is creating new meanings of his own. It is that the reader, as his own experience deepens, is understanding more and more of what Shakespeare managed to weave into the web of his verses.

The challenge to a text-based director is how to get that endless richness and ambiguity onto the stage, in anything like its wholeness. Dryden said of Shakespeare *He had the largest and most comprehensive soul,* and that's the problem. I have never seen a Shakespeare production that has come anywhere near actually comprehending all that is in the play, and it goes without saying that I have never directed one. Perhaps that is the nature of his greatness, and if we felt we had come to the bottom of him, there would be no further need to produce his plays. Peter Brook said of *King Lear,* in a radio interview, *The play is a mountain. Anyone who gets to the foothills is doing well.*

All good playwrights, though they may not contain such riches, deserve this detail of attention, a determined attempt to tease out every nuance of meaning, whether it has been consciously put there by the playwright, or nudged in when he wasn't looking by the *zeitgeist.* Then, when the range of the piece has been comprehended, or as near comprehended as each individual director can manage, the imagination can begin to work, and the production process can begin.

A good play from the past is like the most fabulous treasure-house, securely locked against the ravages of time. The director's job is to find the key that will unlock this legendary hoard, and reveal all its splendours to the amazed spectators. The real problem is that for every director, in every different venue, with each different group of actors, a new key is required.

It might be tempting to say at this point that there is surely no other way of directing an author's play than by trying to convey his intentions as powerfully and as richly as you can, but in the modern theatre there are other ways, which can be and have been startlingly successful, and it is important to try to describe them.

Transformations

When I first began directing, as a student in 1956, I would have regarded any director who consciously ignored the author's intentions as a charlatan or self-publicist, and so, at that time, would most other theatre people, in or out of the profession. But then, like most others, I was pretty ignorant of European developments, and I had certainly not heard of Meyerhold.

Thirty years later, when directing *The Government Inspector* for Sir Anthony Quayle's Compass Theatre, of which I was then co-director, I studied the accounts of Meyerhold's famous 1920s production, but rapidly found they were quite useless for my purposes. Meyerhold had completely transformed Gogol's play, giving Khlestyakov, the play's comic central character, a wan *doppelganger,* who said nothing, but followed him everywhere in attitudes of despair, and he had made dozens of other equally extraordinary transformations, none of them suggested by Gogol's text, all of them the product of Meyerhold's imagination when reading it. The production doesn't appear to have been very funny, and was very long. It caused a sensation in the Russian theatre, but it was no help in my planning at all. I wanted to try to direct Gogol, not a play by Meyerhold based on Gogol.

My own production was, as Khlestyakov reports of Pushkin's health, *only so so.* The play is very hard to pull off in English, because in Russian it is very funny and terrifyingly grotesque at the same time. This conjunction of qualities is at the very heart of the Russian character, as countless works from Gogol and Dostoyevsky to Prokofiev and Shostakovich will demonstrate, but it is very un-English. Our great comedy, though it is sometimes melancholy, is not usually tinged with terror or nightmare, so productions of Gogol's classic in English usually go one way or the other. Mine was funny, but not really terrifying, and to work properly the play has to be both.

It was perhaps in an attempt to get at the heart of this that Meyerhold produced his extraordinary version, though being a Russian, and living when he did, we might feel he hardly had to work hard to convey terror. He also intended to do a production of *Hamlet* with two actors playing the Prince, one playing all the active, vengeful lines, the other all the passive, uncertain ones. It might have been interesting to see that great director's production of the supreme Shakespearean tragedy, but Meyerhold never managed to bring his plans to fruition. He had other tragedies of his own to deal with. In

1940, the secret police took him to the Lubianka, smashed his glasses, broke his left hand, and killed him. Three weeks later they went to his flat, gouged out his wife's eyes, and shot her.

So almost from the beginning there were directors who were prepared to impose radical changes on the texts they were directing, but they were all in Europe, part of that European avant garde that hardly made any impact at all in England. The first English directors, Barker, Basil Dean, the actor John Gielgud, the actor-playwright Noel Coward, and a little later, Tyrone Guthrie, were all text-based, as the English theatre had always been, and non-naturalistic design, much influenced by modern painting, which established itself in Europe between the wars, made very little impact in England. Almost all the new drama by living playwrights was created within a harshly commercial world that lionised the unadventurous Coward, Lonsdale, Rattigan, and a whole school of milk-and-water English Chekhovians, and, though it did tolerate J. B. Priestley's milder experiments with commercial form, it drove Sean O'Casey's restlessly inventive and imaginative genius out of the theatre altogether. When the breakthrough into a more imaginative English speaking theatre came, it came in America. There was no playwright in England in the 1940s to match the theatrical and poetic genius of Tennessee Williams nor the moral seriousness of Arthur Miller, both of whom demanded directors who would break out of the shackles of naturalism, and use the stage as an imaginative space. So English directors tended to be highly professional and commercially-minded text-men, and taking a play and remaking it in the way Meyerhold had done with Gogol, was simply not an option. Shakespeare, during the great Anthony Quayle Stratford seasons in the early 1950s and in the hands of directors like Glen Byam-Shaw, Quayle himself, Guthrie and the young Peters, Hall and Brook, was richly spoken, and sumptuously set, usually in a colourful and rather romantic intensification of period costume, and mostly entirely faithful to the text. I remember very vividly seeing Tyrone Guthrie's 1950s production of *Troilus and Cressida* at the Old Vic, set in the 1880s, with the Greeks as dour Bismarkian Germans and the Trojans as gloriously frivolous Ruritanians. It caused a great furore in the theatre world, especially Helen, played as a flapper, and Pandarus entertaining her at an ivory piano, but that too was a production which was extremely faithful to Shakespeare's text and structure. It simply used its outrageous, and, at that time, completely original, updatings, to illuminate Shakespeare's poetry and characterisation, and it remains in my memory as the best version of the play I have ever seen. It was, in fact, what we would now call a concept production, not the kind of transformation I am discussing.

That came late to England, but was certainly present when the American director Charles Marowitz helped to pioneer fringe theatre in London in the mid 1960s. His most striking productions were certainly transformations, the use of an existing text as a pretext to create modern variations on the original playwright's theme.

For a transformational director a play is material. He may or may not love the text for its own sake, but that will not be relevant to his project. Much more to the point, he can see in it something that he can take and use to make a particular statement. He will therefore be prepared to cut the playwright's text quite savagely, to leave out whole aspects of the work if necessary, and even to insert material from other works, and he will ignore the playwright's structure, being quite prepared to overlay it with a new structure of his own. He will probably still call the play by its original name, and assign it to its original author, part of the point of his experiment being to set up a creative tension between the original work and his treatment of it.

In rehearsal, he will be prepared to do anything, and follow whatever scent his artistic nose suggests to him. All good directors do that, of course, the rehearsal process being always a quest or an adventure in which anything can happen. But the text-director's imagination is constrained, disciplined by the text and structure of the play, whereas for a transformational director, anything is possible. It really is crossing Niagara on a slippery rope in a high wind without a pole. The possibilities for disaster are obvious and visible in every direction, but the rewards for success are considerable.

Principal among them, at the present time, is being noticed. Directing plays is, after all, a profession, and a very competitive profession, in which there are very many competitors and very few prizes. The rewards for success can be enormous, international fame, a great deal of money, and perhaps most of all, power to do the kind of work you want to do. In such circumstances, anything that distinguishes one particular director from the crowd is of the greatest possible value. It has been a matter of observable fact that directors who have taken the most imaginative liberties with their texts have created the most stir both in the press and all the other media that turn their attention to the theatre. Shakespeare produced with great integrity and attention to detail by a self-effacing young director who wishes to reveal the full ambiguity of a well-known text, is not news. Shakespeare produced in the costumes and setting of Star Trek, incorporating Star Trek-style rewrites, film clips, and filling the stage with aliens, is.

A young director with a career to carve out knows that the more extraordinary his productions are, the more likely he is to get noticed, and he may already have learned that it is very frustrating to do a first-class production of something in an out of the way venue with unknown actors that no critics bother to come to see. He may have satisfied his artistic conscience, but he will be just as broke and with just as little opportunity to do his next production as he was before he started. This is not to say, in my late fifties, as I would have said in my early twenties, that transformational directors are all charlatans, bent on creating lucrative careers for themselves. Most, self-evidently, are not, though some, equally self-evidently, are. It is to say that the temptations exist, and all directors, whether they succumb to them or not, are aware of them. It is in the nature of the theatre that it always attracts a certain number of self-publicists and egomaniacs. Shakespeare called them mountebanks, and there were probably roughly as many of them, hanging around the Globe and the Mermaid bar, talking earnestly to actors about their plans for a really new sort of revenge tragedy, or buying both the Burbages a drink, as there are now.

How does a transformational director work? Practically, in rehearsal, much like any other. The differences occur during the planning period. While the text director is burrowing ever deeper into his playwright's world, the transformational director is letting his imagination loose, starting with the text before him, but from that point imposing no limits at all to his creative theatrical processes. He will already have had the original idea, what we might describe as his initial creative metaphor, the realisation that he can use this particular play to say something that matters about the contemporary situation. The initial idea, say *Venice is the city of London*, or *Troy is Bosnia*, to give two obvious examples, will contain within itself all the possibilities for development that will create his production. Beyond that point, there are no rules. The play in itself no longer exists, only as a stimulus for theatrical development.

To look at our original example, *The Merchant of Venice*. The director might wish to use the play to make a savage critique of the unrestricted London financial world of the late 1980s. So the Rialto will become a dealing room full of computer screens, Gratiano, Lorenzo and the Salads will have Essex accents, wear brightly coloured braces, and shout a lot. Love will always be subservient to money, Bassanio and Lorenzo will be young financiers looking for the best way to make a quick million, and Shylock will merely be one shark eaten up by another. Irrelevancies, like the lyric poetry in the garden in Act Five and the whole clash of moral and ethical systems that underlies Shakespeare's text, will simply be dumped, as not relevant to the project in hand. The result, theatrically, might well be quite stunning. Shakespeare's play will have been used as a starting point, or a theme, upon which to play brilliant variations.

As a concrete example, in 1994, an American University did a production of my translation of *Iphigenia at Aulis*, a shattering anti-war play, the product of Euripides' disillusioned old age, as Athens slid towards final disaster in the Peloponnesian War. American Universities often have very sumptuous facilities, and Drama departments that match the best British Drama Schools in their standards. The theatre in which *Iphigenia* was to be performed was the Chichester Festival Theatre and there was a studio theatre and a concert hall in addition.

The two women, members of the Faculty of Theatre Arts, who were directing the play, had a very clear idea of what they wanted to do, and they carried out their intention with great skill, and, considering the cast were all students, some professionalism.

It soon became clear, though, that I would not be seeing a version of my translation of Euripides. To begin with, though about seventy per-cent of the words spoken were mine, lines, sentences and phrases had been incorporated from five or six other translations of the play, including one by a very distinguished American poet. All these translations were written in quite different styles, so that the clash of language from line to line was, to say the least, striking.

The purpose of the two directors seemed to be to create a powerful feminist tract, which was both anti-war and anti-men. Whereas in Euripides' play it is quite clear that the two female characters, Clytemnestra, and Iphigenia herself, become corrupted by the violent atmosphere of the Greek military camp, so that they become as savage as the men, no such investigations were to be pursued in this production. Most of the choruses were cut, and replaced by dance sections, very powerful interludes of Physical Theatre based on Japanese dancing styles, and the last fifth of the play was scissored, so that it ended with the death of Iphigenia. In the received text, there is a messenger speech, describing, probably ironically, the Goddess Artemis' miraculous rescue of the child Iphigenia from the sacrifice planned by her father. Some scholars have argued that this final section is spurious, so there is a case for removing it, as Gilbert Murray did in his translation. But the directors wished to say other things too, about America, and war, particularly the Vietnam war.

They had incorporated a chorus of soldiers, costumed as American Marines, who participated with the Women of Chalcis in the choral sections. During the chorus describing the fall of Troy, one of the poetic gems of the play – all the words, but for a few random phrases, were cut – the chorus of soldiers proceeded, in semi-dance form, to rape the women of Chalcis, so that the stage was full of savagely heaving bodies. After Iphigenia had made her famous speech accepting her sacrifice, she was not marched off to the altar. The soldiers opened up with machine guns, and she was cut down where she stood. So too were the chorus, all the women of Chalcis, who have come to watch the Greek army assembling, so that within a few seconds the stage was full of smoke and massacred bodies.

It was powerful and shocking. We were all forcibly reminded of the massacre of My Lai, and the dramatic point of the men raping and then murdering all the women was made quite clear.

None of this had more than the most tenuous connection with what Euripides is trying to convey in his play. The play was used to drama- tise a quite different agenda, pretty nearly the opposite of Euripides' own. In his old age, he had become convinced that war corrupts everyone, men, women, and even children, so that gender, as such, is not an issue. Of course, a powerful man sacrifices a powerless woman, a father sacrifices a daughter, for the most degraded political motives, but that is only a part of the general degradation of every heroic virtue presented in the play. Agamemnon is a liar, a coward, and totally obsessed with his own glory, Achilles is a prancing fool, more sick of self-love than Malvolio, Menelaus impenetrably stupid, and Clytemnestra, who arrives as a sophisticated political Queen delighted at the impending marriage of her daughter, is quickly trans- formed by the savagery which broods over the Greek camp into a half-crazed mother-as-protective animal, and vengeful murderess-to- be. Even the innocent girl, Iphigenia, is degraded by the war hysteria which has possessed the Greeks into making a ranting speech of self- sacrifice which would not have been out of place in the Third Reich. Like Wilfred Owen, Euripides realised that in war old men, for their own political purposes, always sacrifice the young. But this striking production said none of those things. It said that all men are bastards, cause wars, and destroy women.

It was a powerful evening, skilfully presented, but it wasn't Euripides. It was a new work, built on his foundations, and as reveal- ing an example as I have seen in recent years of transformational theatre at work. Euripides' plays are in the public domain, and direc- tors can do exactly what they like with them, as playwrights have done again and again in the last three hundred years. Nor do I make any restrictions on the use of my own Greek translations. I reckon the old Athenians, having survived for two-and-a-half millennia, can look after themselves.

There are two obvious dangers inherent in the transformational approach. The first is that the new creation, though striking, will seem a great deal less subtle and relevant than the original play presented straightforwardly. But that is a chance all transformational directors are aware of, and one they are prepared to take. Transformational productions, when they are good, have great immediacy and political relevance, but they are rarely designed with the expectation of a life beyond the original presentation.

The second danger of transformational theatre is that if you try it with a living playwright, you might get your shins kicked. Playwrights are dangerous and irrational creatures, and when someone mutilates their children, they are not always answerable for their actions.

Plays without playwrights: auteur directors

Since World War II a new kind of director has emerged, with the ambition to take responsibility for the entire creative process. This approach characteristically involves downgrading the playwright. If there is a playwright at all, and there may not be, he or she becomes just one element in the creative team, rather than the *fons et origo* of the whole theatrical process. Often, but not always, directors of this kind have less interest in words than has traditionally been the case in the theatre, and more interest in movement, mime and informal, expressive dance. A certain kind of non rational, non argumentative dramatic situation can be most powerfully conveyed through a language that is predominantly physical, expressive movement, mime and music, with very little verbal content.

A director will start with a venue and a group of actors, who are very often a group the director has worked with before, or whom he particularly trusts. The actors are going to be required to be far more creative, and creative in different ways than is normally the case in a straightforward performance of a play text, so the director needs to be sure that his actors will enjoy working in that way and can do the job well. The subject may already have been chosen, but perhaps that too is going to be allowed to arise out of the interaction of this particular group of people in a specific place. The uniqueness of the occasion is perhaps the central, indeed, the only credo of this kind of work, the realisation that this chemistry of personalities within a particular space, will produce something which has never been presented before. The prospect is extremely exciting, if you are the kind of director who is prepared to start with absolutely nothing, and trust the creativity within the group to imagine and enact the whole experience.

Once the subject is chosen, the actors begin to relate to each other and to the director, through discussion, theatre games and various kinds of improvisation, and they will perhaps be involved in research outside the rehearsal room, in libraries and among archives, or simply going out into the community, and observing, or even living with, the kind of people to be presented in the play. Then the experiences are pooled, and under the director's guidance, by improvisation, odd bits of scripting, perhaps quite a lot of scripting, if a playwright is involved within the group, the play begins to take shape. Day by day ideas are reworked and developed, scenes grow, or shrink, or change their nature completely. The group gets deeper and deeper into the work, always questioning what has been done, and what can still be done, till a final shape begins to emerge, which may well be completely different from what was imagined at the beginning of the process. The closer the first performance gets, the more traditional the rehearsal processes become, as a script is defined – though it may not be principally a verbal script – and the project moves through final rehearsals into a technical and a dress rehearsal.

Many different kinds of drama have been created in this manner in the last forty years, by very contrasted directors. At their head stands Peter Brook, who has been working in this way for many years and rarely directs a conventional play. By now he has become a kind of theatrical alchemist, distilling essences of theatre practices and skills, combining his alembics and retorts in different ways, to create a kind of theatre entirely his own, in which playwrights play no discernible part at all.

At another extreme, there are community plays being performed all over the country, stories put together locally, usually concerning the daily life or history of a certain village or area, in which a huge number of local people takes a creative part, as actors, writers, researchers, musicians, stagehands and costume-makers. Occasionally they hire a playwright to interpret their community to them, but more often a group effort is involved, growing out of the combined creativity of a large number of mostly non-professional people. The director in such a case has something in common with the director of the Royal Tournament or the Edinburgh Tattoo, and perhaps even more with the logistical organiser of a huge public event, like the Notting Hill Carnival, or the World Cup!

In between those extremes there is room for the work of people like Mike Leigh, who carefully encourages his actors to improvise scripted plays for him, though nowadays more often on film than in the theatre; Peter Cheeseman, whose local documentaries at the Victoria Theatre Stoke-on-Trent, seemed almost to have created a new genre in the late 1960s; Simon MacBurney, the chief modern exponent in England of Physical Theatre, and of course Joan Littlewood, who was every kind of director, text, transformational and auteur, as it suited her purposes. For some directors movement and staging becomes *in itself* the principal method of defining reality. The ways in which the actors, move, gesture and interact, whether they are dancing or building a house on stage, are themselves the truths the production is seeking to illuminate.

Language, whether the fact is recognised or not, remains at the heart of the problem. Actors and directors, when they improvise or otherwise create whatever text they require, inevitably use the tired language of every day, and most often fall into the kind of clichés playwrights spend their lives trying to avoid. Writers of all kinds place a particular value on the unique word, but actors rarely have that degree of interest in language for its own sake. For them, it is always a way towards another kind of truth. But for writers, words themselves are truth. Actors will ask, *is that what this character would say in this situation?* whereas playwrights would add a further question: *is it worth saying?*

Structurally, a good director, with his wide and continuing experience of every aspect of theatrical work, can create as unsinkable a vehicle as the best playwright, but when it comes to words, a good playwright is indispensable. The consequence is that almost all auteur theatre pieces are brilliant one-offs, restricted to the life of the original production. Of course, all theatre is ephemeral. That is one of its greatest glories, a paradox which film buffs, who pursue the chimera of the perfect cinematic performance, rarely appreciate. Theatre people know productions exist in time, they flourish and are gone, as life flourishes and disappears into memory. It is only playwrights who can make theatre live beyond its original birthday, and they do that by creating a text-blueprint, like a freeze-dried version of a theatrical experience, something that can be brought to life at any time, even thousands of years into the future, with the application of the warmth of real actors and living imaginations. No one is ever likely to do Peter Brook's *U.S.* or *The Ik* again. They were his creations alone, of no value as texts, part of the theatre history of their time.

Joan Littlewood, inevitably, is the glorious exception. Working with a radio script by Charles Chilton, most of which she eventually rejected, a wonderful collection of songs, and some first rate improvisations by a terrific group of actors, she created in *Oh What a Lovely War*, the one imperishable masterpiece of auteur theatre so far. No one who ever saw her great original at Stratford East – I am one of that privileged group – will ever forget it, the almost unbearable intensity of grief and joy combined in that small theatre, as we saw the unsinkable comic spirit of humanity triumph over the horrors of the trenches. Twenty years later, I directed a cast of eleven-to-fifteen-year-olds in the play, which made their parents and friends weep openly at the spectacle of those young and untouched lives celebrating the indestructible spirit of their great-grandfathers; and all over the country the play is permanently in production, creating its unique mixture of laughter and horror. It joins *Journey's End*, *The Long and the Short and the Tall* and *The Accrington Pals*, as one of a small group of plays that give unforgettable expression to the sufferings and triumphs of the English – public schoolboys, poor bloody infantry, irreverent squaddies, and the women they all left at home – in the terrible wars of the twentieth century.

Confronted with the phenomenon of auteur directors, and indeed transformational directors too, it is difficult to avoid the obvious thought that, like film directors, they come to feel that the whole creative process should be their own, and not be put at the service of a playwright. If they want to express themselves fully in the theatre, then it must be their own vision that is put on the stage, not someone else's.

True or not, there is more than mere arrogance behind this. The best theatre directors, in whatever style, have become complete masters of all the techniques of the theatre, both technical and artistic. Like great pianists, there is nothing they cannot do with their chosen instrument, they have complete command of every expressive nuance or colour that can be created on a stage. Very few playwrights, except the very greatest, who by virtue of their fame, have written many plays and seen them into production, can have anything like the experience of the theatre that a top-class director has. It is natural for some of these directorial masters to wish to express everything their insight and experience has taught them, and natural too to think that will be far more sophisticated than anything even an experienced playwright can contribute. Characteristically, directors of this kind rarely direct new plays. They spend their time devising their own shows, doing radical and extraordinary versions of classics, or doing musicals, where a given text can still give them the maximum room to display their talents.

The fact is, though, that playwrights bring weight and truth and relevance to the theatre, and that great directors without them too often seem like virtuoso pianists improvising. We are stunned by their brilliance, but we soon feel the need for more substantial food. Good playwrights, because of their mastery of words, can define a feeling, or a thought, or an age, in a way that is and remains unforgettable. We write the history of the theatre, even in the twentieth century, largely through the history of its playwrights, so that in a hundred years time we can be quite sure that Shaw, Brecht, Tennessee Williams, Arthur Miller, Samuel Beckett and Harold Pinter will loom larger even than Peter Brook. Their plays will still be performed, whereas Brook's theatre, though it will continue to influence other directors, and stimulate their own investigations, without Brook himself, will be nothing.

What comes first, the chicken or the egg? Did directors begin to regard plays as material they can do what they like with because of the structuralist ideas of the 1970s, or did the ideas arise because of what directors and other artists were already doing?

My own view is that not many directors spend their time relaxing in the pleasant fields of philosophy, though some quite clearly do. Their art is primarily a practical one, concerned with what can be done in a given circumstance with given people, and abstract justifications tend to play little part in the processes of creation.

It seems, too, that the patterns of ideas that have dominated the last twenty years have deeper roots in social and historical change than in anything artists do. Artists react to and chronicle these deep movements in society, as they have done throughout history, but they rarely create them. Technological advance, the creation of an immensely lucrative industry designed to serve and channel popular taste, and the world-wide triumph of free-market capitalism, with its need to destroy any system of values beyond its own, seem to me to be more to the point. The work of art created by its reader rather than its author, is the ideal art object for multinational consumer society. No truths can be expressed from one person to another. Each reader creates what suits himself, as each consumer buys the clothing, car and general lifestyle to his taste and his pocket. It is, to say the least, a coincidence, that such ideas should arise at such a time, and if you give any credence at all to Marx's subversive idea that society determines consciousness, that ideas are the product, not the creator, of economic and political power-centres, then the reality seems clear enough. It is the sort of take it or leave it attitude to the arts you would expect to arise in an age when international buying and selling is all that matters, more than justice, more than equality, more even than the ecological survival of the planet.

When I was teenager discovering theatre, there was a welfare state which was intended to look after everyone's needs, all sorts of social-democratic curbs were in place to restrict the brutality of the free market, and only self-publicists messed about with plays. The two ideas are related. The spirit of the age, which now tells us that if you can sell it, it's good, has created the situation where the consumer is king, art is whatever you call art, and directors can do what they like with scripts with no other justification than that they want to. A freedom has been granted to directors, which was not granted in the 1940s and 1950s, and some directors have made good, even great use of it.

By now, my own position in this debate, which covers the whole world of the arts, not just the craft of directing, has become clear enough. I am a text-director through and through, as, being a playwright with more than fifty works behind me, I am almost bound to be. If I didn't think there was some special quality contained in the art of playwriting which is beyond what directors can do, I would not practice it. I know perfectly well what I am trying to say in my plays, and I can point it out in detail, word for word and action for action, but I know too that there are things in my plays that I did not put there, and that each director and each actor will bring to my work something uniquely his or her own. That process is in fact my profoundest joy, the greatest reason for being a playwright, what makes my works come to life. The theatre is a living collaborative art form. Every new generation, even thousands of years into the future, has something of its own to contribute, and yet somehow the essence of a good play remains the same, century after century. I am sure that Sophocles would recognise *Oedipus the King* as his own play, even in a language which didn't exist when he wrote his text. The fact that a play changes with every passing day, but remains the same is, of course, a paradox. But in the age of quantum theory, when the speed and position of a particle cannot both be measured, and the universe may contain thousands of alternative quantum worlds, perhaps that little contradiction is allowable, even to be relished.

In fact, I am one of a particular sub-group, of playwright-directors who are equally practised in both skills. Though I began writing at fifteen, I had been a busy professional director for seven years before my first play was staged, and even now, when I consider myself perhaps more of a playwright, I have directed very many more plays – about a hundred in all the media – than I have written. The modern theatre, in England at least, is producing a good many playwrights who are also skilled directors, Alan Ayckbourn the most senior perhaps, but including Harold Pinter and David Hare, all of whom are as much at home directing other people's plays as their own. As to the virtues and vices of directing your own work, they are fairly evenly balanced. A playwright knows far better than anyone else the subtleties of what his script contains, but he is limited by what his own imagination has created, and knows perfectly well that another imagination might add all kinds of glories of interpretation to what he has written. Most playwrights feel, and I certainly do, that if they could be certain they could find a director who would respect their intentions, and seek to express them with the full range of his imagination, they would always be very happy to let him do the work, and watch the play slowly developing, and help to improve it where they could.

But such directors are not easy to find. I have found four in my thirty years of seeing my plays produced, but I have also had one play whose original production, in the West End of London, was completely destroyed by a director who substantially rewrote my play against my wishes, and two others which were spoiled by a director insisting on doing things I specifically asked him and her not to do.

But that is a whole new subject, which doesn't belong here, and is part of the craft process of direction. It is to that craft, and that process, we must now turn.

2

Selecting your play

The process begins with the selection of a play to direct. All kinds of external pressures might qualify the choice, and to some of them we will return later. Whatever the reasons that influence the decision, the act of choice is crucial. If you get it wrong at this first stage, the chances of success shrink alarmingly, if they aren't already negligible.

It really amounts to two necessities, knowing your subject, and knowing yourself: and if you have to judge between the two, the latter is probably the more important.

For a director, there is no substitute for knowledge, the fruits you have harvested from going to the theatre, thinking about theatre and reading about it over a long period and as your principal interest. Some find a virtue in confronting a play and coming to it raw, saying, *this is all quite new to me, I am going to interrogate this text with spontaneity and freshness, so that my approach will be vivid and uniquely my own,* but they usually end up making the same old beginner's mistakes. There is no virtue in ignorance beyond naiveté, and that soon palls. The danger of making catastrophic howlers, so that people who **do** know what they are talking about laugh at what a fool you are making of yourself, is a very real one, and a sensible director takes every possible precaution to avoid it. However learned you are, there will always be someone who knows more about the subject than you do, and the more you study the world of a good play, the more you will find in it, and the more you will be able to reveal in your production. The task is bottomless of course, more than lifelong. We all feel beginners, however long we have been at it. But we are not beginners, we do have some knowledge and experience to fall back on. Without it, you fall back on your bum, which is painful, and you get up full of bruises.

It is, of course, crucial to retain your freshness of response to any text, that instantaneous relationship you entered into during the first reading, but that ought not to be spoiled by increasing your depth of knowledge. If it is spoiled, it is likely to have been wrong in the first place, and is best forgotten.

I do not include a close knowledge of theory among the necessary requirements. Read Craig and Artaud if you like, on the principle that it is always better to read than not to read, and anything germane to the subject contributes to the widening of your theatre mind. Far more important is to go to plays, any plays, anywhere, from the Royal National Theatre to the local school, as often as you can, and to read the basic texts. It is better to read plays, any plays, plays in enormous numbers and from every culture, than to read people theorising about the nature of the theatre. If you do read theoretical material, read the practitioners, Brecht, Peter Brook, Arthur Miller, people who have the weight of long experience in the mainstream theatre behind them, and whose lives and livelihood were and are genuinely on the line every time they practice their art. It is among such people that all the secrets are to be found, and it is in such company that a young director should make himself familiar, and feel in his blood and bone how the processes work.

For an English director, a close knowledge of Shakespeare is essential, even if you hate him and never intend to direct him. He towers so completely over English dramatic culture that an ignorance of his stature makes it impossible to relate truthfully to any other works. Shaw, for instance, made a fetish of an attack on Shakespeare, but it was because he exerted such a total, and in Shaw's day, an almost entirely baleful influence on theatre culture that Shaw felt he had to try to destroy him. English writing could never be free if it couldn't emerge from under that giant shadow, and Shaw, seeing imitation Shakespeare tragedies all around him – does anyone at all now remember Stephen Phillips? – understood that English writers had to begin to think in a non-Shakespearean way, stimulated by Ibsen, Strindberg, Chekhov and the German Ibsenites, writers who were trying to come to terms with the real turn-of-the-century world, not writing verse tragedies about medieval kings.

Any decent director should have at least a working knowledge of all Shakespeare's plays, as well as some understanding of the social and political world that produced them, and for my taste at least, the classical Greek tragedians are almost as important. Their significance is not only in the lasting quality and relevance of what they created, and their seriousness, at the heart of the public debate of their times, but in the fact that they were the first, and that the particular dramatic form they invented, its non naturalism, its poetry, its music and dance, its wonderful fusing of all these elements into a complete art work, is still full of tremendous implications for the modern theatre. It is a rich paradox that, though nobody, except possibly Racine, has ever successfully imitated Greek tragedy, or even managed to find a way of making a contemporary version of the Greek chorus, their influence is perhaps still the most powerful creative force playing on modern playwrights from the past. Eliot returned to them in his largely unsuccessful attempt to revive the poetic drama, and both Arthur Miller and Edward Bond show evidence in their works of the continuing fire that warms us from Athens. There has probably never been a playwright who hasn't thought at some time or other what a marvellous device the Greek chorus is, and wouldn't it be wonderful if he or she could think up some modern dramatic technique that would do all the things Greek choruses do so economically. None of us has really managed it yet. That particular mixture of poetry and music and dance, allied to the ability to comment seriously on a dramatic situation, and develop and define it in the most direct or the most lyrical, or the most philosophical terms, still remains unique to the Greeks, however we try to learn the lessons they have taught us. As with Shakespeare, a director who isn't on familiar terms with the Greeks is like a child with no family, someone who is lost in the modern world without any idea who his ancestors were, or where he came from.

Beyond those two great bases, every director will pursue his or her own course of study, depending on personal taste. Plays from any period can be approached in almost as many ways as there are directors, but the director who doesn't know everything he can find out about the play he is seeking to present is asking for trouble. Knowledge is everything, the foundation upon which imagination can begin to build. Ignorance always ends up in making fools of the actors, and selling the audience short. They are paying for their tickets, and they have a right to be addressed by someone who knows what he is talking about.

That essential background knowledge should not be purely theatrical. The development of theatre studies as a university discipline is very much to be welcomed, but in some courses it does result in a removal of theatre from the culture of its age, as though it existed on its own. Theatre, wherever it is found, is always a part of the literary, and very often the musical, culture of its time and place. Playwrights are often men of letters too, poets, and novelists and short story writers, as well as dramatists, and a director needs to have at least some working knowledge of the literary and musical culture within which the plays he intends to present were created. A director of Shakespeare who doesn't have some knowledge of Spenser and Donne, or some acquaintance with the music of Dowland, Morley and Robert Johnson, is working with one hand tied behind his back. He doesn't have to *use* that knowledge practically in production if he doesn't want to, just as he may choose not to use the authentic Robert Johnson settings of

Shakespeare's songs that survive. But the music of the age, and its poetry, must be in his ears all the time, part of his perception of that culture and its characteristics, so that if he decides to reject them in his own work, he will know quite clearly what he is rejecting, and be better prepared to define what he is trying to create to replace them.

Then, it is a question of being honest with yourself, and seeking to make yourself expert in some area which instinctively appeals to you. The world of the drama of the past is so wide and various that no director is likely to have an equal taste for all of it, and if he or she pretends to, for money, or for the main chance, or to do a favour to a colleague, the risk usually outweighs any advantage that might accrue. I know by now that I don't have much taste for French culture, particularly light, airy, Gallic sophistication, and I have two grisly failures in my CV to prove it, lost battlefields on which I learned my lesson. Every director must learn to recognise what he loves, what he can tolerate, and what he hates. No one will need encouraging to grasp the chance to do what he loves, but the temptation to do what you hate is sometimes very strong, in the presence of a fine actor, a good venue, a handsome cheque. It is a temptation to be resisted, a risk that is likely to end in tears, or scenes in the breakfast room of the Grand Theatre Brighton on a Tuesday morning. It is not a part of a director's professionalism to assert that he can direct anything, even traffic. The real pro knows what he won't touch in any circumstances, and fends it off with a barge pole.

So, you have educated yourself in the fundamentals of theatre literature, you have seen dozens upon dozens of plays, and nine times out of ten come out thinking *they've got it all wrong, I could do much better than that*, the young director's healthy response to almost everything, and you have some idea what suits you and what does not. There is still the question of which particular play you choose to direct.

In fact, it is very rare that the choice will be totally untrammelled. We all dream of the producer or theatre-owner who says, *here's the space, and here's the money, now do what you like*, but most of us never meet him, except in dreams. It is much more likely that someone will ring you up with a project already more than half-formed, or a social discussion will start in a pub or at a party that will develop into a production idea, or together with a group of like-minded friends you will suggest a project to some theatre, financed by hope, idealism and unpaid actors. Whatever the circumstances of each particular production, propitious and well-funded, or very hairy and budgeted on a shoestring, a director must have some burning reason that drives him to want to do a particular play. If there isn't some sort of hunger, some picture in the head that demands to be realised, some sort of feeling about a scene or a character that makes the emotion swell in your chest and the adrenalin run in your muscles, then you'd do better to take up some less-demanding and better-paid task.

It doesn't necessarily mean that you must *only* do a play you know well and have already prepared for production in your mind. If that were the case no director would ever do a new play. There is nothing quite like that exhilarated feeling that sweeps through you as you read for the first time a play that you know you like a lot: in the case of a new play, it is surely one of the most exciting moments in a director's life. I shall never forget reading David Turner's first play, *The Train Set*, when I was twenty-four, or the sense of awe with which I read the typescript of David Mercer's *For Tea on Sunday*, quite sure that I was reading some kind of masterpiece of that now-defunct form, television drama. Such moments are to be cherished, not only because they are moments of unique personal joy, but because they are the clearest indication that you have something to say about a play, and ought to try to direct it.

It is important to experience something like that feeling the first time you read any play you are likely to direct, even if it is an established masterpiece that you happen not to have encountered before. If you don't feel immediately that you see why the play has the reputation it has, if the jokes don't make you laugh, or the poetry doesn't move you, then you should probably give it a miss. You need not get everything in the play on the first reading, indeed, with any kind of complex and high-quality drama it is unlikely that you will. The play that gives up all its secrets at the first encounter is not likely to satisfy for long. But there needs to be a sense of bonding with the play, the knowledge that, even if you know you have only lifted the corner of a great sheet, under which the body of the play is lying, you sense what is there, and you know with great certainty how to bring it back to life.

Trying to define exactly what that feeling of commitment is, the idea that a director has about a play that moves him, brings us close to one of the more controversial questions in the life of a modern director, the concept of The Concept.

Concepts

The word is much used, particularly by dramatic critics, and there are very many productions, particularly of plays from the classic repertoire, which it aptly describes. It is probably true to say that in recent years in the professional theatre, the non-concept classic production has been something of a rarity.

What it means is simply that the director has some unifying idea which every aspect of the production will be harnessed to express. A further implication is that it will be a new idea, possibly outrageous when juxtaposed with the text it is designed to illuminate. Like a Craig Raine metaphor, it will most characteristically yoke together two seemingly alien ideas, a play and a context that would not normally be imagined to belong together.

Concept Theatre started among directors who felt a need to find new ways of staging Shakespeare. When Shakespeare plays were usually staged within the play's historical period, or in a kind of idealised Renaissance setting, and this seemed to have gone on for many years, which was the situation in England in the mid 1950s, the desire to make the plays feel new and relevant led directors into all kinds of experiments with the period, setting and costuming of the plays. The idea of 'Shakespeare in modern dress' – the very phrase is illuminating, with its implication that Shakespeare should not normally be 'modern' – had been around for some time, of course, and there had been more than one Nazi *Julius Caesar* in the 1930s. Yet the concept idea, as it has become more sophisticated and ubiquitous in the last thirty years, is rather more than that, what one might define as an overall social design idea. Characteristically, it has meant the location of a play in a fully realised and detailed social scene alien from its own, which gives rise to the design and costuming ideas that will best express it. Among many hundreds of examples we remember the RSC British Raj *Much Ado About Nothing*, and Jonathan Miller's television *Merchant of Venice*, with Olivier playing Shylock as a nineteenth century Jewish banker, respectable frock coat and black topper, rather than a Jewish gabardine. The same director's *Rigoletto*, set in the world of the American gangster movie, has been immensely successful all over the world, and there have been many other genuinely illuminating examples of plays and operas seen in a stunningly new light. Not all of them have opted for a detailed social background, some seeking more abstract metaphors to express their vision. The necessity for a fully realised society in a play was probably a result of the absolute mania for Brecht and Brechtian staging ideas which swamped the English theatre in the late 50s and early 60s. Not all directors bought that manifesto however, perhaps the most striking example of one who didn't being Peter Brook, whose extraordinary *A Midsummer Night's Dream* saw the world of the play as a kind of metaphysical gymnasium, and magic as a phenomenon of trapezes and plates spinning from wand to wand.

At its best, and there have been many fine examples over recent years, the concept production can illuminate a text in a quite unfor-

gettable way. At its worst, and there have inevitably been even more
of those, it can be a flashy and self-promoting substitute for thought
on the part of the director.

Guthrie's *Troilus and Cressida*, though forty years in the past
now, has always glowed in my memory, not only because I saw it
at an impressionable time in my youth, but also because, for all its
startling imagery, it served Shakespeare with absolute integrity,
enriching and revealing his work in the way only the very best
productions do. It has always been axiomatic in literary criticism of
the play to point out the striking difference between Shakespeare's
portrait of the pragmatic and Machiavellian Greeks and the romantic
and heroic Trojans, and how cleverly he uses this distinction as a
structural device, following one with the other to the most telling
effect. Guthrie's concept of the Greeks as post 1870 Prussians and
the Trojans as Ruritanian aristocrats expressed Shakespeare's idea
with great theatricality and precision. The Greeks were dressed in
long grey greatcoats, wore spiked helmets, and debated long and
earnestly over their plans to take Troy. The Trojans wore tight white
or red trousers, golden breastplates, and golden helmets with huge
white plumes, and after debating whether to return Helen, and
deciding, persuaded by Hector, that honour demanded they should
keep her, they drank a toast in champagne and hurled their glasses
into the fireplace. Like all good concepts, that idea of the doomed
unreality of Trojan honour paid off later in the production, when the
unarmed Hector, caught off-guard by Achilles and a band of
Myrmidons – rather French-looking infantrymen, with long barrelled
rifles – was unceremoniously cut down by a volley from the brutal
Achilles' rankers. That stage image is in my head till I die, and so are
many others from that production: the openly homo-erotic nature of
the Achilles-Patroclus scene – at a time when that idea was startlingly new, not the dreary cliché it has now become – with the
gigantic Achilles stripped to the waist, wearing gabardine trousers
and a brightly coloured dressing gown, cuddling the thin and
callowly youthful Patroclus, dressed in the cheap uniform jacket and
trousers of an infantry private: Troilus and Cressida playing their
passionate farewell scene in an upstairs bedroom while Cressida
pulled her heavy skirt on over her corsets, while downstairs in the
hall the Greek officers smoked moodily and looked at their watches:
most of all perhaps, Pandarus' final speech, with the greying flaneur
wearing an expensive overcoat and homburg hat, carrying a suitcase
with labels from Paris, Monte-Carlo, Rome and Berlin pasted upon
it, the universal social butterfly, the man who always manages to
wangle a seat on the last plane out before the city falls. There were

no vulgar effects in that great production, although it was full of the most startling things. Shakespeare was being served, and his meanings illuminated in the most unforgettable manner.

But concept productions, when they are created by directors with less mastery and integrity than Guthrie, far from serving a playwright's text, can distort it beyond recognition, or fail to come to terms with it at all. Two dangers in particular must be recognised by any director, however pure-hearted and full of integrity he may be, when he sets out to realise some startling concept of a classic play. Ignoring them can lead to productions of callow shallowness or vulgar self-advertisement, as well as, it must be regretfully admitted, a great deal of attention in the press.

The first danger of a strong concept, especially if the director brings it with him fully worked out to the first rehearsal, sets designed, costumes sketched, the whole thing cut and dried, is that it completely blocks all the other alternative meanings the play in this particular context might possess. The production of a play is a unique meeting of a text, a place, a group of actors, and a director and his co workers, and by its very nature is unrepeatable and *sui generis*. In the best circumstances a spark of collaborative energy is generated that might catch fire into the most enthralling flame of creation. If the right orientation between text, actors and director is achieved, very many pathways into the country of the play are revealed, and a good director will lead his actors down all of them, to see what treasure may be revealed at the end of the journey. A concept production that has been totally imagined by the director is in danger of cutting off all these paths of exploration except one or two. The actors' imaginations will no longer be free, they cannot pursue the poetry, and follow wherever it takes them, because they will soon come up against the brick wall of the director's idea.

A distinguished actor friend once told me of a production of *Macbeth* in which he was playing the name part. He was told it was to be a Japanese production, and thinking of memories of Toshiro Mifune and Samurai swords and black top-knots, he was rather excited. On the first day he saw the costume designs, and realised he would be playing Macbeth from inside a kind of walking bamboo cage. The production, from that point, was about the costumes, not the text, and never got off the ground.

When a concept is purely visual, concerned with the look of the stage above everything else, so that the costumes and sets are the touchstone against which all decisions are measured, the alarm-bells ought to start ringing. Plays are about poetry, and characters and actions first and foremost, and the visual dimension should stay where

Aristotle put it, as a powerful ornament of a production, not its *raison d'être*. Physical Theatre, its whole nature growing from certain perceptions about what can be conveyed through the visual dimension, is another matter, with its own quite different parameters. But in the staging of a classic text, the spectacular elements in the setting and costumes need to stay where Aristotle in the *Poetics* put them, sixth and last of the crucial elements in the creation of a tragedy. When I was twenty and writing tragedy papers, as well as my own first plays, Aristotle was an old Greek fart who was hopelessly out of date. As I grew older, he seemed mysteriously to become more relevant, till now, in my late fifties, it seems to me that he got most of it just about right. Sons go through much the same experience with their fathers, and when it comes to dramatic criticism, Aristotle is everybody's father.

The organisation of theatre administration too has had some part to play in this process of encouraging the development of an overall concept. In the English theatre, rehearsals rarely last for more than four or five weeks, unless you are doing a major new production for one of the flagship companies, in which case you might have a little longer. In whatever case, production schedules have to be met, if a set is to be built on time, and costumes are to be ready to wear. A designer who does not have his drawings and models ready by the first day of rehearsal is likely to be very unpopular with the theatre's construction and costuming departments. The pressure is therefore on all directors to make their decisions early, to do the work in their imaginations and to come to the first rehearsal with everything more or less settled. Experienced directors have to learn to work with the system, to decide what has to be decided, but to leave as much fluency and ambiguity as possible within the planning process, so that the real business of rehearsal, the exploration of a text within the minds and bodies of an unique group of actors, can have a chance to flourish.

In an ideal world, it ought to be possible to choose your actors, take them to the empty stage where your production is to take place, and say, *now let us begin our process of exploration, with no preconceived ideas, even the shape and layout of the stage we wish to use*. Then, as the actors begin to explore, and the meaning of the poetry in action for this particular group emerges, the production will begin to take place. Perhaps a very strong concept will emerge, and then the building and sewing can begin, knowing that they are the outcome of the actors' needs when confronted with this text, not the arbitrary product of one imagination working in a vacuum. On rare occasions something like this does occur, and it is a joy for all concerned. But most people working on a classic theatre production never get within striking-distance of such an opportunity.

The second great danger of the concept process lies in what ought to be one of its virtues, following the idea through to its logical conclusions. To illustrate what I mean, let us create a couple of hypothetical examples.

We have decided to do a *Julius Caesar* set in the World War I period, and we are looking at the quarrel scene. Brutus, we have decided, is a public school man through and through, probably Winchester and New College, Oxford, whereas Cassius is a natural outsider, a brilliant self-educated military leader and politician, but definitely not, 'one of us'. The scene is set in a large room in a ruined château just behind the front line, where Brutus has set up his headquarters. There are staff-officers marching in and out, and a corporal is working permanently on a field telephone. There is a tray of tea, newly made by the batman for Cassius after his journey, and the usual drinks and cigars available in a half-smashed cabinet. Cassius arrives, with his staff, and the scene begins.

It all sounds vivid enough and the images immediately strike home. But decent actors in that circumstance will automatically begin to play Brutus and Cassius *as* British officers, working on mannerisms typical of such men, the way they speak, their habit of understatement, the way they pour a drink or cut a cigar. It is the attention to this kind of detail that marks out the first rate actor from the second. But none of this is at all necessary to Shakespeare's scene, in fact, if it is not very carefully controlled, it can become a hindrance to the exploration of what the scene actually contains and says about the two men and their dilemma. It shuts down most areas of possible exploration, and leaves only one, Shakespeares's verses in the way they might be spoken by British officers. There would be a great deal of pouring-drinks-acting, tightly-belted-Sam-Browne-acting, understated-English-stoical-acting, quite a different thing from the Roman stoicism Shakespeare tries to express, or the rich language and subtle Renaissance verse he uses to express it. After all, when you come down to it, the play is *not* actually about World War I and British Officers. In its detail, it is republican Roman, seen through late sixteenth century eyes, and archetypically it is any revolutionary civil war. Politically, the metaphor doesn't fit without fudging, and for the sake of a few striking stage pictures, something crucial is being compromised. Things designed to enable the play to speak more clearly, become in fact barriers, ensuring that the true speech of the play will remain unheard.

Let us imagine an even more striking example. We are doing a Romanian *Macbeth*, with Macbeth and his lady as the Ceaucescus. We remember the stunning film image, when the first flicker of terror creased the dictator's face, as he realised he was beginning to lose his power. It is one of the icons of the present age. That has been the germ that started the production in our mind, and we will use the idea in *Tomorrow and tomorrow and tomorrow,* the report of the Queen's death. We shall see Macbeth look into the pit and face his final demise in that speech, and we are quite right to judge that something like that happens in the verse itself. We will find other things while working it in detail with the actor, but that is our starting point. However, that logically means the scene must be public, and we must see it being recorded on film. It is the dictator's statement to the media, his sound bite for the six o'clock news after his wife's death, with all the journalists taking notes, and the video-camera recording. All very fine and exciting, except that if you create those circumstances, there is only one way a good actor can play the speech, like a politician making a public statement to a camera. Otherwise the actor will be dishonest to the situation, acting one play while another is performed all around him. But the speech, being one of the great moments of English drama, contains a great many more possibilities than that, melancholy, tragic self-knowledge and irony among the most obvious, and they must all be sacrificed to the clever directing idea, if you carry it through to its logical conclusion. But if you don't carry the idea through to its conclusion, it loses a great deal of its force. So you make the actor play it that way, surrounded by all the paraphernalia of the scene you have created, and what you end up with is a cheap and flashy stunt, that comes nowhere near expressing anything of the grave beauty and moral horror of that sublime speech.

How many times have we seen concepts of that kind strutting our stages in the last twenty-five years, and thought *what a shame we have to spend our evening watching a smart-arse director instead of a great poet?*

But all directors are not smart-arses, and concepts do not have to be thin, flashy and not-thought-through. They can be moments of profound illumination that change your life. In Peter Brook's *A Midsummer Night's Dream*, which seemed to me to fail with some aspects of the play, the young quartet's love poetry in particular – that old business of the largest and most comprehensive soul again – there was one of those moments. Shakespeare describes the Mechanicals as *hard-handed men who work in Athens here,* and casting aside the usual mummerset traditions, Peter Brook made them just that, a workmen's amateur dramatic society, in their first scene having a meeting during their lunch break, some of them bringing their sandwiches with them, as Peter Quince handed out their parts and told them about the project. In the fifth act performance before the Duke, Snug the joiner, a skilled craftsman in wood, wore a most beautifully crafted and joined wooden lion's head, made in the shape of a box with a side panel cut out so that his face could be clearly seen inside it, exactly as the workmen-actors have described it in the rehearsal scene, so that the ladies shall not be afraid. It is that sort of vividness of imagination and attention to detail that marks out the great director, and the concept that serves the needs of the play. Every time I approach the scene myself now, however and with whomever I do it, it is always with Peter Brook's precise vision at the back of my mind.

But all plays are not classics, and all playwrights are not dead. The question of selecting your play when you are dealing with the works of the living, and perhaps the unrecognised, raises a whole host of new problems, and at least one ethical dilemma.

Living playwrights

It is not possible to teach literary judgement, only to acquire it. When confronted with a previously unread text, every director is on his own, his powers of judgement on the line. An educated director who has read a great deal may be at an advantage: experience may help him to recognise the difference between good writing and bad. Or education may prove to be a disadvantage, if a director has allowed it to fossilise into dogma, so that plays cannot be good unless they are like other plays. New writers often do quite new things, treating new subject matter in new forms, and the fact that you can find nothing like them in your previous experience of plays may be the main point.

There are certain safety checks you can make. Precise, concrete, economical writing, that clearly defines what it is talking about, is always likely to work better than windy generalised metaphysical writing, full of large abstracts and undefined absolutes. If the metaphors are genuine discoveries, or have some kind of personal signature, the audience will probably listen, whereas if they are the usual cliché comparisons of everyday journalism, they are likely to nod off. Action which is direct and moves inexorably from scene to scene is likely to play much better on a stage than if the structure is confused, keeps taking odd turnings and you can never be quite sure where you are, how you got there, or why. But again, you must beware. Sometimes remarkable artists invent new structures of action that appear to break all the conventional rules, but work. Sometimes, indeed, smashing up accepted ideas of form is the main point the artist is making, the only way a new vision of reality can be expressed. *Waiting for Godot* contains no action in the accepted sense – indeed that is the metaphysical point Beckett is making – so that a good many people, myself included, were bemused when they first read it. In fact it does have a tight line of action, which emerges very clearly when you act it, as I did in a rehearsal cast within a year or so of its premiere, or when you see it played. Beckett had discovered a new kind of action that was not in the dramatic text-books, and those who rely on such things were caught out.

Look for precise writing and tight action, try to judge whether you know the characters as you read their lines, or if they are flat and two-dimensional, and if you want to guard yourself against all the evils of bad playwriting, read the last act of *The Critic* again and again till you know it by heart. Otherwise you must rely on your instinct, as you always do when choosing a play, that feeling that you can see and hear exactly how this will go on the stage. If you can't see and hear that, you shouldn't do it, because, for you at least, it will not be good enough.

There is one danger easy enough to avoid, which trips up many directors and producers, particularly in television, where the grue-some production system they now work under makes it almost inevitable. That danger, which is extreme when you are dealing with a synopsis rather than a finished play, lies in judging the idea instead of the play. Dozens and dozens of people can come up with brilliantly striking ideas, but very few of them are good enough writers to make them into a play. If you get this wrong, you will end up with compelling pre-publicity, and dreadful writing – a commonplace of modern television drama – and of course you will fail, because in the long run people will not sit and watch rubbish, even compelling rubbish. It is much better to trust a writer whom you know can write, who mumbles something incoherent about a sort of idea for a sort of play with a wild glance in his eye and keeps spilling his beer, than to be taken in by some smart operative who talks about gender politics or Aids or the homeless, or the international money market, or any other immediately fashionable and important subject, and then writes pages of dramatic duckspeak. Duck dialogue is everywhere, because there are always an enormous number of bad writers and very few good ones. Don't be taken in by even the most terrific theatrical idea, if it quacks. Quacking is quacking, however you try to disguise it. Make sure your chosen playwright can actually write the idea in a way that is as original and compelling as the idea itself, before you chuck your hat in the air, open the champagne and start spending money. Or you might find yourself hatless, drinking lager, and broke.

Having found your new play, you must learn how to cope with your new playwright. Ninety percent of this is a matter of personal relationships, and for that there are no rules, or none at least that are specific to the art of making plays. If you are going to create something worthwhile, the relationship will need to be close, for a time at least, with complete honesty between the two of you, with no fears or criticisms held back. In all human relationships that is a counsel of perfection, but when you are producing a new writer's play there is no more certain recipe for disaster and angry tears than one holding back and not telling the other his thoughts, or even worse, when both are doing it. It is hard to be honest, but it is much safer.

That said, the relationship doesn't necessarily need to be personal, as long as it is closely and honestly professional. For four years, between 1960 and 1964, I worked very closely with David Mercer on his first six television plays. It is hard to imagine that any two people could have been in closer contact as artists than we were. We discussed everything, we spend evenings together, lunched together, chatted in pubs together, went to dinner in each others' houses and involved our wives in the discussions – mine had always been at the heart of everything to do with my work from the beginning – and shared all the joys and disappointments of making drama. But I played no part in David's vivid personal life, nor, though I broadly shared his politics, the details of his political life, in CND and the New Left. We both talked about everything, but when either of us was in trouble outside the world of our shared work, I wasn't the first person David rang up, and nor was he the first whom I phoned. With other writers it might be necessary to have that complete personal involvement, but in the work I did with David it was not. We were the perfect artistic team, but our personal existences were separate.

Nor must you assume that this relationship will last for ever, or even for longer than one play. No artists have rights on each other, however closely they have worked together. As each one of you develops, it will eventually become essential that you should move away and work with other people. There are few lifelong teams in the history of the theatre, more often brief glorious flowerings. Our four years of close co-operation was rather long, as these things go. Then David went on to work with other directors, Alan Bridges, Anthony Page, David Jones and finally Alain Resnais, and the results, with their subtle differences of emphasis and tone from director to director, are there for everyone to see.

The nature of the professional relationship between writer and director has changed since I worked with David Mercer thirty years ago. Then, it never occurred to me that I should do anything other than exactly what he wished me to do. That didn't mean I abdicated my directorial responsibility. A director must never do that. Ultimately, the responsibility for the production is his, not the playwright's. If I felt something David intended wasn't quite working, I suggested something else, but it was never to attempt to change his meaning into mine, only to try to convey his meaning in a better way than his original text had conveyed it. In fact, this hardly ever happened. After his first play, which needed substantial re-writing, I can remember only one half-page scene in the eight plays of his I did which I didn't like, and which I encouraged him to change. He did so, unwillingly, certain he was right, but prepared to go along with me. Otherwise, with as much honesty as I could, I tried to do his plays exactly as they were written. When he wrote difficult things that were complex to communicate I didn't try to simplify them, but coped with the responsibility of presenting the complexity he intended. It never occurred to me to work in any other way with a living writer.

But there are now directors' courses in university Theatre Studies departments that tell their students that they must always ignore the author's stage directions, and at one such department, I spoke to a worried student who told me that his production of one of Pinter's short plays had been heavily criticised and marked down, because he hadn't taken an attitude to the play, and had simply done what the author said.

It is a piquant story referring to that particular author, whose views upon people who tamper with his plays are well known – and fierce. Quite right too. I imagine there isn't a living playwright who doesn't agree with him on that matter, one hundred per cent.

At bottom it is an ethical problem. When you have the responsibility of giving concrete form to a play that has never been performed before and exists only as a text, you must do everything you can to present your playwright's vision to the world exactly as he intends it to be presented. That seems to me to be a moral question, a sort of moral copyright is involved, a matter of ownership that is nothing to do with money. The director is still entirely responsible for everything he sees and hears on the stage, and he must encourage the playwright to change passages if he thinks they do not work. He must even be prepared to disagree with the playwright about how to stage a particular scene, if he is sure his way will present the playwright's meaning more clearly. The ethical issue arises when there is a doubt whose meaning is being presented. If the director is tempted into presenting his own vision by means of the playwright's play, then some sort of moral line has been crossed, and the playwright has justified cause for complaint. *Write your own play*, he can cry, *don't muck about with mine! If I'd wanted to do it that way, I would have written it that way!* It is a problem I can honestly say doesn't often arise with me, because I *can* write my own works to express what I want to say, and I don't feel the compulsion to change other people's. But with a lot of directors who feel themselves to be especially creative but are not writers, it can be a problem.

The fact of the matter is that if you change a new play fundamentally, you are changing forever the way in which it is presented to the world, and what you do to it will be judged by both audience and press as being the author's intention, not yours. Of course, the playwright, if he is lucky enough to get into print, can publish his full text, but that doesn't have the impact of the first production on the stage. If what you do as a director changes the play's meaning, as almost any significant modification must, then the playwright, if he has not agreed the change, has a right to feel that you have stolen his work. He may even feel tempted to withdraw your permission to perform the play, or take other legal action, though in practice playwrights hardy ever do, because it is a form of suicide. When Peter Coe, without telling me, savagely cut and paraphrased the first and completely rewrote the second act of *The Exorcism*, for his production at the Comedy Theatre, so that its meaning was horribly vulgarised and completely changed, I told my agent, the legendary Peggy Ramsay, that I wanted to withdraw the licence and stop the production. She quite simply replied, *Darling, if you do that, and close the production before the curtain goes up, no producer will ever touch you again.* An obvious truth. So I had to grin and bear it till the play closed, which, because of the death of its star, Mary Ure, wasn't long. Playwrights always lose in these circumstances. If they complain to the press it is always assumed they are merely whingeing, and they probably make the situation worse. It is always best to suffer in silence, and hope that you will have the pleasure of working with the kind of director – the great majority, of course – where the question of legal action never arises!

In the commercial theatre, both in America and England, there has been a long standing tradition, half theatre legend, but certainly half fact, of the play being completely rewritten during the out-of-town tour, of 'play doctors' arriving in Boston or Philadelphia, or tense scenes in Brighton or Bath. In this scenario the playwright is usually cast as a neurotic fool or wide-eyed innocent, who doesn't really know what he is doing, and who has to sit up all night with cigarettes and ice-packs writing a new second act, to please the producer, or the director, or the star, while the director is cast as the hero who saves the show. This certainly happens, in the real world, as well as in Hollywood musicals but it should not happen, and with serious playwrights and good directors, on the whole, it does not. There is a certain area of the commercial theatre, the home of the carpentered boulevard light comedy, thriller or farce, where the play is being constructed to fulfil some interpretation of what the audience wants, as a kind of market-researched product, and in that context there is no doubt that substantial rewriting during production will take place to ensure that the product will hit its target market fair and square; but this isn't really very much to do with the art of the theatre, and good playwrights and directors try to avoid becoming involved in such games. The playwright should not present his work till he is sure it has reached its final form and will work as he intends in the theatre. The producer and director should not accept the play until they are quite sure they like it and want to see it produced more or less as it stands, and if they do want changes made, as a condition of producing the play, they should make sure the rewrites are completed to everyone's satisfaction well before rehearsal begins. The need to rewrite substantially during rehearsal, and even more, during performance, is a sign of incompetence on someone's part, either the playwright, or the director, or more probably, both, and always causes great anguish within the company. The acid test of a play's viability always occurs when it meets its audience. Good playwrights and directors are people who can imagine this outcome in detail, and bring it to reality, on the page and on the stage. If what they imagine proves to be quite unlike what actually occurs, then they have done their work badly. If it happens regularly, they should seek another profession.

In recent years, a creature called a dramaturg has emerged in some theatres which have to consider a large number of plays and can afford to pay an extra administrator. This is a form of life which has existed for at least thirty years in television, bearing the much less romantic title of script editor, and mostly held in contempt in that medium by playwrights and directors alike. In large organisations like the BBC, the Royal National Theatre, RSC and Royal Court, which must expect to receive very large numbers of unsolicited scripts, the dramaturg performs an essential function of administration, encouragement and development. He or she must sort out the plays from established playwrights, which will always be more than any theatre can perform, even if they are all fine plays, and more importantly, he or she must sift through all the new plays by unknown writers, sent in by agents or unsolicited through the post, and try to recognise the gleams of real talent that will certainly be there, hidden among all the mud and gravel. Few busy directors running large theatres ever have the time to do this and they must find someone whose taste they can trust to go through the initial winnowing process, so that the plays that do show some talent can swiftly be passed on to the directors who might eventually stage them.

A good dramaturg can do other crucially important things too. He can go to hundreds of plays in performance, to find out where the new talent is lurking, and by creating workshops, introduction sessions and part-dramatised private readings can help new playwrights to see how their own work will function in performance.

What he should never do, is to start telling the playwright how to write his play. When a dramaturg begins to offer a raw talent discursive criticism of his work, and detailed suggestions as to what he should have done instead, the alarm bells should begin to ring. At that point the wise young playwright will walk away. A dramaturg who brings a playwright, particularly a young playwright, into his office, and lectures him on what he should have included, and what he has left out, of themes he would like to see developed further, or others which bore him, is simply crossing the line of his competence, and likely to damage the playwright's talent more often than improve it. To be a good dramaturg you need to be a cross between a genius and a saint, with the ability to understand plays and playwrights, and the self control to resist the temptation to start telling creative people how they should write. Any play can be written dozens of different ways, but a playwright picks his own way, which must be respected, because it is that individuality of personality in the long run that creates the good writer. The good dramaturg, sensing talent, maybe even raw talent that needs refining, should hand the playwright over to the director who is actually going to stage the play, and leave the two creative people to get on with it.

The giving of critical and creative power to the theatre dramaturg is the first step down the slippery slope which has destroyed television drama, towards the hegemony of the committee, where five, six or seven people have their say about the script, over the despairing writer's head, and the script gets blander and blander with every revision. Individuality is the key to all good art, and the fewer people who interfere with it the better. The director must interfere, because he is going to be the crucial partner in the play's creation, but like a good marriage, the relationship works when two people are involved, not three, or more. A playwright will respect changes from a good director, if trust has been established between them. The more people who meddle in his work, the less respectful he will become, till he might end up as one of those stony cynics who earn their living writing for television, who expect to be treated badly by self-regarding incompetents, and are seldom disappointed.

Naturally, small changes, to both text and action, occur all the time in the production of new plays, and playwrights, even if they don't like them, have to learn to put up with them, as part of the price of working with genuinely creative people. With a good director, even if he is persuaded to do some rewrites against his will, the playwright is probably still getting a good deal. Large changes, which change the play's structure or meaning, are a different matter, and it seems to me that a playwright has a right to have his own way over such things, even if, in the last analysis, the director thinks he is wrong. If he is, he will soon find out, and learn by the process. And if he is right, and the director's changes spoil the impact of the play, then the director has the play's probable death on his conscience, which, as far as playwrights are concerned, is as bad as any other kind of murder.

In Woody Allen's *Bullets over Broadway*, the playwright of genius, the hoodlum Cheech, shoots the actress who is ruining the play, and throws her in the river. The action is a brilliant comic metaphor for what all playwrights feel in their hearts about people who maltreat their imaginary children.

In the real world of the theatre, if the big disagreements occur, rights don't usually come into it. It becomes a question of power, who has the greatest pull. Usually it is the producer, or the artistic director, who provides the money and carries the responsibility, or the star, who brings the audience, who will get their way. Only rarely, in opposition to such powerful forces, is it the playwright

With an established modern play by a living or recently dead writer the situation is slightly different, morally, if not legally. An established playwright can legally compel a director to follow his wishes by the simple act of refusing a license to perform the play when it is requested. The estate of Samuel Beckett will not allow any changes at all to the text of the plays, and insists that the stage directions are minutely complied with, as Deborah Warner found out to her cost with her production of *Footsteps,* where some changes in the action, not the text, brought the full force of the Beckett estate down on her head.

I don't think there is ever much of a case for more than small practical cuts, dictated by the nature of the space and the resources of the performance, in an established modern text, but a case can be made for an imaginative interpretation, provided the playwright will allow it, and that will be a question of the character of each particular writer, or, more often, whether there is any genuine trust between the playwright and director. After all, a strong concept production is not likely to damage an established modern play, any more than it will damage Shakespeare or Euripides, and a good many playwrights – I am one of them – find it very exciting when a director applies a vivid imagination to their texts, *provided* it is done with integrity, out of a desire to make the text strike home more powerfully. In the case of Stephen Daldry's expressionist version of Priestley's *An Inspector Calls*, far from damaging the play, the director's work gave it a new lease of life. Each case will be judged on its merits, and if the playwright is prepared to trust a good director, all kinds of exciting things might be discovered, by the playwright about his own play, as much as by anyone else.

A particularly interesting case arose when I directed Edward Bond's *Bingo* on BBC Television in the summer of 1989. I regarded, and still regard, the play very highly, as one of the best written in English since the war, a very much more subtle creation than the Shakespeare-was-a-Tory-really simplification that the critical press usually presents. What Bond has actually achieved is a subtle metaphoric exploration of the despair of the man who has created King Lear but is himself fatally aware of his own complicity in the bleak world he has imagined, so that he can no longer even write about it, only play games with his fool in the snow, and die.

Because I was doing the play on television, where it had not been performed before, and because the tape was likely to last, and be seen by millions of people who had never been to an Edward Bond play in the theatre, I felt particularly responsible to the author, and told him I intended to direct the play in accordance with his wishes. The rehearsal was intense, difficult at times, but very exciting. Edward is a very demanding presence at rehearsal, not letting you get away with anything less than the fullest examination of his text, and again and again we found ourselves forced to look more closely at something we thought we had got right, only to find greater subtleties, and profounder depths.

When we came to the confrontation scene between Shakespeare and his daughter in the snow, in which the poet excoriates his child in the most terrifying manner, the actor, David Suchet, and I both decided to try to investigate what it means, in terms of character, to say things of this kind to your own flesh and blood. Both of us being fathers of girls, we felt the full horror of what the poet was saying, and began to investigate the pain which must lie behind such a confrontation. When Edward saw the scene, he said we had it completely wrong, that he was not concerned with the personal relationship between the two. Their relationship was entirely economic, the scene was taking place in a snow field. Yes, we said, we understood that, we realised the play's sub-title was 'scenes of money and death' but we wanted to explore the other path, to see where it would lead. *You can do it that way if you like*, said Edward, *but it's wrong*.

The actor and I talked quietly together. We both felt very strongly that it was the very antithesis of theatre work not to explore a path to see where it would lead, to say *no, that way is forbidden*. We wanted to follow our artistic instincts, to see what they would reveal. But we finally decided that we had a great respect for the playwright and his play, and we would act it in the icy way he asked, because, when it came to the point, it was his work, not ours, and when it was being preserved on tape, perhaps for very many years, he had a right to have the play done in the way he wanted. We did as he asked, the two characters became as frozen as the field which surrounded them, and it worked very well indeed. But I have often wondered what we would have discovered if we had pursued our investigations as far as we could. Perhaps it would have worked very well, seeing the characters suffering at what they were being compelled to say. Or perhaps, when we had completed the work, we would have realised that we had sentimentalised the scene, and found our own way back to what the playwright wanted, by doing the opposite, and recognising that it didn't work. I shall never know the answer to that.

I have often brooded since on Edward's dictum, *You can do it that way if you like, but it's wrong*, so against everything we are all taught to believe about the theatre. One's first reaction can't help but be outrage, to say *I must be free to follow my instinct, to try something, to fail if necessary, and in that way to learn*. But the more I have thought about it over the years, the simpler it seems to be. A play is a text, it cannot be defended, short of recourse to law, so that practically anyone can do what they like with it. But the living playwright knows what he intended, and if you violate that intention you are not allowing his play to live its own individual life. You are forcing your own will upon it, like a kind of rape. Like an art object, I turn the dictum round again and again and look at it from many different angles: and just as a play both changes as time passes and remains the same, so it is clearly wrongheaded and obviously true.

Not all playwrights adopt such an uncompromising stance, some invite you to explore their plays and find whatever you can in them: and with playwrights from the past you can never be so absolutely sure of the details of their meaning as to follow such an undeviating line. But when a director is confronted with a living playwright whose work he respects who makes such demands of him, he has to have extremely good reasons to reject them.

Some time later, I thought of the great scene in *Oedipus at Colonus* in which the old Oedipus curses his son in terms that make your flesh creep. It is clear enough that to soften or personalise that scene would destroy it. There is no forgiveness in Oedipus's tirade, nothing Christian, just the stark outline of choices in the ancient world, and political crimes too great to be forgiven. Bond, who has always had something of the Greek tragedian about him, in his seriousness about public issues and his refusal to compromise his bleak vision, shakes hands with Sophocles across the centuries, in his picture of a social nexus which has destroyed the natural relationship between a father and child, and by entangling it in the destructive network of money, turned it into hatred.

As a brief comment on the whole question of playwrights and directors, two examples from the American theatre.

In *The Crucible* (1953), Arthur Miller wrote a short scene, between scene two and three, in which Proctor meets Abigail in the forest. It was removed during rehearsal, but printed in early editions of the play. With the author's permission, I included it in my 1981 television production, but in the theatre it it not usually played.

Elia Kazan insisted that Tennessee Williams should write a new third act for *Cat on a Hot Tin Roof* (1955). The playwright was unhappy, but, with characteristic generosity, afterwards wrote, *No living playwright that I can think of hasn't something to learn about his own work from a director so keenly perceptive as Elia Kazan.* Now Williams's original third act is usually played.

We have come a long way from selecting plays, and making relationships with living playwrights, and we could go a good deal further. The choices made at this stage will qualify everything else that happens in the production, and if fundamental errors have been made at the start, it will be almost impossible to rectify them later. If you have chosen the wrong play, the wrong playwright, or the wrong production idea, you are very likely to be stuck with them and must do the best you can in the circumstances.

In fact, many other less artistic considerations will probably qualify your choice of play. What the theatre space is like, how much money you have and how many actors you can afford, whether the theatre has a regular audience or must create one for each play, are all questions that will have to be seriously considered. In addition, you may be working for a theatre that is following a particular policy, which will restrict your choice to a few popular plays. You can be sure that if you are brave enough to be presenting a new play by an unknown writer, you will have to struggle to find any audience at all. The English public is very conservative at the moment, unwilling to go in anything but the smallest numbers to see a play by a writer it has not heard of.

However, the play will eventually be chosen, the production process will begin, and a whole host of more practical problems will confront the director. They may not have philosophical and aesthetic implications, as the questions we have been considering so far certainly do, but they are no less important to the eventual success of the production.

3

Preparation

Direction is a juxtaposition of two very different kinds of talent, the creative-imaginative, and the practical-administrative. A creative genius who cannot plan is likely to be a quite disastrous director, and a brilliant planner with no creative insight will be just as bad. There are, of course, plenty of examples of both, making prosperous careers in the theatre.

One of the key qualities a director requires is the ability to be aware of problems and to create strategies for solving them before they happen, not as they are happening or after they have happened. The theatre is a powerful metaphor, because the opening night, like death, will certainly happen. Even more frighteningly, it will happen on an entirely predictable and unchangeable date. For theatre workers, unlike people in industrial management or finance or administration, there is no changing of schedules, no excuse accepted for inefficiency, no late delivery of raw materials or administrative cock-up to blame. If the play is a shambles, for whatever particular reasons, it will still open, and be seen for what it is. There is nowhere to hide. This concentration, this sense that a great deal must be done, and will be done, in a finite and usually too-short time, means that pre-planning becomes a crucial part of the process. If you can go some way towards identifying and solving all the problems, artistic and administrative, in your head in the silence of your study, you will have a much better chance of solving them in the rehearsal room or on the stage, when the clock is remorselessly ticking its countdown to curtain.

So, the text of the play is in your hands, it has been agreed between you and the writer that it is in its final form, or at least the form in which it will go into rehearsal, and all your background reading and research is done. What next?

By this time you will have had your principal ideas about how and why you are going to produce this particular play, and how you are going to release the playwright's vision on the stage. These ideas you will have communicated to your designer and costume designer, and you will now have worked through the processes I shall consider in Chapter 4, so that you will probably have in your hands a theatre plan, and a fully three-dimensional model-box, containing a scale model, made in balsa wood and cardboard and probably painted, of what your set is going to look like. A thoughtful designer will also have provided you with a series of to-scale human figures, which don't fall over as soon as you put them onto the model stage and your costume designer will have provided you with most of the required costume sketches. In spite of the ideal situation I outlined in the preceding chapter, in the real world this work will normally have to be done in good time for the beginning of rehearsal, and perhaps well before. The director, unless he is going to lead an experimental adventure into the text, will need to have sufficient time before rehearsal with the model and plans in his hands, so as to allow his own imagination to work.

How much work the director does at this stage, and how detailed it is, depends upon the complexity of the play and the personality of the director. Some do no conscious preparation, or at least none that will be committed to detail on paper, and they rely on the thoughts they have accumulated emerging in a coherent form when rehearsals begin. Others go into the most meticulous detail, planning the play almost to the last move and stage effect. There is no right way or wrong way. What will suit each director best will be the method that for him or her delivers the goods, has the play ready, creative and alive, on opening night.

But some points might still be made.

It can be useful to produce the whole play in your mind or on your model, taking care to solve all the problems of blocking and structure, and understanding all the tensions in the text, speech by speech, as comprehensively as you can. It is particularly important when you have a large scale play, with a lot of characters and some spectacular scenes, and this is where your little model actors will be very useful. You can move them about the stage, and get some idea of how your blocking will look, what the lighting will do for you, and what stage pictures you can create. Movement of large numbers of people in relationship to each other is very difficult to plan, even with model actors, because the exact relationship of many movements to each other is impossible to imagine in a precise manner. In your head you may see your swirling crowd, streaming across the stage, and it will create a great emotional turmoil within you, but you will not see your inner pictures in detail, in terms of the exact relationship of particular characters to particular stage objects. On your model with your plasticine

actors, you can set out a series of static approximations to those
moves, but quite without the emotional charge the inner eye gives
you. Neither method is adequate as a description of what will actually
occur when you begin to manipulate your real people on your real
stage, but both techniques represent a useful preparation.

Even when you are dealing with a play that concerns no more than
two or three characters in a room, it is good to work out a complete
scenario in your head, or in your production note book, though you
are well aware that you are likely to change the whole plan in
rehearsal, when the actors will make their own demands. When I
directed my play *Retreat from Moscow,* with no more than four characters in a single room, I produced a complete production plan, move
for move, and climax by climax, but working with four very creative
actors whose contribution was as positive as I had expected it to be,
I threw all the pre-planning away during the first week-and-a-half,
and together with the actors, created a new blocking scenario. That
doesn't mean the work was wasted. The intellectual discipline of
having created the whole finished production within my head before
meeting the actors, stood me in very good stead when I did meet
them. I knew the play extremely well, and I had formulated in my
mind workable solutions to all the major problems of staging, so
when those problems came up in rehearsal, I knew the parameters of
choice that were available to me, and could make the decisions,
which the actors required in order to make their own contributions
true, quickly and honestly. I was never left stumped, not knowing
what to do next, or abdicating my responsibility and letting the actors
get on with it, both disastrous situations for a director in rehearsal.

The actors, too, will have done some preparation, and some of
them will have done a great deal, but it will usually have been solely
to do with their own part, not the play as a whole. The director's job
is to co-ordinate all those individual contributions, and then to fuse
them into a single statement, by contributing the warmth and passion
of his own interpretation.

But however detailed your planning has been, even in the case of
large scale spectacular scenes, it must be tested, even to destruction,
in practice, and you must be prepared to sacrifice it to actors' needs
or staging imperatives, or what is the process of rehearsal for?
Directors who stick rigidly to their pre-planning are usually bad directors. The pre-planning is a starting-point, a foundation, and in most
cases, the stronger and better set the foundations, the stronger the
house that rises upon them will be.

However, making all your decisions in rehearsal can be an equally
dangerous process, because you may be allowing practical consider-

ations only to inform your choices. In a defined space, with a particular group of actors, an obvious way of doing the scene will usually
suggest itself. The shape of the stage, or the personality of the actors
will indicate ideas, which may be very good ones indeed, and the
ones you will eventually follow. Certainly, only a crazy director takes
no notice of the nature of his theatrical space, or the personalities of
his actors. But it is equally foolish to let the space and the people
produce the play for you. The obvious way is by no means always the
best way. There needs to be some vision, some imagination at work,
so that the meeting of imagined pictures and emotions and the real
space and people creates the tension and excitement of a genuine
theatrical event. You must use your imagination in your pre-planning,
if you are not to let the obvious moves and effects be dictated to you
by circumstance. But you must equally be prepared to throw all your
planning away, even your most cherished effects and ideas, if the
reality of rehearsal suggests something better. The meeting of pure
imagination and practical experience is the very essence of what the
idea of theatre means. That clash, and the spark it sometimes
produces, creates the most exciting kind of dramatic illumination.

But direction, like anything else worthwhile, is not all blinding
insights and creative epiphanies. There is a great deal of mundane
organisation, list-making and day-structuring, in a good director's
routine work. The time certainly isn't wasted. If you have made sure
that everyone arrives when they should and that your own and your
actors' time is used to best effect, the epiphanies and insights are more
likely to arrive. If your rehearsals are a confusion of people not being
present when they are wanted, or sitting around all day doing
nothing, and rehearsal plans not completed when they should be, you
can be quite sure they won't.

A schedule of scenes or sections to rehearse is almost the most
important thing when you sit down to consider how you will work on
the play. You may not feel you wish to communicate the whole
schedule to the actors at the beginning, so as to leave the opportunity
to make changes in the last week to suit the progress of rehearsal. But
you should certainly have a detailed pattern clear in your own mind.
If you do decide to issue a fully detailed rehearsal schedule on day
one, the actors will love you for it, but however much you insist that
the schedule is provisional they will invariably assume it is definitive,
and you may find that if you do want to change it, at least one or two
of the actors will have arranged something else, a voice-over or an
audition, on the assumption that they had a certain day free. Of
course, they are contracted to you, and your show must come first,
but they will feel annoyed if they have to cancel work or the possi-

bility of work, and you will feel a heel for asking them to. It will be an extra cause of tension you can well do without.

If it's a mistake to be too generalised, and have actors sitting wasting their time because you have not been specific enough about what you intend to rehearse when, it is even more of a mistake to be too detailed. I once knew of a director who would have his rehearsal schedule mapped out like a train-timetable, or an invasion-plan. An actor would be told he would be required to rehearse a scene at eleven twenty-eight, and the next actor would be called at eleven forty-four, or whenever. Rehearsal is not a mechanical engine whose movements can be accurately predicted. If something genuinely creative occurs during work on a scene, it is sure to take time to explore its full implications, and if you have the next lot of actors turning up precisely to the half minute, your schedule is soon going to collapse. You should look at your scenes, try to estimate how much juice might be in them, make sure you allow sufficient time to squeeze all of it out, and then allow a little further time for a second pressing. You will soon learn what your own working methods are like, and how best to accommodate them. Rehearsal time is the most precious resource you have, and should never be wasted waiting for actors you have not called early enough, or trying to hurry work that needs longer to come to fruition, because half a dozen grumpy actors are sitting behind you looking at their watches.

On the last run-through, before you move into technical rehearsals, the play should be ready to meet its audience, fully-rehearsed, and running as sweetly as you had originally imagined it would. It will be too late to make major changes before the audience arrives, and all the big questions should have been thought through and solved a week before, so that cast and director are ready to see how the play goes in front of its first spectators. To achieve this, you should have been able to run the play two or three times complete, and without pause, in the last week of rehearsal. The actors should, from about the Tuesday of the last week onwards, be able to give a full performance of the play to the empty rehearsal room or theatre, perhaps to a few observing technicians, or even, in carefully chosen circumstances, trusted friends. There must still be time for detailed rehearsal in the last week, and the opportunity to re-rehearse and even substantially change details of any scene, but unless the play is extremely long, that should not be a problem. Even if you decide that, for the sake of fluency, you want a fully-performed run-through every day – and there is a great deal that good actors will learn about a play and their own parts simply by playing it through – a run will not normally take more than a morning or an afternoon, and in either case you will have the other half of the day for detailed rehearsal. If something is always going wrong at the same place and in the same way, it will probably not solve itself merely by running, and you will have to work on it to get it right. Otherwise, it is remarkable how many things you note in your book as needing rehearsal will mysteriously get themselves right in the process of running the play through.

In order to be able to run the play fluently in the last week – I am assuming the professional norm of a four week rehearsal period – all the work of breakdown of the text and action and discovery of its meaning for this particular production, will need to have taken place in the previous two weeks. The week before that, the first week of rehearsal, will have been devoted to blocking the play, and if you can complete the blocking, even sketchily, by the end of the first week, so much the better. Let me emphasise that this is the normal and conventional rehearsal schedule. Each director will modify it to suit his or her own needs, and directors who employ theatre games and improvisation techniques will modify it very substantially. In some visually-oriented or non-script-based productions, the final pattern of moves is often one of the very last things to be decided.

Whatever your method, when planning your schedule, consider your actors. Don't call them at ten o'clock, and then make them stay around all day to deliver a single line at four. Don't, unless there are particular reasons for doing so, or the cast is very small and on hand more or less all the time, necessarily rehearse the play in scene order. Scene order rehearsals can be very useful in helping you and your actors to see how the play grows organically, but you will have a much happier company, and probably work more efficiently yourself, if you schedule all the scenes played by a particular group on the same day, rather than calling them four days in a row to do one scene each day. Don't shackle your work by being over-considerate to your actors, but do remember they are artists, not navvies, and if you treat them well and have their interests at heart, they will perform better for you. There are directors who believe in disturbing and upsetting their actors, breaking them down in order to get more out of them, but I am not one of them. It's surprising how quickly you can get through a scene and solve its difficulties with a fresh actor who is keen to work, and how like wading through treacle it can be if the actor has waited five hours for his scene, and his brain is tired and bored.

Good actors will usually master the words in the first week unless the part is very long. Always encourage your actors to get the words at least loose-learned as soon as you can. No one can really begin to act, or discover what their part might contain, while they are still chained to the book. Always be suspicious of the actor who consciously refuses to learn the part till late on. Some of them will say that they don't want to learn it, because they want to keep their options open till the last minute, but this will make life difficult for you, and for all the other actors. It's usually a selfish actor who takes that particular line. Acting, unless it is solo, is at least fifty percent how you relate to the actors you are playing with, and an actor who doesn't know his script is not only unable to get his own timing with the other actors sensibly rehearsed, he is also preventing them, although they may be dead-letter-perfect, from sorting out their timing too. And of course, from the director's point of view, the orchestration of scenes becomes impossible if the actors cannot work at the speed, intensity or particular timbre you require. If an actor refuses to learn early, then the director has a problem, which can only be solved as all such problems are solved, with tact and cunning. If on day one you clearly announce to the actors when you want them to put their scripts down, there will be no room for misunderstanding.

However, it isn't only the actors you have to consider. The costume-makers will need to call the actors away from rehearsal for fittings, and so will wig-makers, if you have any. Directors always find such necessities infuriating, especially in rehearsal time, but the jobs are important and must be done, and it is the director's responsibility to schedule his rehearsals so as to include time for wardrobe and make-up appointments, without wasting the valuable time of either side.

Stage technicians and lighting designers will also eagerly seize on every element of careful pre-planning you can give them. You will, at some stage, at least a week before you go into the theatre, convey to your lighting designer what lighting effects or simple illuminations you require, and the more precise detail you can give at this stage, the more subtle and sophisticated your lighting is likely to be. Challenge your lighting designer's imagination if you can, so that you enthuse him or her with your vision of the play. Do drawings and sketches by all means if you are good at them, and if your visual imagination is sufficiently precise. But evocative words and moody descriptions can as often inspire your designer into coming up with something special. Don't, unless you are an experienced lighting designer yourself, try to do your colleague's job. The theatre is a collaborative art, and you are more likely to get a startling result, if you can inspire someone else's imagination, than if you dictate lamp by lamp what you want. A typed schedule, detailing each scene as you want to see it, and whatever changes you envisage within or between scenes, will work wonders. If you are lucky enough to have a widely experienced or particularly distinguished lighting designer, pay him or her proper respect by giving them a great deal of room for an original contribution. The final decision is the director's, of course, but as with a great actor, you don't work with the best and then dictate to them as if they were beginners. There is, throughout the theatre, a deep respect for great talent and wide experience, something which is, perhaps, now not shared by society as a whole. In the theatre we know who our great people are and how much they are worth, and it is a very foolish director who ignores the respect conferred by proven genius and long experience, in the technical fields, quite as much as among actors and writers.

All technicians tend to feel a little outside the play, particularly if they are a part of a regular theatre team which does many plays, and you are just the next on the list. It is always good to make your fly men or stage hands feel as much a part of the production as the leading actors, however hard-bitten they are, and it will help if you can produce for them too carefully worked out and detailed sheets of what they are required to do and when. Then, even if you have to change it all during the technical, they will have a solid basis from which to work.

Preparation of this kind, trying to foresee and help solve everyone's difficulties, not just your own, is what marks out the really good director. He is the captain of the ship, the leader of the team, and it is his job to see that everyone working under him, from the star to the humblest temporary worker in the box office, is happy in what they are doing. For those working on the production itself, this will mean giving them confidence that the show has been thought through, and proving it by showing them detailed schedules of how it will work. Administrative and imaginative pre-planning won't create a show full of directoral genius, but if you have any of that true fire within you, it will ensure that it gets the opportunity to blaze.

Casting

By far the most important element of preparation the director must undertake is casting the play. After the script itself, the actors are the most important element of the production, more important, when it comes to the point, than the director. The actors, if they have to, can perform the play without the director, but without actors there is no play.

Sometimes a director will not have a choice of cast. If you are directing a play for a standing company, you will know when you sign your contract that you must work with an existing set of actors, and your skill and experience will then be devoted to working out which particular members of the group should play which part. If the company has a resident artistic director, even this choice may not be available. The artistic director, responsible for the not-always-easy task of keeping a group of actors happy over a season, may well have cast the whole play, and present you with a fait accompli. If that is the case, he will almost certainly have been experiencing some difficulties, and he will put a word in your ear where the tensions are likely to lie, who feels their part is not the one they wanted, and who is snapping at whose heels. If he tells you that a certain actress is a fearful old bitch, or the leading man eats ingenues for breakfast, keep a corner of your mind open, but be prepared to believe him. That sort of insider information is always worth listening to.

Working in the commercial theatre you may well be presented with a package, a play and a star, or several leading actors, already contracted. If that is the case, they are probably more important than you are, and you take it or leave it. However tempting the offer, you must always make sure that you can get on with the leading actors in question, and that you are going to be able to have at least some of your own way. You must find a good social opportunity to meet them, to talk to them in private, and attempt to establish a rapport. It is as well to remember that it is unlikely to be a one-sided business. You will probably be attending an audition yourself, as much as finding out about your actor. Sometimes you may find yourself saying *oh yes, I can work with him,* only to find that he thinks you are a revoltingly opinionated little shit, and has told your agent so. Some star actors are self-centred brutes, whose only consideration is that they should emerge with their own version of their reputation enhanced. With such an actor, unless you are very subtle in your approach, or can employ the cunning learned by years of dealing with such people, you will only be able to do what the actor will let you do, and you must weigh up that situation with the greatest care. If it comes to a power struggle, you will probably lose, because you will be sacked before the actor. You, unless you are one of the select company of top flight international directors, are not going to fill the theatre, and the producer thinks the star is, which is why he has hired him. If you go into a commercial production without that situation quite clear in your mind, you are likely to run into trouble. On an artistic level too, a production which has only been half-directed, because the star insisted on going his own way, can never do more than limp along, and will never give you any satisfaction, even if it pays the bills.

Most stars, of course, justify their great reputations, and it is a privilege to work with them, something you will remember and treasure all your life. They will never let you get away with anything sloppy, and they will give your ideas the most rigorous examination. That is why they are stars. You should welcome that sort of testing. If you can manage to release their great talents in the service of the play, you will have the happiest and most satisfying time a theatre director can have.

Casting the rest of such a play may well be left to you, in consultation with your producer, who has hired you after making up the initial package of play and star. Your choices will probably be rather restricted there too, because high profile commercial plays tend to be cast from a fairly small circle of known actors. But you will know all these things when you take on the job. Directing a play in the commercial theatre has something in common with riding a tiger, and most people can recognise a tiger when they see one. They have yellow and black stripes, and they eat people. If you don't recognise the tiger you are riding, and think it's a donkey which will go exactly where you tell it to go, you may well end up a gnawed bone in a cage.

In most cases, though, you will be responsible for casting the whole play, and it is a process most directors dislike intensely. Meeting actors is always a delight, though it can be a tiring process when you are meeting fifteen or twenty a day. It is the necessity to make a choice between a group of human beings that is the problem, particularly as the choice, which you know might make or destroy your production, has to be made based on insufficient information. When the choice is finally made, it is as often as not an inspired hunch or gut reaction that makes it. Most times you will eventually feel that you made the right choice, that you found a way of making the part live through a particular actor, even though your intellect will tell you that you could probably have been as successful, in different ways, with any one of a hundred actors. If you don't feel that your choices have turned out well, and if this is a regular feeling, you had better pack up being a director, or employ a casting director you can trust to do the job for you.

There are some purists who say that any good actor can play any part, within approximate age ranges. Theoretically that is so, and each good actor will illuminate the part slightly differently. But all directors have within themselves a kind of half-defined feeling of what sort of person the imaginary character is, and there is a sense in which that essence of character is not finally actable, can only be, and you must cast the right person as well as the best artist. If an actor's personality is outgoing, aggressive, brash and upfront, he might well be able to act a fine Hamlet, but you might feel that an actor of a naturally philosophical nature and sharply probing mind might be an even better one. These things are a matter of the very finest shades of instinct, not mere type casting. After all, in the English profession, with its very high standards, you will probably be faced with ten actors, all of whom look right, and all of whom are good enough actors to illuminate the part. But only one can play it. Inevitably you will have to make a fine psychological judgement, on almost no evidence at all except for instinct – or reputation, if you know the actor's work – as to which of the ten actors has the qualities you have imagined as necessary for the part most deeply within his nature. Finally, you take a chance, and you jump, hoping that you will land where you want to be – or at least, somewhere.

So where do you find your actors ?

As part of your training as a director you should have visited hundred of productions, so you will have seen thousands of actors working. Television and the cinema will broaden that experience further, though very few actors work at all regularly in those media, and there are great numbers of fine actors who have never done a television play or film in their lives. There is no substitute for personal knowledge, seeing actors work, and getting to know some of them as your friends. But however conscientious you are, that knowledge will never be comprehensive enough.

The acting profession in England is organised around the agent system, and *Spotlight,* the actors' directory – the director's indispensable database and permanent torture-chamber. All directors hate turning the pages of *Spotlight* for the thousandth time, and they all know it is the one indispensable book without which they cannot do their work. What it does is to remind you. A posed face with an agent's logo or a personal phone number is no use to you on its own, and if you don't know who the people are they very quickly blend into an all-purpose actor/actress image as you wearily turn the pages. But the faces jog your memory, remind you of a fine performance, or an odd play, or just an actor you have already worked with, or met socially, but who has temporarily slipped your mind. In certain cases, if you are looking for a particular kind of face above all, the photographs alone may lead you to the person you want. But you must always take care, and particularly consult the date beneath the photograph, if there is one. Some actors do not change their photographs as often as they should, and it is by no means only actresses who sometimes present an image of themselves which is not at all in accord with current reality. I am not the only director, I am sure, who has on occasions hardly recognised the person coming through the door as the photograph on my desk. The thing not to do on these occasions is to say, *hallo, who are you?* Faces remain fundamentally the same, they simply age in different ways, and you will soon see that the person on the page and the person in front of you are one and the same. If you are in any doubt, ring the agent before you arrange an appointment, and discuss your needs, tactfully but frankly, or even, if the actors have no agent, speak to them on the phone. That can be a little embarrassing, but is a great deal less embarrassing than saying, *oh, come in, but I'm afraid you're much too old, you really do look much older than your photograph.* Certain artists, at this point, might kick you in the groin, and you would deserve it. Actors and actresses are their appearances, their looks are an important part of their livelihood, and a director who cannot handle them with the necessary tact, and respect the pressures of an actor's life, is not up to the demands of the job.

Photographs can deceive in other ways too. That aristocratic young girl, who has all the hauteur and beauty for the Princess you are casting, may turn out to have an Essex accent you can cut with a breadknife. The days when all actors would have received pronunciation English in addition to their own native accents, are, I'm afraid, no longer with us. Actors who send photographs through the post usually accompany them with a detailed CV, which will give you some idea of what kind of actors they are and what they can do, but Spotlight photos rarely contain much real information, so if you are arranging to meet someone based upon their photograph alone, it is as well to remember that photography, like film-making, is a wonderfully sophisticated form of lying, and you will only know what you have really arranged to meet when a human being walks through the door and begins to speak.

The other great instrument of a director's working life is the agent system, which grew up in the theatre during the 1930s and 1940s and is now world-wide. As you begin to work as a director you should build up close working relationships with at least half a dozen agents. They will always be available to chat to you on the phone in great detail about your needs, or your current problems, or indeed, about life in general in some cases. Of course, they want to sell you the actors and actresses they personally represent, but the best of them, and indeed, in my experience, the majority, are not hard-nosed salesmen. They will happily tell you who they think is right for the part, even if it is not one of their own, and the others, the ones who barely listen to what you say, and then send you a standard list of their clients, whether they are suitable for the part or not, you will soon learn to recognise, and avoid. The good agent will listen carefully to your description of the part, and then send you the two or three people among her clients she thinks best suited for the role. I

use the female pronoun advisedly, because very many of the best
agents are resourceful and knowledgeable women. With the ones
who are really helpful, who won't waste your time by sending you
wildly unsuitable people, and who will occasionally make brilliant
suggestions that hadn't occurred to you, you rapidly build up a close
and continuing relationship, which can last, in some cases, for thirty
years or more. The odd thing is that these are usually entirely tele-
phonic relationships, a voice at the end of the phone, with whom you
can be relaxed, chatty, flirtatious and even quite intimate at times,
though you both know that this is merely a way of oiling the wheels
of a professional relationship, making work a more pleasant process.
Of all the agents with whom I have had the closest working relationships, I have met only one or two face to face, by accident, at a party,
or a first night. It is always a surprise of course, because they never
look at all the way their voices sound. I wonder if they get as much
of a surprise when they see me?

Not all actors, of course, are in *Spotlight* or have agents, and in these
disastrous times for the theatre profession, when even actors who have
been in the business forty years will sometimes agree to work for
nothing, and young actors entering the profession will be lucky if they
have more than one or two properly paid jobs in several years, some
of the best among the new intakes do not have Agents, and can only
be found among the anonymous quarter page photographs at the end
of *Spotlight* sections, if there. You will only find such actors by great
patience and hard work. If you see as many fringe shows – where the
actors are almost inevitably unpaid – as you can, and plays in the less
well known regional theatres, you will get some idea of who is new on
the scene and what they can do. Otherwise, if you publicise your
productions through *The Stage* and *PCR*, you will receive a great many
letters, which you must conscientiously wade through. Some will clearly
be unsuitable, from their photographs and CV's, but you must see as
many of the rest as you have time for, in the certain knowledge that
though most of them won't be very good, some of them will be the real
thing, perhaps even great actors in embryo, and it might be you who
gives them that first chance.

The actual process of holding auditions always represents a crucial
moment in the creating of any play. Deep down, it is an uneasy business, and I am sure I am not the only director to find it one of the
most demanding aspects of the profession. Not only is someone's
livelihood at stake, but their self respect as well is on the line. In my
first few professional productions, when I was a very young director,
I found the whole process uncomfortable and almost demeaning,
feeling the nakedness of the needs sometimes expressed at me across

the desk particularly starkly. After a time one develops a thicker skin, a professional manner, a way of putting both the actor and oneself at ease, but it is never an easy business, and is always to be approached with great care. After all, however thoughtful and courteous you may wish to be to the actor before you, the success of your production, and ultimately your own livelihood, is on the line too.

An audition is, in fact, a little drama in itself, a kind of conflict which can resolve in different ways. The actor wants the job, and if not the job, a job. Having decided he is good enough to be a professional, he has to think he is the best person you could possibly find for the part, and that self-belief is at stake every single time he confronts a director across a desk. The director, on the other hand, has to make a series of very important judgements in a very short time, and upon very flimsy evidence.

All directors conduct auditions in their own way, but I shall outline my own technique, before trying to comment upon some others.

Assuming this is an actor whose work I do not know, or know only by discussion with an agent, I usually begin by chatting generally about the play, or asking the actor to tell me something about his work. This part of the audition is important, because it will help to put the actor at ease. Most actors sitting across a desk from you will be nervous; young or inexperienced actors will be very nervous, and if you can't help them to relax you will probably not get a clear idea of what they can do. If an actor does not do him or herself justice at an audition, you, as director, have failed as much as the actor has. You have not created the situation where the actor can relax and demonstrate the qualities he has. You have missed a chance.

The chat might be about anything at all, some general subject of theatrical interest, a mutual friend or acquaintance, or a new play. Eventually you will bring the conversation round to the play you are doing and the parts uncast, and the actor will screw up his concentration, knowing that you are approaching the point. You must tell the actor all you think he or she ought to know about a play before confronting him or her with a text. When I am auditioning for a leading part, I always talk for some time about the play, the story line, the characters, and what the author is trying to express in his work. This is not wasted time or a director's ego trip. All the time you are watching and listening to how the actor is reacting to what you say. Quite often, with more senior actors who will not be expected to read from the script, but will come to meet you, there is nothing beyond this fairly generalised chat, and you must gain as much information from how the actor reacts to what you say, and his own contribution to the conversation, as you need to enable you to make a decision.

With other actors you will then ask them to read a scene, or maybe several scenes from the play. Don't, as a rule, or without great confidence in your actors, ask them to sight-read. That tests nothing but their sight-reading. You must give them adequate time to read the scene through to themselves, and be prepared to elucidate details or larger ideas about the play before you ask anyone to read aloud with you. Nine times out of ten you will know within a few words whether the actor is any good, though not necessarily whether he is suitable for the part you are trying to cast. Be prepared to stop the actor within the scene to offer him direction, perhaps even in some detail. There are many ways to play most parts, and the actor may not automatically light upon the one that suits you. A good actor will see the point of what you are saying, and try to do what you ask. From this process you will learn a lot, not only about whether the actor can do the part in the way you want it done, but also about how flexible he is, and how he takes direction. Top-rate actors, though they have their own opinions about a role, which will come out in rehearsal, can, like top-rate musicians, perform with equal skill and commitment in whatever way the conductor/director requires of them. If, after you have made a detailed comment on an actor's reading, described a new way of doing the part, to which the actor has eagerly assented, he then reads it in exactly the same way, with every nuance and timing unchanged, you will know this is a limited actor, and on the whole, to be avoided. Bad actors are rarely absolutely incompetent, though a sad few are. They are more often simply dull, they lack width of imagination, they read only, and even that they do with no insight. You never dismiss such an actor summarily, even if you are clear at once he is no good. It is a human being you are dealing with, not an animal. Always let the actor finish the scene you asked him to prepare if you don't intend to go any further with him. Then when he finishes, you can thank him for his reading, and for coming to see you, and promise to let him know your decision as soon as possible. Only with an actor you are very interested in should you interrupt after a few lines. You may see at once that this person is an exceptional talent, and want him to read something more central to the role. In that case, the actor will enjoy being interrupted. You must always bear in mind that any actor, simply by being interviewed, is in something of a humiliating position, and you should go out of you way not to add to the humiliation. Every actor you meet should tell his or her friends that they enjoyed the audition with you, and think they did pretty well. No one should ever leave an audition you conduct hot with shame and humiliation. Some will, inevitably, but it should not be your fault. Being rude or aggressive to actors is something only second-raters and charlatans do, or a small group of sadistic directors who convince themselves they can learn something by upsetting and disorienting people. They may well be learning something about themselves, but they rarely learn anything useful about actors. You don't expect a clarinettist to play well for you if you smash him across the lips with the back of your hand, nor should you expect an actor to reveal what he has locked up in the depths of his psyche, if you go out of your way to bruise it. The people before you are artists, which means they have set themselves the task of doing one of the most difficult things a human being can do, express the truth of themselves and the world around them through art, and actors, to make it worse, use as their expressive instrument their own bodies and personalities. That demands respect, and should always get it from a director.

If you can tell whether an actor is good or bad within a few words, how is it done? There is no absolute touchstone, but a good actor, when reading, immediately makes you unaware of the script in his hand. He memorises a line or two, so that he looks you in the eyes, he modulates the words through his voice, using tone colours and little pauses, so that he sounds to you as if he is saying the words for the first time, not reading. Average actors read well, intelligently, with some feeling, but they read. There is a detachment, no spark or flame leaps across the desk. You, as a director, must always read as well as you can, with as much acting truth and technique as you can manage. Acting is an interactive art, actors feed upon each other all the time in performance, and if every line you say hits the floor, then what chance does the actor have, trying to pick up the scene every other line? If you are a very bad reader, get an ASM who can read well to work with you, or you won't give your actors a chance.

On some memorable occasions, there is a true fire passing back and forth across the desk, you read with a good actor, and something real is created, there and then. Those are fine moments, and to be treasured. My first meetings with Juliet Stevenson, very early on in her career, and Michael N. Harbour, stand out, among many others, as occasions when I knew at once I was in the same room with a considerable talent.

Reading auditions, of course, have their dangers, because some people are very fluent readers, but can't really act, and some fine actors stumble and sound most uncertain at a first reading. There is no way of coping with those dangers except by exercise of your judgement and instinct, vital qualities, without which you cannot be a director at all. You must judge whether the fluent reading will go any further, or simply be the same on the stage as it was on the first day, by which time all the other actors will have long overtaken it.

Similarly, you must try to hear the truth behind the stumbling sentences of the good actor who can't read well. You must listen hard, and look penetratively, and you will still make some mistakes, which will serve you in good stead the next time. I have more often made mistakes by overvaluing the fluent reader who can't really act, than by failing to see beyond a stumbler. But that is perhaps a fact about me, and my principal concern with texts, rather than a general truth.

The audition process should never take less than about a quarter-of-an-hour, and in the case of an actor you are interested in, it is more likely to be thirty minutes than twenty, and might stretch to an hour. I realise that some directors will not agree, that they will feel that they can happily wheel actors in and out, giving them not much more time than it takes to say their name and read a few sentences. Of course, directors are always pressed for time, because no play ever has as much rehearsal or preparation time allocated to it as it needs. But if you can only allow three days for auditions, it is much better to see twenty-four actors and give them a chance to show what they can do, than to drag in forty or fifty, and be conscious of nothing more than an emoting blur. It is up to you to choose the people you really want to see, and be prepared to live with your choice. We are not working in a meat market, but in the most subtle profession, in terms of human relationships, there is. Time, courtesy and respect are the least qualities actors should demand from a director, and if they don't get them, then the director should sink in their estimation.

There are, of course, many other ways of conducting auditions, and my own way, which was probably pretty universal in 1960, when I started, I would guess to be in a minority by now. Younger directors are much more concerned with movement skills, improvisation and mime than I am, and these qualities cannot be judged sitting at a desk. From my own point of view, I assume that any decent professional actor knows how to use his body expressively, I loathe mime more than I can say, and being a writer, I have not much time for improvisation, which seems to me more often than not a sloppy use of language without a writer's guiding sense of decorum and taste.

But many directors nowadays prefer this workshop approach, they will call actors for auditions that last half a day or longer, and they will get them to play theatre games, use improvisation techniques, both verbal and non-verbal, and sometimes do very little work on the script they are to present, even if at that stage it exists. Their idea, I imagine, is that by observing actors in a much freer situation than being confined behind a desk, and seeing how they react to all kinds of unexpected stimuli, they will learn a great deal more about them than in any other way. As in almost every other aspect of theatre, there are no right or wrong ways, only successful and unsuccessful. It doesn't matter how you decide to evaluate your actors, as long as you treat them with dignity and courtesy, do not ask them to do things they do not want to do, and come out at the end with the right result, the good and suitable actors in your play, the bad or unsuitable ones rejected.

I do feel, though, that to keep an actor working for too long without the assurance of a job at the end of it can be a kind of directorial indulgence, a using of actors as director's toys. When I began in 1960 it could not have happened, or not very often. Actors, with a strong Union behind them and guaranteed rates of pay, had more power and dignity then, and a young director would not have dreamed of asking them to subject themselves to long drawn out processes of judgement, let alone workshops lasting a whole day. You were expected to meet an actor, either for an audition, or informally, and after a brief time, to be able to make your decision. But this is perhaps indicative of how the balance of power has shifted in the theatre, away from the actor towards the star director. Actors now, far less protected than they used to be, and finding it much harder to earn a sustainable living from acting, will do pretty much what a director asks them, for the chance of a job. Young actors in particular, who are barely protected at all, many of them outside Equity and working for a pittance or nothing, are likely to find themselves from time to time confronted by directors who will certainly exploit their weakness. From my point of view, it shouldn't take a workshop of half or a whole day to sort out the actors you want to work with from the ones you don't. But these things are a matter of opinion, and mine is no more meaningful than anyone else's.

However, there is still a quite strict but entirely undefined decorum about how you treat senior actors, and even good middle-range actors who work a lot. A director is expected to know which actors you can call in to read for you, which you call in for a talk, which you send a script to before making an appointment, which you send a script to and wait for their reply, and which you simply go down on your knees to. If you hope to work with Sir John Gielgud or Paul Scofield – I have had that great privilege with both masters – you speak respectfully to their agents, hope they might have a gap which fits your play, send a script with a covering letter, and pray to whatever Gods of the theatre you believe in. The problem, for young directors at least, is that there is no clear line of demarcation between the various grades of actor: actors shift from one group to another, as their careers prosper, and a director is expected to know the right thing to do in each particular case, as if by telepathy. An actor, and more especially an actor's agent, is likely to get quite shirty if you make an approach which is not in accord with the actor's status, or what he thinks of as his status. You learn by experience, and your mistakes.

It can be frustrating, and cause nights of agonised thought, even when you are dealing with a great actor, wondering whether he or she is exactly right for the part. The great ones, of course, need cause you no pain. They will make the part their own, whatever your first idea was, and, what is more, you will stand by with wide-eyed admiration, wondering how you could ever have conceived it differently. With good middle-range actors, where you cannot ask them to read and need to make an offer on what you know of their work, you must simply make a judgement, and stick by it. I have to say that I have hardly ever regretted that sort of decision. English actors, whatever their level, are mostly fine artists. If you trust them, they will usually deliver the goods.

And of course, you can always sack them, if you have to, but that is usually far more a sign that you have made a mistake than that the actor has. I have, in fact, never sacked an actor, though I can think of at least one occasion where I should have done. In all the cases where I might have done it, and they have been very few, it has been less from the actor's incompetence or my own miscasting, than that the actor has been a troublemaker, a self centred monster who was making it impossible for me and all the other actors to do our work. There are such people in the profession, indeed there are quite a few of them, and they can cause far more havoc than a poor actor who isn't really competent. Every actor or director who reads this book will have his own list of such people – as I have mine.

Producers

The other principal figure who must play a big part during the preparation period, is the producer, if you have one.

To clear up a common confusion, a producer, as in the film world, is the impresario who makes all the financial and administrative arrangements that make the play possible, while the director does the artistic job of putting the play onto the stage or screen. A producer may be an independent figure, like Bill Kenwright, Duncan Weldon or Michael Codron, running his own play-producing company, raising the money, finding the play, matching it with the star and booking the theatre, or he may work for a larger organisation as television and film producers do, while still fundamentally performing the same function. In large, multi-production theatre organisations, the artistic director, responsible for the overall direction of the theatre and the subsidised or sponsored budget that sustains it, may well act in a kind of producer role towards his director, participating to a considerable extent, or he may remain very much at arm's length, allowing the director to work as he pleases. What every director must remember is that, whatever the method of work, the producer bears the final responsibility and has the ultimate power. If it comes to a fight, without the possibility of compromise, the producer will usually win, because he has the cheque book in his hand.

A good producer can be a priceless asset to a director, whereas a bad one can be a nightmare. If you are lucky enough to work with a congenial producer who, while being efficient and workmanlike at his job, shares values and a common outlook about the work you are doing, the relationship will be very rewarding and will contribute a great deal to the final quality of the work. Working in BBC Television with Louis Marks, over a ten year period, I shared in exactly that sort of creative relationship. Louis took all the financial, executive and administrative weight off my shoulders, fought all the political battles for me, and made it possible that our collaborations, on *The Crucible, The Critic*, my own play in verse, *The Testament of John,* Bulgakov's *The White Guard,* and four Greek tragedies, could happen at all. If you had asked me five years earlier, I would have imagined that at least five of those projects could never be presented on BBC Television. He left all the artistic creation to me, but questioned everything that needed questioning, made useful suggestions of his own, and was an invaluable companion against whom I could bounce problems and ideas. Ultimately, he left me to my own artistic devices, making it his business to see that they were financially feasible and could be brought to fruition, and in ten years of near-continuous work, I cannot remember that we ever had a cross word.

I have never had the good fortune to find that sort of long-lived relationship in the theatre, but I do not doubt that such relationships exist, and that they are as fruitful as ours was. There is no easy formula for finding such a working partnership. Like so many things in the theatre, it is simply a question of constructing a personal/artistic relationship that works – about as easy to achieve, I suppose, as a good marriage, and as likely to end in a bloody divorce.

All a director can do is to use his judgement of people, and to respect the fact that the producer is responsible for a great deal of money, which may or may not be his own, may well have had the first idea and set it up from the beginning, and that the buck stops with his judgement. If he thinks you are going to lose him a fortune, he will dispense with you, and you will be left to consider where you went wrong, whether it was a project you should never have taken on in the first place, whether you did it the wrong way, or failed to recognise that in our game, at whatever level of artistic seriousness you aspire to operate, you must fill the theatre if you are going to succeed on any long term basis.

The most common cause of trouble between producers and directors is when they are revealed to have been following different agendas from the beginning, the producer seeing the work as one kind of play, and the director as another. When a play goes off at half-cock or fails to live up to expectation, an honest retrospective look will often reveal that the differences were present from day one, and that one or both of you tried to avoid seeing them. I am not the only director, I am sure, to have thought in such circumstances, *well, I can give him more or less what he wants, while still doing what I want, and anyway what I want will be so stunning that he will be won round when he sees it.* Alas, in those circumstances it hardly ever is, and he usually isn't. There is no substitute for the plainest kind of honesty on these occasions, for saying *well, you see it that way and I see it this way, and do you still want me to work for you?* But it is very easy to give such advice and very difficult to follow it. Sometimes the situation simply isn't talked through enough for the small hairline differences to emerge before they become large cracks, or, more often, neither side knows with absolute clarity what they think when the contracts come to be signed. Perhaps all directors, particularly young directors, should be issued with a kind of directorial highway code. On page one it would say, in very large letters, *do not think you are so smart and talented that you can bamboozle an experienced theatre producer into giving you your own way in spite of himself and against all his commercial instincts.* You can't, the most likely outcome is that you will be off the play before it opens, and your name will be plastered over on all the billboards. Always a sad ending to a voyage that started out with such excitement, and to be avoided, if you employ the most open-eyed honesty, both with the situation to which you are committing yourself, and your own directorial intentions.

There is no way of preparing yourself for these subtle processes of personal relationships except by living, and the problem with lived experience is, the more of it you get, the less time you have to use it.

4

Design and Designers

The biggest external influence upon your finished production will be the space in which you perform it. That space, though it will impose its own demands upon you, can be modified, and the process of modifying the space is the essence of what we mean by design.

Design isn't a necessary part of drama. All great plays, and probably all decently competent ones, can be performed in a bare room, with the actors wearing their ordinary clothes, on whatever furniture is available, with bits of cardboard, milk bottles, plastic cups, ashtrays and sheets of paper standing in for props, and such performances can be unforgettable. The final outside rehearsal run-through of my TV production of *Oedipus at Colonus*, with Sir Anthony Quayle, Juliet Stevenson and many other fine actors, on an empty sound-stage at Ealing Studios, with the live band present, and a few technicians and the producer as the audience, was one of the finest performances of anything I have ever been associated with, even better, if the truth be told, than what finally ended up on the tape. I like to think of it as one of the long list of great performances that took place in those studios, and probably quite unlike any other. In addition I have staged performances of Greek choruses with teenage girls in their school clothes on a bare patch of floor in the school hall, that have held the audience spellbound.

All a play *needs* is a good script, good actors, an empty space and an audience. That is why Aristotle put spectacle sixth in his list of the constituents of tragedy. But reason not the need, or none of us would 'scape whipping. Design is the most powerful and the most magically effective enhancement of the processes of drama we have, and used well it can become a positive aspect of the performance in its own right. In a good concept production it will be the key element in whatever interpretation is being attempted, and in the hands of a director and company committed to the ideals of Physical Theatre it is likely to become very much more, a central motif of the dramatic meaning of the performance. In whatever field, it represents one of the most

important decisions a director will have to make on a production. If
he gets it right, his production is already half way to success. If he gets
it wrong, failure is probably inevitable.

Theatre Space

There has been a revolution in the use of theatre space in the last fifty
years. Before that time, the tradition of theatre spaces was a rather
simple one. The small Athenian Theatre of Dionysus, became the vast
Hellenic Theatre, like the one at Epidaurus or Pergamon, which was
modified by the Romans, who cut down the chorus floor, and
enlarged the stage, but left the space as a whole unchanged. The
Renaissance simply put a roof on the Roman theatre, as in the magnificent Teatro Olimpico at Vicenza, and in England, where the visual
arts were at a low ebb, the practicalities of working in an Inn Yard
gave birth to the Elizabethan platform stage, surrounded by seating
galleries, a pattern which remained the same when plays moved
indoors to the Blackfriars and Salisbury Court Theatres. Meanwhile in
Italy, the Renaissance painters, commissioned to create great public
entertainments with music and verse, had developed the proscenium
arch and painted scenery, and when Sir William Davenant combined
these elements with the Caroline Theatre he had known in his youth,
he created the type of the Restoration playhouse, which the eighteenth century, by bringing the proscenium forward and shrinking the
forestage, developed into the picture frame theatres which held sway
in Europe till the early decades of the twentieth century. The line of
descent is very direct, and it is striking, over two thousand years, how
similar the basic way of presenting plays has remained.

But alongside that great tradition, there was another tradition of
both private and popular theatre, which was performed anywhere, in
monasteries, nunneries, churches and great houses, on the back of
carts in the English mystery plays, and on street corners, in squares
and on portable stages by the Commedia del Arte strollers. Since the
middle ages, that popular theatre tradition has tended to be obscured
by the main line of theatre development, but it is that kind of variety
of staging that has been rediscovered in the twentieth century.

At the present time, the first question that confronts a director,
probably even before he chooses his play, is what space he will work
in, and the choice available to him is dizzyingly, bewilderingly, wide-
ranging. Traditional theatres still exist in large numbers in England,
and most directors, though not all, still consider it a high point of their
careers to work in one, but there are many other kinds too. New main

house theatres can contain many different kinds of theatre layouts, from the modified indoor Greek amphitheatre of The Olivier to the custom-built theatre in the round of The Orange Tree, and almost every possible variation in between. Perhaps the most striking comment on the great change that has occurred is to realise that in, say, 1900, if a new theatre was built, everyone knew what its stage arrangement would be like. All the magnificent Frank Matcham Theatres, jewels in the English dramatic crown, are the same in stage layout. On the other hand, for the last thirty years at least, when new theatres have been built, the precise layout of the stage has been a choice made by architects and the theatre people for whom the building was being constructed – or more often, unfortunately, the local council – and there has been no universally accepted pattern to be followed. Some of the new theatres can be re-arranged to create a picture-frame stage, a platform stage, or a thrust stage, and the small studio theatres, that have been attached to most municipal arts centres or theatre complexes, are usually a simple black box building, within which the seating and theatre space can be re-arranged to whatever staging configuration the director requires, one end, in the middle, thrust, in the round, traverse, circular, or whatever.

The Fringe theatre adds to the amazing variety of choice, sometimes by utilising the most unpromising spaces, like the Gate at Notting Hill, or the Finborough Arms in Chelsea, and showing just what can be done within severe limitations by an imaginative director and designer working together. Almost every Fringe theatre is *sui generis*. There are a good many rooms above pubs, but they each have their own characteristics, and add to them the number of basement rooms, sheds, warehouses and churches, together with locomotive roundhouses, tramsheds, shipyards and deserted factories that have become venues for theatre, even, in the case of New End Theatre in Hampstead, a mortuary, and it is easy to see that absolutely any space at all can be used for theatrical performance, if you are determined to discover its potential. One of the most stunning such things I ever saw was a performance by the Polish avant-gardist, Tadeusz Kantor, and his company, on their home ground in Krakow, a weird experience that took place in a vaulted gothic basement under the medieval city. In the open air, Roman ruins, Country houses, London parks, village hillsides, anywhere where a large number of seats can be put together in front of an appealing vista – in the Minack Theatre, Cornwall, the backdrop is the Atlantic ocean, no less – theatrical events can be performed, and in recent years we have seen yet another development, the promenade production, where the audience is led from place to place, with a new scene being

performed in each new location: as, most recently, in Deborah
Warner's promenade experiment, with the audience, two at a time,
being introduced to a series of happenings and scenarios while
walking round the deserted St Pancras Station Hotel in London. That
too is a re-interpreting of a past tradition. In the medieval mystery
plays the audience walked from cart to cart to see the drama of
creation and redemption played out all round their own town, and in
a fairground ghost-train, over no more than a minute or so, the paying
customers are wheeled into a succession of frightening 'scenes.'

What this means, as with so many other aspects of theatre, is that
there are no rules anymore. Fifty, even thirty years ago, I could have
written a paragraph or two on the dynamics of stage space, that could
have been assumed to apply to any theatre a director was likely to
work in. Such precepts and suggestions – they are no more than that
– can still be offered for picture-frame proscenium theatres, platform
stages, and even in-the-round theatres, but beyond those basic staging
set-ups, the possibilities become so various that no useful detailed
advice can be given.

What must be emphasised though, is the overwhelming importance
of getting to know your space, whatever it is. Go and stand in it on
your own, face the audience, wherever it is to be, look at your
entrances and exits, see how far they are from the main performing
space, so you can judge how long an entrance will take, and try to
work out where the strong spaces and dynamic moves are within your
particular area. If you want to identify your strong spaces, go and sit
in the empty seats, not just in one seat, but in every part of your auditorium, and look critically at your performance space, so that you see
where your eye naturally gravitates. When you have done this from
most areas of your seating plan, you will find that certain spaces recur
in your imagination. You will define these as your strong spaces, and
make a mental note that your most important events must occur there,
or on the way to or from there.

Then try to think of your empty space as a picture, or, if your audience is on many sides, a sculpture or sculptural group. You will most
times want to fill every part of your theatre space with important
theatrical events, or with significant emptiness, and to do this you can
begin no better way than by studying the first masters of theatrical
grouping, the Renaissance painters. Mantegna, Piero della Francesca,
Raphael, Leonardo and Michaelangelo spent their artistic lives solving
the problems of grouping human forms in space, it was one of the
principal concerns of the Renaissance artistic ideal, and a director's
sense of grouping should always start from an understanding of what
they discovered about the tension and movement within groups. From

their beginnings each director will go his own way, but if he is wise their great achievements will always have a permanent place in the back of his brain. Grouping of figures is a passionate and emotional business, and nowhere more so than on the canvases of the Renaissance masters.

Working in a many-sided space, a director should remember how Michaelangelo's *David* reveals new wonders from whatever side you view it, that Rodin's *Burghers of Calais* or *The Kiss* create harmonious groupings and forms from every angle, and attempt to remember those forms and harmonies when he considers his own space. Of course, actors are not frozen in time like paintings and sculptures, but many of the basic principles of grouping still seem to apply to figures in action. Great film directors like Eisenstein, Bergman and Bunuel have a painter's eye for the beauty of grouping and grouped movement, and it is no surprise how often their films seem as beautiful as paintings, frame by frame, and sequence by sequence. Visual artists, from the Greeks, Egyptians, Indo-Persians and Sino-Japanese down to present day painters and action photographers, have discovered a great deal about the beauty and truth of form and movement. All those discoveries are available, and should become part of a young director's mental furnishings. If a director is at a loose end in a strange town for a few hours, he should always ask his way to the local art gallery.

Don't, unless you have a very good reason indeed, imitate famous paintings in your groupings. For one master like Buñuel, who makes Leonardo's *Last Supper* serve a savagely ironic purpose in his *Viridiana*, there are dozens of second-rate directors who imitate the groupings of famous paintings, for no other reason, apparently, than to prove that they have seen them. If there is some good reason within the play why you should group a scene so as to look like *The Night Watch*, or *The Arnolfini Marriage* or *The Anatomy Lesson*, then by all means do so, and make your ironic or melancholy or comic point. Otherwise you become no more than a tourist showing the audience your postcards. What should always be in your repertoire of stage grouping, are the *principles* upon which the masters constructed their groups. So you might decide that your play should employ the colour-palate of a Veronese or Titian, the dramatic chiaroscuro of a Caravaggio, or the logical interlocked groupings of a Raphael. That can be a creative impulse to inspire your own work with your designer, whereas the imitation of famous paintings for their own sake is really nothing more than a silly grin directed at the audience.

Confronted by the unique and sometimes bizarre theatre spaces of the present day, a director can only rely on his studies in painting and the plastic arts, and his own instinct, and of the two, his instinct is by far the most important. Your studies in painting and sculpture should complement and civilise strong feelings that already exist within yourself about the power and emotional implications of grouping and movement. Without that powerful instinct, what you learn from the masters will never be anything but wooden reproduction. When you confront an unusual theatre space, the excitement generated inside you should be your principal indication of how to begin work. If the theatre space doesn't excite you in that way, then you had better look for another.

Certain simple principles can be stated about conventional forms of staging, the product of the collective experience of actors and directors over many years. On a picture frame stage, or one with a forestage that is not more than about twenty feet deep, downstage centre is always the strongest position, closely followed by downstage right and downstage left. The mid downstage positions are slightly weaker, probably because they are felt to be on the way to or from the stronger positions, rather than places where an actor would choose to linger. Upstage positions are always weaker in emphasis than downstage positions, if an actor is alone on stage. If you give an actor a very important speech standing upstage right or left, don't be surprised if it loses some of its force. But if two or more are playing a scene, the dynamic is reversed. It is not without reason that actors talk about being upstaged. If one actor is upstage of another with whom he is having a scene, the other will normally have to turn and face him, so that our eyes too will naturally go to the upstage figure. Perspective also will tend to draw our eyes upstage, even if both actors are looking downstage. In such a situation, you must always be sure you put the dominant character in the upstage position, or your scene will not come off as it should. If one actor has a long impassioned speech to the other, and the other merely interjects, and you put the interjector in the upstage position, the scene will go off at halfcock. Actually, what *will* happen, is that the downstage actor will gradually manoeuvre himself upstage of his colleague, even if he has to climb through the backcloth to do it. Basic stage mechanics will always assert themselves, and it will soon be made clear to you if you have got it wrong.

Upstage positions can be very powerful indeed, in a crowded scene, if they are raised high above the stage, whereas if the actors are upstage on the same stage level as all the downstage people, they will simply not be seen by anyone in the stalls. Messengers and sudden dramatic arrivals of any kind will always normally wish to enter on a rostrum or down a set of steps upstage, so that everyone is compelled to turn to look at them, and there is perhaps no more powerful move in the theatre than to come diagonally down from such an upstage rostrum to downstage centre, or to downstage right or left, particularly if you are talking as you come. Even if you are not, all eyes will probably be on you, and the poor actor who *is* talking will plead that you do the move on one of your own lines, not his. Generally an audience will always watch movement rather than still- ness, even if the still actor is speaking, so that actors who are not doing anything important should not normally have full moves, or fidgety movements that distract from what the still actor is saying. Some old-fashioned actors will insist that no one moves on stage during an important speech, but in the modern theatre directors hope to choreograph movements in such a way as to allow other actors to keep their own characters alive, not frozen, while not detracting from an important speech or moment. Like everything else, its a question of skill and tact. It is possible to keep an audience focused on a single actor speaking, even if the whole stage is a swirl of movement around him, if you know what you are doing: just as it is possible to make stillness and silence the thing that everyone looks at, if the stillness and silence is intense and concentrated enough.

Diagonal moves, because an actor is moving down and across stage at the same time, are usually more compelling than lateral moves, and the direct move downstage from back to front is always powerful, in any part of the stage, because the actor, in approaching an audience directly, is dominating them with his presence and getting larger and easier to see as he gets closer. Conversely, moving away upstage, either directly or diagonally, is always a weak move, and should never be used for a character who is saying or doing something important. Of course, if the actor doing such a move turns just before the exit and delivers a good line, it is very strong, an exit line technique that has probably been in regular use among actors since Shakespeare's day. Exit lines are considered old-fashioned nowadays, but I suspect that in itself is a fashion. It is such a basic and effective staging device, that I cannot see it ever leaving the theatre repertoire for long.

These simple precepts are not rules, rather the dynamics of a conventional stage, as they have been observed by generations of actors, from whom the first directors learned them. You can ignore them if you wish, and create powerful lines of force of your own. Indeed, if you fill the stage with any large amount of scenery, walls flats or buildings, which cover up large parts of the stage floor, you will change all the stage dynamics anyway and create new ones with your shape. But on the basic stage floor the old lines of force generally apply, and if you ignore them, particularly if you ignore them out of ignorance, your production will suffer from a lack of focus and clarity.

Theatre-in-the-round too, though its history in the modern theatre stretches back no more than a few decades, is beginning to develop certain dynamic precepts of its own. Picture making in full theatre-in-the-round, with the audience on all four sides, is clearly impossible, and the director has to think in three dimensions, sculpturally. He has to remember too that the price he pays for the intimate sense of the actors being in the same room, is that someone in the audience will always miss something that is extremely important. For someone, the actor will always be presenting a broad back at the tenderest moment of emotion, or another actor will be blocking the view. When the audience is sitting at 360 degrees to the action, this is quite impossible to avoid, and directors of theatre-in-the-round must be aware of the problem, and do their best to minimise its effects. When I saw Helen Mirren give her much-admired Duchess of Malfy at the Roundhouse, she had her back to me for *I am Duchess of Malfy still*, and throughout the strangling. It couldn't be helped. She had to have her back to someone, and I, and those sitting near me, drew the short straw. Good theatre-in-the-round directors, as far as possible, keep their actors moving, so as not to anchor them on one place for too long, but this tactic inevitably has its limits, set by the verisimilitude the scene requires. There is nothing sillier than the theatre-in-the-round director who keeps his actors running round in circles all night, so as to keep showing their faces to everybody. There are times when stillness is required, and the strangling of the Duchess is one of them.

Logically, this theoretical failing ought to put theatre-in-the-round at a permanent disadvantage compared with other forms of staging, but in practice it does not. There is no doubt that its audiences find their proximity to the actors exciting, and their sense of being within the same space where the action is being played gives them a frisson of involvement in the drama which can't quite be experienced in any other form. All live theatre creates a sense of audience involvement missing from the mechanical media of film and television, but theatre-in-the-round takes this process to the extreme. The audience finds itself facing its own opposite side, and the drama being acted in between, against a background of watching and listening faces. Even when a particular member of the audience is contemplating the back of one actor, another actor, in addressing the first, will be speaking almost directly to that particular audience member, as though playing the lines to him. As Sam Walters, the director of The Orange Tree Theatre, has said, *when they come here, they are as far from watching television as they can get.* No pictures can be created and they miss things, but it does feel rather like being shoulder to shoulder in a crowd within which something exciting is happening. Reporting it, the audience is tempted to say, *I was there when it happened,* rather than *I saw it in a play.*

The overall point that grows from this consideration of theatre space is that the large variety of spaces now available has enormously enlarged the experience of playgoing. Each particular space has its own characteristics, and modifies to some degree what the audience experiences within it. Human beings can be moved and stimulated differently in each, so that new creative possibilities emerge for both director and playwright with each new space they work in.

The design

When you have made yourself familiar, as far as you can, with the dynamic patterns and lines of force indigenous to your chosen theatre space, you will then meet your designer, followed closely by your costume designer – who may sometimes be the same person – and your lighting designer, who, these days, is almost always a specialist. A few directors design and light their own shows, but most directors do not possess those multi-skills, and the ones who do are in a minority.

Whatever the personnel, the meeting with the designers is one of the most crucial moments in any theatre production. The decisions taken and acted upon at this time, though they cannot ensure the success of a badly-written and badly-acted play, can certainly ensure the failure of a well-written and well-acted one. Powerful theatrical weapons are involved, and no director should underestimate their significance.

The director will presumably have had some say in his choice of designer. On rare occasions, or if the engagement is with a theatre that employs a resident designer, the design team will come with the package. Whether this is the case or whether the choice is yours, it is important to have a very clear idea of the sort of artistic personality you are working with. Directors and designers often strike up long-term partnerships which last for many years, perhaps more often than directors and playwrights do, and it is easy to see why. If you are lucky enough to find a colleague who thinks about the theatre in broadly the same way as you do, then the confidence can grow which will enable you to test each other, so that you will both feel able to try more daring and experimental things together.

The marriage of director and design team is quite as important as the marriage of director and playwright, and in some ways even more so. A director and playwright can spark each other off by striking at their differences. There is room for quite a wide tolerance of ideas and intentions between director and playwright, which can still be unified into a striking artistic statement, but if the director and designer are at odds, and don't have a clear unity of view about the play and the way it should be staged, disaster can be very close.

Designers, after all, are artists as well as technicians, with powerful creative ideas of their own, and they are as various in their attitudes and beliefs about the theatre as directors or playwrights are. As with directors, there are those who will always want to transform or recreate a theatre space with every production, and who will never feel satisfied if they cannot do that, and there are others with a deep love and understanding of texts whose principle wish is to create structures within which a text can be most richly expressed. On another level, designers can be located on a wide spectrum that ranges all the way from the pure painter, who sees canvases on the stage, to the total theatre mechanic, who can solve every problem of staging practically, with a power saw, some paint and canvas and an electric screwdriver. The ideal designer possesses both talents in abundance, has the visual creative imagination of the painter allied to the technical know how of an architect or civil engineer. If a choice has to be made, the director should always trust practical experience and perhaps a little less vision, rather than a profound artistic vision and a complete inability to make things stand up or understand how they work. Putting it down nakedly on paper, that seems a depressingly unimaginative thing to say, but I guess most theatre directors would stand by it, if they have to make the choice – which most times, God willing, they won't. The theatre is a severely practical business. Things must perform as well as people, and if the flying doesn't function because the designer hasn't worked out his engineering properly, the revolve is too slow because he hasn't checked out weight and motor speed, or if, as happened to me once with an experienced designer, he hasn't taken account of the differing angles of stage rakes in different theatres on a tour, then all the artistic visions fly out of the window while the director contemplates the disaster of a production that simply isn't functioning. In the case I quoted, the technical rehearsal, instead of being a careful preparation of how the play would look and sound on the stage, was a three day nightmare of wondering whether the play would ever be able to open at all. It did of course, successfully, but not without a great deal of fast creative thinking on my part, unnecessarily hard work by the actors, and far too much compromising of the original artistic vision.

So the first thing a director must do, if the designer is not an old friend and collaborator, is to examine his mind in as much detail as possible, to find out what excites and horrifies him, and to try to get some idea of whatever visions are flashing through his head on a permanent or temporary basis. It will soon become clear whether there is a sufficient match to make a creative collaboration possible. Of course, you don't have to agree about everything, and you can afford to have a good many intellectual and artistic tensions at stretch between you. They can often produce striking and individual work that surprises you both. What can't be tolerated are diametrically opposed views about the play or the theatre in general. However good the intentions of both parties, they will have their way in the end, you will fall out, and the production will suffer for it.

As with my comments about producers, this is a counsel of perfection. If we could all fathom the mysteries of other people in a few brief meetings, there would be no wars, no divorces, and no theatrical ventures that end in angry tears and disaster. No one can ever discover enough about a new person to be sure that any kind of relationship with them will work. But it is important to be aware of the necessity for an artistic meeting of minds, and to use whatever sensitivity you possess – if you are hoping to be a director, that needs to be your most highly developed skill anyway – to predict what degree of genuine collaboration you are likely to be able to achieve. If you have any niggling doubts fidgeting at the back of the brain, call a halt at the start, part good friends, and find a new designer who doesn't make you nervous at three o'clock in the morning.

The first working meeting with the designer is one of the most important you will have over the whole production, only giving place to the later meeting to consider the finished model box. You should not come to that meeting with a closed mind. If you have chosen well, you are going to be working with a creative talent at least as great as your own, and that talent must be respected, and given the opportunity to express itself. But you will certainly hope to bring with you a very good idea of the way you want the play to be done, at least in broad terms, a living idea that is going to inform your production. Vivid pictures should be glowing in your head, of what the stage should *feel* like, rather than what it should look like, and if you are lucky your designer will accurately translate that feeling into cloths, flats and rostra. Certain detailed pictures will probably be alive in your head too, alongside the less precise ones, scenes where you can describe with great clarity to the designer how you want to stage the play. If you meet a good designer *without* a clear idea of how you want the play to look, then he will probably direct the play for you, at least in terms of staging. It isn't a competition, its a co-operation, but the final decision, with design, just as much as with acting or music or costumes, must rest with the director. If you don't make your decision, you must expect other people to make it for you.

If a designer arrives at this first meeting, having read the play, with a complete design fully worked out, warning bells should sound. This is a designer, you will feel, who has a very clear idea of what he wants, before he has met anybody else, even the director and the actors, and who may not be a very amenable colleague. Of course, as with everything else in the theatre, there is always an element of suck-it-and-see. You may feel very miffed if a designer turns up with full plans and model box, complete with furniture and little actors, when you have a quite different conception clear in your own mind, but you should nevertheless study very carefully what he has done. It may be that the designer has become quite possessed by the play, has seen it with intense clarity, and has had to get it down on paper even before meeting you; and it may be, too, that such an intense vision has created something really good, even, *mirabile dictu,* very much better than anything you have thought of. If that does happen, don't let *amour propre* stand in your way. If you really think the designer has cracked it, then throw away your own idea and joyfully appropriate his. He will get the credit for the look of the thing, but you will get the credit for the whole show, and even if you know in your heart that the whole success is based on a brilliant original design concept, critics probably won't, and you can bask in undeserved glory. Directors so often carry the can for other people's failures, it's quite reasonable that they should earn some undeserved praise now and again.

The ideal situation for the first meeting is that the designer should come full of enthusiasm and tumbling over with ideas, which at this stage may be rough sketches, a few details sharply imagined, or just a feeling, but which show that he has fully responded to the play. Then you can tell him what your own ideas are, and if you are well-matched your two enthusiasms will fuse, and diamonds will begin to form. A really good designer will be able to show you vistas of staging implicit in your own ideas which you hadn't realised, practical ways of presenting your concepts which are entirely his own and which have grown as passionately in his imagination as yours have in your own creative processes.

If you do find yourselves on the same wave length, it is important that you should give the designer every scrap of information. Every staging idea about every scene or fragment of a scene that you have had, you must convey to him as passionately as possible. Even if you have visualised nothing, but experienced a powerful emotional feeling about a scene, try to convey it. Direction is ninety per cent a job about your powers of communication. Just as your choice of the right word might unlock an actor's performance into greatness, so the right words, the right metaphors, offered to your designer, might inspire him to surpass himself. Throughout the production process of a play, the whole group of creative people, all in their different ways, are trying to stimulate each other into making new discoveries about their work, entering and exploring new countries, whose very existence they had only dimly heard of before. The theatre is a collaborative art. We are not poets sitting alone in our garrets composing verses in solitude. Theatre poetry is made when a group of people works together, and the divine fire, because of their interrelationship, touches them all.

What part should an author's stage directions and descriptions of design, if there are any, play in this part of the process? That depends not only on the individual play in question, but also on the type of play it is. Shakespeare's plays, not having been written for a theatre that employed anything we would recognise as a design, give no instructions, so the director and designer can with good conscience do exactly as they like. But in some plays the design is a kind of extra character in the play, and in such cases it is perilous to ignore what the playwright says. Ibsen is perhaps the most obvious example. His plays, over most of his long career, are demonstrations of the appalling price paid by individuals living in a society as repressive as late nineteenth-century society was all over Europe. In play after play sexual and financial guilt tears the characters apart, or destroys them over many years, and it is noteworthy how in his mature plays Ibsen usually describes in great detail not only the exact architectural settings of the plays, but some of their dressing detail as well. This, on one level, is merely a description of the customary scenery his characters live in, but on another it is a physical manifestation or symbol of precisely the oppressive society that is exacting such a toll on their lives. The heavy velvet curtains, the ornaments, the woodwork, the dangerous mountains visible through the window, the sea, the fjords, are powerful manifestations of the bars which constitute the characters' prison, or the freedom they yearn for, and to remove them from your design, just because you are fed up with staging Ibsen as he has always been staged, is a dangerous, and perhaps ultimately rather frivolous tactic. That heavy furniture and those oppressive rooms are there for a purpose, and to remove them is like removing a character from the play. There has been a fashion for open stage performances of Ibsen in recent years, without the nineteenth-century clutter, but, for my taste at least, it has been as though one of the weightiest chains has been removed from the characters' shoulders. Hedda's dilemma is not only the man she is married to, and her own self-destructive character. It is also the house she has to live in. It is significant that when Nora Helmer asserts her freedom from her husband, it is by going out and slamming the door. That sound echoed all round Europe, and was one of the most striking instances in modern European theatre of what is basically a design idea taking on profound theatrical meaning, particularly when we remember that the theatre in which Ibsen spent his youth was one in which doors, windows and even furniture, were painted in two dimensions on the backcloth.

As a small illustration of the importance of the kind of naturalistic stage descriptions Ibsen employs, *The Pillars of Society* is set in a large room in Karsten Bernick's house, which is described as having four doors, one of them a window door looking onto a garden. When I directed the play, I found that my theatre space, and the budget available, would not easily accommodate four doors, so in consultation with the designer I cut one, and made do with three. As soon as I began serious blocking, I realised I had made a mistake. Ibsen had been serious, and very precise, about his four doors, and the various confrontations and meetings the play consists of could not really make architectural sense without all four of them being operative. I simply couldn't work out with my actors a coherent understanding of where people had come from and where they were going to. It was too late to change the design, and we simply had to fudge it, make a few entrances and exits that didn't make sense in terms of real people inhabiting a real house. We deceived the audience, and they didn't notice the anomalies, but we did. Ibsen was right when he had asked for four doors, and in changing his instructions we had transformed sense into nonsense.

I am not suggesting for a moment that every time a playwright details a naturalistic set and furnishings in his stage directions, the director must automatically follow them. That is the direct path to fossilised, theme-park theatre. But all playwrights write stage directions and set descriptions for a purpose, not just to fill paper or pass the time, and a director should study a playwrights' instructions with great seriousness, discussing all the possible reasons why he might have written them as he did, before deciding to cast them away. Even if a playwright is working entirely within the naturalist tradition, and director and designer decide they must follow his instructions closely or else fatally distort the play, it is still possible for a good designer to express his design personality while giving the playwright exactly what his directions describe, indeed, it is absolutely necessary that he should do so. It is easy to see this kind of artistry in action by comparing photographs of the sets of the same naturalistic play created at different times during the century. Nine times out of ten there is not the slightest doubt which design comes from which period, because the designs so perfectly express their own time as well as the author's intention: which is exactly as it should be. Whenever a director and designer sit down to create a production together, however closely they follow the playwright's instructions, their purpose is to create a work in their own time, not in the past, and each age has its own signature, as recognisable as handwriting.

The director's powers of judgement and foresight are required to be at full stretch when the designer brings him his finished idea. If we have to pick out one meeting, or one work-session absolutely crucial to the production's success, this is probably it.

Nine times out of ten, if you are working with a designer you know and trust, or one you particularly admire, you are going to be so overwhelmed and delighted at what he brings you, that there is a danger of your critical faculties being swamped. But a director should be well aware that his talents are never going to be subjected to a more profound scrutiny than they are likely to be in the next few hours. Whether the designer has followed your instructions and suggestions with scrupulous accuracy, or gone off on a wonderful flight of design fantasy, you must interrogate what he has done with the profoundest scepticism and disbelief. The most dangerous thing you can do is to be so delighted by the magnificent colours, the striking shapes, the wonderful stage spaces your designer has created, that you uncritically accept them and give the go ahead for immediate building. It may indeed be that the designer has solved all your problems with one brilliant conception. It does happen, and when it does, producing the play can be a very exciting experience. But even if you feel he has, a feeling isn't good enough, you have to be sure. After the meeting, you will give the designer the go-ahead, and building will begin. You will be committed then, and significant changes will probably not be possible. Even if they are, they will cost money, and your stock as a director will go down if you are perceived to be someone who can't make a decision and get it right first time.

You must take your time, look hard at the model, measure it up with your scale furniture and human beings, and study the way in which the design plan modifies the lines of force and energy within your chosen theatre space. One of the first questions you will ask yourself, is whether the set reinforces the natural strengths of your space, and develops them so that there are even greater possibilities of movement and emphasis than there were on the bare stage, or whether it weakens them, and cuts down what you can do. There is nothing worse than the kind of set that only contains, say, three feasible moves. It is even more disastrous if you don't spot the limitation before rehearsal begins, and you find yourself permutating the three possible moves over two and a quarter hours of drama. It is difficult to imagine who will be more bored, you, the actors or the audience.

As you look at the model, you must try to run through in your head, or even overtly with the script, all the scenes you have to stage. If the set is a multi-patterned flexible one, with changes to be made each scene, or even a series of different sets for different acts, go through all the changes in detail with your designer, and brood deeply on each one, making quite sure that you will be able to direct the scene as you want to direct it in the modified space of the design. If you are lucky, your designer will have had some brilliant staging ideas you hadn't yourself thought of, which you feel will add immeasurably to the play. These you must interrogate with particular care, because you have not lived with them in your head, as you will have done with your own ideas, and simply *because* they seem so impressive. Carefully argue through in your mind all the possible virtues or disadvantages, and try to foresee every difficulty or disaster that might arise at any time during the process of producing the play. Do not allow yourself to be rushed. If you want to live with the design for two days, tell your designer so, and make the builders wait a day or two, rather than rushing yourself into a decision you might regret. Carry the design around with you in your head, and keep on questioning it. Only when you are sure it is giving you all the right answers can you congratulate your designer and tell him to go ahead. If you need significant changes, don't be afraid to say so, or to make clear what they need to be and how soon you will need them. However difficult the situation between you, or however close or past the deadline is, do not be forced into accepting a set you are not sure of. If you do, you will have to live with your decision, whatever it costs your production, and you will have no one to blame but yourself.

Lurking behind the whole process is the unavoidable realisation that the designer can be your best friend, or your worst enemy, and that bad design, or even good design wrongly applied, can destroy a production as completely as good design that serves the play can contribute towards its success. We have all heard our own horror stories, and the common tale of actors complaining that a play has seemed to go very well in rehearsal, but somehow never quite got off the ground in the theatre. It is almost always the design that is at fault when that happens. Barriers have been put between the openness and freedom that the actors felt in the empty rehearsal room, which have stopped them doing their work. I once saw a particularly striking example of this in action. A designer, following the wholly admirable trend to design the complete theatre space of a proscenium theatre, so that the upper parts of the stage picture are as relevant as the stage floor, had created a wonderful network of scaffolding, platforms and ladders reaching right up to the grid, that probably looked sensational as a painted picture, or even in a model box. However, the problem was that the actors, playing on small platforms, half way up ladders, or even hanging from or climbing up scaffolding, had no opportunity to relate to each other. You can't have eye-contact with someone twenty feet away from you, and fifteen feet above your head, however sensational the stage picture looks from the auditorium. So the actors duly ran about this three-dimensional maze, like a group of programmed mice, and nothing really occurred. The play was spoken, but there was no performance. They all said their lines, but the huge and intricate set was preventing them from acting. Speaking to one of the actors after the show, an old friend, I heard the usual litany. *It was fine in the rehearsal room. Something went wrong when we went into the theatre.* Sets must always serve the actors' needs, whatever else they do. If they don't do that, in the race to a successful production, they have fallen at the first fence.

If you find a designer who really has a close understanding of the needs of actors, and a deep interest in them and their doings, as well as artistic vision and technical skill, clasp him to your bosom and never let him go. Such people are gold dust, close to the very centre of what makes good theatre. Cast your mind back to the beginning, and the twenty-year row between the poet Ben Jonson and the designer Inigo Jones, both grimly pursuing totally opposed visions. Stage designers are always some species of visual artist, moved and excited by different agendas from those which stir a poetry-based text director. In a good relationship, each will attempt to live at least to some degree within the other's agenda, so that the director will be prepared to think pictures and visual emotions as well as text and actors, and the designer will understand that his visual fantasies have to be inhabited by real people with lines to speak and relationships to create. Never trust designers who, like the enormously overrated Craig, in their heart wish to get rid of actors altogether, and substitute marionettes, even living ones, so that their visual fantasies can come to life. Theatre is about people, not puppets, and the kind of designers – and directors for that matter – who have a secret desire to be puppet-masters, should make their way to the film studios, where they belong.

Lighting and Costume Designers

Lighting designers and costume designers, though they must have paragraphs to themselves, are in no sense an afterthought. Lighting designers, in particular, can be as crucial a part of the central design concept as the set designer, and sometimes even more important. It is possible in the modern theatre to design a show entirely with space and light, inside a plain designer's box, or with a few movable screens conceived as surfaces to receive and reflect light, and any decent production in a well-equipped theatre will expect to see its set dramatically and imaginatively lit. If possible the lighting designer should be in on the earliest discussions between director and designer, because the light will not only enable you to see the set or not, it will also have a profound effect on what you feel about it.

The electrification of theatre lighting was one of those watershed moments in the history of the stage. The theatre had been adequately illuminated by candlelight, oil lamps and sconces, and finally by gas light, but it was only the coming of electricity that enabled the lighting designer to use the stage space like a three dimensional canvas, and to begin to paint with light. Electric lights were not only more powerful, their power made it possible for them to be focused in a much more precise and directional manner, and because their brightness was controlled by an electric current, they could be faded up and down, singly or in batches, to create lighting states that varied from the brilliantly bright to the barely visible. Because there was no live flame involved, the use of coloured glass, and, eventually, plastic gels, made it possible to create every conceivable colour and colour combination in stage lighting, and there was sufficient light available on the stage for the audience, for the first time in theatre history, to sit in near darkness, and give all their concentration to the illuminated wonderland before them. No longer could audiences see and be seen, flirt with each other, make assignations and even fight duels, as they had done in the Restoration theatre, or eat, drink, play cards and chat, as they had done during Mozart's operas. Darkness finally civilised theatre audiences, turned them to the attentive and respectful spectators they usually are in the modern theatre. For the first time actors could be sure every word would be listened to, and if they were not heard, it was their fault not the audience's. *The Sun*, said J.M.W. Turner, *is God*, and there is no doubt that in the modern theatre too, light is God. The first necessity is to be able to see what is on stage, but theatre lighting not only illuminates what is being played before us, it qualifies it in profound ways, and controls to a very great extent what we feel about what we are seeing.

Within the confines of naturalistic drama, precise lighting can create a dramatic power simply not available to the pre-electric generations. A street lamp can illuminate a single door in an otherwise darkened street, or shine through a gently blowing curtain. A woman can stand in silhouette in a doorway, with light behind her blazing into a darkened room, where her husband sits at a table, his face only half-lit from the lighted door, watching his wife's elongated shadow fall right across the room. Scenes can be lit as though directionally, as if the only light appears to be that generated on stage, from lamps or through windows. Stage light very rarely is fully directional. If it is, it looks much starker than it ever does in real life, and a good lighting designer will touch in lighting fills from other directions, so that it *appears* to be directional light we are watching, but in fact is not.

In non-naturalistically staged drama, the function of light can be even more powerful and central. Like impressionist or expressionist paintings, the stage can become a series of powerful statements in light, broad washes, vivid colours, jagged lines or whatever, that will convey powerful states of feeling about the play. In addition, the modern lighting designer has all kinds of other lighting effects within his repertoire, from stunts with holograms and lasers to the vast palate of gobos and projectors that can transform the stage almost at will. Gobos are small patterned cut-outs slid into frames in front of a particular lamp, so as to break the light up into a magnified version of the pattern cut into the gobo, and they are most regularly used with, say, leaf shapes, so that the stage surface can be transformed to a forest floor with light shining through the trees, or broken up into any other expressive pattern the director might call for. There is no limit to what gobos can do, from the shadow of a window frame falling across the floor, or projected onto a cloth, to moons, star-clusters or geometrical shapes in light which make the stage floor a living cubist picture. Projectors can create slow moving clouds on a backcloth, snowstorms, stormy seas, or pictures, photographs and verbal texts. There is almost nothing that can be imagined into existence through the use of light that cannot be achieved by a resourceful lighting director, if he has the creativity, the technical skill, and the money to pay for it.

The greatest mystery about stage lighting, indeed, about all lighting, whether in films or in your own drawing room, is its powerful emotional charge. This isn't the place for me to go into the psychological reasons why this might be so, but the fact is that the most powerful way to control an audience's emotions in the theatre, apart from through the speech of the actors, is by the use of light.

And in real life, if a young man wants to seduce a young woman, or vice versa, low-key lighting is more than a romantic cliché. Indeed, it has become a cliché because it works!

At first sight light seems to function according to a simple scale, the darker the more emotional, but that isn't quite the case. Pitch-black scenes might well generate a feeling of mystery or excitement, but it is vivid or half light that screws up the feelings. The simplest of experiments will prove the point. If your actor has a powerful emotional speech to play, and you play it in brilliant white light, the audience will observe the actor, in a kind of detached way, but its feelings will remain under control. But if your actor is speaking on a half-darkened stage, with a powerful, directional light from the wings slashing across his face, so that only one cheek and half his mouth is visible, and his eyes are a gleam within a dark hood, the audience will empathise with his pain much more, because the light will be intensifying their own emotional state. They will participate, be drawn in, as an audience is drawn in while watching a film. This is precisely the reason why Brecht, in his epic theatre, wanted his scenes to be played in bright white lighting. He was very suspicious of emotional involvement in an audience, and went out of his way in his production style, to avoid it, and to create a standing back and judging temperament in the spectators, the alienation effect. Moody lighting, he realised – the very adjective is revealing – would work most powerfully against what he wanted to do, so he outlawed it.

Conversely, if you are playing comedy, particularly high verbal comedy, and you go in for all kinds of half-shadowed or richly-coloured lighting effects, you won't get many laughs, because you will be programming your audience's feelings another way. To create a real comedy relationship between actors and their audience, you must ensure that the actors' faces can be clearly seen, so that the audience will be able to pick up every word and every nuance of expression, and their emotions will not be involved, only their sense of humour. As with everything else, these precepts are not rules, just the results of observation. You can go against them all at any time, play your comedy in the dark and your emotional scenes in bright daylight, but it is as well to be aware of the likely consequences *before* you make such a decision.

Beyond that, as with any theatrical weapon of such power, it is a matter of taste. Personally, I hate to go into a theatre and see before me an unlit set, or an unilluminated backcloth. When the audience comes into a lighted auditorium which has a stage without a curtain, the scenery should be subtly illuminated with a pre-set light, so that the shapes and planes are alive and if there is a sky cloth or cyclorama, there should be some restrained light on it, so that it glows, and is not moribund cloth. There is nothing deader than an unlit set or shadowed backcloth. A set before a play is about to begin should contain a suggestion of the magic that is about to be enacted on it, and without light it contains nothing at all except flat paint. Of course, you may argue that you require your audience to experience just that quality of deadness as they enter the theatre and before the play begins, and in that case I can't argue with you. For my taste, though, you can't beat the subtle illumination that tells you something dramatic is about to happen. Then, as the lights in the auditorium fade and the lights on stage brighten, you are ready for anything.

My other personal bête noir of lighting is the blackout, which seems to me to be a confession of failure. The Victorian curtain between scenes is long gone now, except in the most old-fashioned conventional productions, and for my taste the sooner the blackout follows it into oblivion the better. During a blackout the play stops, nothing at all is being communicated. Even if there is music playing, there is nothing for the eye to look at and we are transformed for a few moments into radio listeners. Designer, lighting designer and director ought to be able to devise a continuous entertainment on a stage that can progress from scene to scene as the play requires, without having to resort to the expedient of saying to the audience, in effect, *don't go away, we'll start again in a minute when we can get everything ready*. Whenever I see a blackout in a play I always find myself thinking it's a shame the director couldn't think of *something* to keep the play moving, rather than just giving up for two minutes. Most scene and lighting changes are a great deal more entertaining done on stage than concealed behind a blackout or curtain. If you think of them as another theatrical moment rather than a hiatus, they can become a positive virtue. In one particular production of mine, the actors got a round of applause when, in full view of the audience, they set up a full dinner party on a circular table in about a minute-and-a-half, and another when they removed it! The theatre becomes like the circus in such moments, and the audience applauds the skill, precision and danger of the way the thing is done, just as they do when they see jugglers or high-wire-walkers.

An experienced director, when he sees pictures in his head before meeting his designers, will see them in colour, shaped and modulated by light. If he is the kind of director who does sketches or story-boards, he will sketch in the lighting effects together with the solid forms, because he will know that how the designer's shapes are perceived will be crucially determined by light. In fact, design in the modern theatre is essentially the creation of a triumvirate working closely together. In a good team that is functioning well, director, designer and lighting designer will be in the closest possible co-operation from the beginning, and the final stage picture will be no single individual's work, but the result of all their talents working harmoniously together.

At least three other aspects of the production will need careful preparation and pre-planning, costume design, sound design, and music, though they may not need to be planned before the rehearsal period, as stage setting and light must normally be.

Costume designers, as a rule, are far less subject to what one might call artistic variation of style than set designers. The best ones know all there is to know about historic costume, including a close knowledge of the materials that were used in the past, and how they were cut and stitched. One of the reasons for the great success of the costume department in BBC Television classic serials and historical plays in the 1960s and 70s was that the costume department in those days possessed its own collection of historical costumes, so that designers could not only look at them for style, they could pick them up, feel the weight, find out exactly how they were sewn, or even put them on to feel how they sat on the human body and moved as the body moved. The kind of costume designer you will want to work with will have all the personal design flair and technical knowledge of a couturier, plus a deep historical understanding, and an instinctive knowledge of the needs and vagaries of actors and actresses. One very experienced costume designer, female, of my acquaintance, always made the first fitting of a costume a little larger than necessary, so that she and her actors could both agree that it needed taking in a little, and the relationship between them got off to a very good start.

Make sure the costume designs, as well as being excellent in their own right, express the character in the way you want to express it. It is no use asking an actress to give you an inward, restrained performance, if the costume designer has dressed her in multi-coloured diamonds, a huge hat and a seven foot cloak. It seems an obvious point, but it is a mistake that can be very easily made when the differences at issue are more subtle. If the costume is at the slightest tangent from the way the character is conceived, it will become very difficult for the actor to give you what you want. With actresses you are usually on safer ground. Most will have an obsessional concern that the costume and accessories will be right for the character they are expressing, and with most actresses, you can trust their integrity and instinct for artistic self-preservation to lead them to the right choice. Not all actresses, however, can be given that freedom. There are a few who will always put personal appearance and image before the character, and in those cases, you and your costume designer will have to gang up on the offending Thespienne, and make sure you get your way. Let it not be suggested, either, that only actresses have the peacock mentality. There are a good few actors too that a wise director and costume designer will keep their eyes on.

Get a good set of detailed drawings from your designer, early enough for the costumes to be made and rejected, or substantially modified, if they have to be, and bring your actors in at the very beginning. They have to wear the things, and they must be consulted all along. I usually ask for drawings by the read-through, and then spend an hour or so after the reading, supervising meetings between designer and actors, listening to reactions, and trying to make sure everyone is happy.

You must always take the actors completely into your confidence on the whole subject of how they are to look, wigs and make up too, if they should be relevant. Physical appearance is so deeply bound up with what an actor is, that its importance can hardly be overemphasised. Some actors start with a few details of physical appearance, and build up the character from that, beginning with the right shoes, or the right jacket or cardigan, and working inwards to an exploration of the character's psychology. Others start from the inner life, and work outwards, till they realise, just a few days from opening night, that this character *must* have a moustache, or wear a shirt too large for him, so that he keeps tucking it in.

A director must always take these obsessional concerns with detail very seriously, because he is treading on sensitive ground, full of mines that might explode if he moves without due care. Actors *must* feel happy with what they are wearing and their whole appearance, and that feeling is nothing at all to do with vanity. Simply, an actor can't act a part properly if he or she feels something is wrong. Never force an actor to wear a costume he or she is unhappy with, because you'll never get out of them everything you might have helped them to discover if you had been more tolerant. Your stage picture might look just as you have imagined it, but if there is no heart in the acting your picture won't matter. If you have extraordinary or bizarre costume ideas, you must be especially careful. Normally actors will go along with such ideas very much more readily than they will with costumes which just slightly miss the mark, but you must always take care, particularly with your actresses. If it comes to tears and an outright row, you will do better, most times, to let the artist have her way. If the changes upset your design concept, then change the concept. Don't take positions simply to assert your authority. Weigh up just what the change will mean to the play as a whole, and nine times out of ten you will be better off selling a costume change in order to buy a happy actress.

In one television play I did in the 1960s an actress tore up her dress in front of me in the studio, rather than wear it. And that was a dress she had designed herself! She may have been a rotten dress-designer, but she was a good actress, and delivered the goods in performance, wearing something the costume designer had rustled up for her at very short notice, but which she *liked*!

Sound and Music

Sound design, in spite of the enormous leap forward in sound technology in recent years, and the regular practice of television and film-making, in which it is a separate and highly regarded part of the production process, is still the Cinderella skill of theatre production. It is rare indeed to find a theatre production that has a sound plot that is anything like as sophisticated as the lighting plot. When there are a lot of sound effects, they are more often than not the practical sounds required by the story, noises of war, an offstage party, passing cars and police sirens, etc. Rarely is sound used for its poetic effect, as an enhancement of the atmosphere and meaning of the play, rather than as a naturalistic ornament.

Yet some playwrights have indicated the way this aspect of the theatre might go. We all remember the famous snapping string Chekhov asks for at the end of *The Cherry Orchard*, though, for my own part, I can't say that I have ever heard in the theatre a sound that matches Chekhov's imagination. Tennessee Williams, too, often suggests intense and poetic soundscapes, one of which was beautifully realised in Peter Hall's production of *The Rose Tattoo*. But consider this, from the opening stage direction of Bulgakov's play *Madame Zoyka* (translated by Michael Glenny):

> Outside, the courtyard of the huge apartment house sounds like a musical box gone mad. A gramophone is singing *The Human race in all the world...*, a voice is shouting *We buy second hand primus stoves!* another *Broken samovars soldered!* The gramophone *worships but one sacred idol!* Tram wheels grind, bells clang, cars hoot. Cacophony. As the noise dies down slightly, an accordion plays a cheerful polka...

And that was in a play premiered in Moscow in 1926, when a gramophone would have been available, but all the rest of the noises would have been performed live! And yet see with what economy the sound script helps to set up the frantic mania of the New Economic Policy period in Soviet Russia, before one character has uttered a word.

The technology now available in our larger and newer theatres means that almost anything can be done if a director has the imagination to think aurally. Sound mixing and generating systems, together with high quality tape recorders and CD players are in most large theatres now, and some even have state-of-the-art loudspeaker systems, though in a lot of established theatres that aspect of sound reproduction lags far behind. I was surprised, the last time I took a play on tour, how many theatres could not adequately separate on-stage sound effects from auditorium sound effects, or could make on-stage effects really directional. In Krakow, in 1976, working on my play *The Exorcism* in the city's third-ranking theatre, I found myself in a sound suite which seemed as well equipped as a top rate recording-studio, and heard one of the most extraordinary sound effects I have ever heard in my life, in a play about the return of Ulysses. At the climax, when Ulysses fires his bow, the sound of the arrow, a fearful and exciting whooshing sound, sped all round the auditorium, via four speakers placed at the four corners of the hall and sounding one after the other, with electrifying effect. I have never heard anything quite like that in an English theatre, nor indeed are most auditoriums well enough equipped to perform such an effect.

Of course, before designing an imaginative and poetic sound plot a director must check on two things, that the play he is directing really requires it – few playwrights think in these terms yet, though they increasingly will, I am sure, as the children of the technological revolution begin writing – and that the equipment in the theatre can accommodate his aural fantasies. Brilliant sound effects, more than most kinds of effect, suffer very badly if they don't quite come off technically. If you have only one very old tape recorder in your fringe theatre, or a cassette deck that cannot be cued up accurately, design your sound score with appropriate simplicity. In fact, it is amazing what you can do with two old reel-to-reel Revoxes, and access to a reasonably well-equipped sound studio to prepare your tapes. If our theatre is still unimaginative in its use of sound, that is because we haven't customarily thought as Bulgakov thought, not because we can't make it work. If our playwrights and theatre directors let their aural imaginations loose, as radio directors do in every production, there is a whole new expressive landscape to be explored, and with the new technology at hand no limit to what can be achieved.

Most directors are likely to have some sort of interest in music, and the use of music in plays is always a very personal business. There is nothing that can be usefully said about *how* a director should use music, or *what* music he should use, because that will always depend upon the play, the particular production style adopted, and what each director wants to achieve by making musical interventions. Directing musicals, or operas, really demands a whole book to itself, and is certainly beyond the scope of this one, but using music in any form in a play is always a great delight, particularly when it is live. Alan Plater spoke for me, and, I suspect, a good many others, when he said *when I go into a theatre and see musical instruments lying around, I know I'm going to have a good evening.*

A director needs to make himself as knowledgeable about music as he can, principally about the European musical tradition and its history, not only because it will help him to use music in his productions gracefully and with some sophistication, but because it will be a useful tool in the whole process of directing, and in working with actors in particular. Singing and acting have a great deal in common. Good theatrical singers, these days, have to be able to act as well as sing, and dramatic speech, particularly within the classical tradition, Shakespeare, the French tragedians, Congreve and the Greeks, has a good deal in common with singing. The actor presents a modulated and coloured voice to express what he wants to express, and will select one pitch of his range rather than another to convey a particular emotion or comic point, just as a singer does. Remember Edith Evans' *a handbag!* which probably contains enough musical sounds within two words to be scored on a stave. The singer works within much more rigid limits than the actor, in terms of what can be done with the voice: the composer tells him or her how fast, with what phrasing and at what pitch, but both actors and singers are vocal artists, and a good director is well aware of the similarities and differences, and uses them all the time in his work.

So music of every kind should be a director's lifelong study and pleasure, and if he can play an instrument, read music and recognise the simplest principles of harmony and counterpoint, so much the better. Some acquaintance with pop music will be necessary too, as it can be a powerful dramatic weapon in the theatre, and a good many younger writers inhabit a world in which it is a shared language. The violent and terrifying noises which some pop musicians make, cannot really be matched anywhere else in the musical world, even by the most uncompromising classical avant-gardist, and if that is what you need to express in a play, you will know where to look. A good director will hope to have some working knowledge of the European musical tradition from, say, 1500 to the present day, including jazz, and a sound collection to back it up. A wide knowledge of books and music is a necessary part of a director's professionalism. Spare money and birthday presents should contribute to building up that basic recorded music library, as important to a director as a library of books.

When I began as a professional director, I was a musical illiterate. I was musical, and had played self-taught cornet in my own amateur New Orleans jazz band for three and a half years before going to Oxford. Purist New Orleans Jazz, of the most uncompromising kind, was my obsession: I even religiously played all Bunk Johnson's wrong notes. But like all obsessions, though it enabled me to find out a great deal about the particular kind of music I loved, it cut me off from every other kind. I used jazz in some of my university productions, of course, but as soon as I became a professional director, doing up to seven television plays a year, I found out that knowing about New Orleans jazz and nothing else was hardly an adequate musical background. At the simplest level, there were times when I knew I needed to use music, and I didn't know what to use. I had hardly ever listened to anything from the classical repertoire, and it meant nothing to me.

The question came to a head when I was directing a play by David Turner about a Midlands garage-owner with a deep love of the arts. I wanted something for the final captions, something uplifting and exciting, which would show how thrilling art could be, and I asked my PA, who loved music, and had frustrated conducting ambitions, to suggest something. He introduced me to the finale of Mozart's Jupiter symphony, a fine choice for the play in question, and listening to that marvellous counterpoint rolling round the gallery at TV centre as we recorded it, I thought I had never heard such a wonderful noise in my life. I went out and bought the record next day, and that week my musical education began. For years I bought records obsessively, two or three a week, and educated myself by listening, and eventually going to concerts. The process still goes on, as it always does with music, however late or early you start.

One of the greatest of a director's musical pleasures is commissioning new music for a play, from a composer he admires. As with every other aspect of inspiring your colleagues' creative faculties, the secret lies in the right choice of words. Give a composer as much hard-edged detail as you can. In my experience they are practical, clear thinking men and women – how otherwise could anybody put together anything as complex as an orchestral score? – and exact timings and clear descriptions of what you require, in colourful words, are more likely to be useful than anything else. Don't, if you want to make a good working relationship, tell them how to write the music, hum tunes, or say you want it in C Major. If you say *I want 35 seconds of grief immediately followed by two minutes of farce,* most composers will know what you mean, and be able to express themselves accordingly. You might mention a specific instrument, if you know what you are talking about, as long as you are not surprised or miffed when the composer brings back the piece you asked for on an oboe d'amore, written for a chamber organ or penny whistle. I often make reference to other composers, *something a bit Ravelly here, or a bit of Vaughan-Williams going for a good walk and enjoying the view,* and I always try to describe what I want through a series of vivid metaphors. With the composers I have collaborated with, these techniques have worked well. Other composers might hate them, and require quite different stimuli. As with your relationship with your playwright and designer, you must make your own, to suit your own creative personalities. Some people can communicate in grunts, and still know exactly what they want from each other.

If you feel the need to use established classics in a play, you must take the greatest care, particularly if they are from the Classical or Romantic age. Music from that period has a clearly audible musical structure of its own, which moves at quite a different pace from theatrical structure, and if once your audience begins listening to the musical form, rather than what your actors are saying, you are lost. Beethoven, Schubert and Mozart have their own things to say, and will not be easily incorporated within anyone else's scheme.

Otherwise, as a good rule of thumb, if, when you are working with music you are enjoying yourself, it is reasonably probable the audience will be enjoying itself too.

Crossing imaginary bridges

The last two chapters have illustrated a particular and important part of a directors talent and discipline: the ability to think ahead, to sense difficulties before they arise, to be aware of solutions to problems that have not yet arisen. Finally, it is a question of precision of imagination. Sitting in the quietness of your study, you must be able to see in your head the finished work on stage, and you must also be able to zoom in to the details and think them through, in the abstract, before they confront you in their horribly concrete reality. Then, when the unexpected arises in the rehearsal or preparation stage, you will smile wisely and bring out your solution. You won't ever find yourself running about in a panic saying *what the hell are we going to do now?* Directing is a great deal to do with establishing a natural authority among your fellow workers, an authority not based on sanctions, but on the respect your fellow workers have for someone who has the whole play at his fingertips and knows what he is doing. Being at a loss, or unable to suggest an answer to a problem within a few minutes of its occurring – certainly in rehearsal the reactions need to be that fast – undermines a director's authority very quickly indeed. A few days of that sort of indecision and he will find the actors or the designer taking over, and his own attendance at the proceedings becoming increasingly redundant.

In every aspect of the production on stage, the buck stops with the director, the final responsibility is always his. If your designer comes up with a set that falls over, or the costumes are unwearable and the actors stamp on them and walk out swearing, the director is finally to blame, not the designers. Of course, a director must trust the professionalism and artistry of his colleagues, but it is his particular task to spot the flaws in what designers and other theatre workers present to him, *before* they open into bottomless chasms that will swallow the production. A great deal of that sense of what is going to work and what is not, comes from experience, from having done a lot of plays and having been in similar situations before, and that can't be learned, only lived. But a great deal can be done by sheer force of imagination. Without that quality, without that feeling that you know exactly how a play will go on the stage, simply by reading and studying it, it is wiser not to attempt to be a director at all.

5

The Rehearsal Process

Directing actors is, for most directors, the most exciting and the most rewarding process in the production of a play. Most of the good and bad memories will be located there, and it is usually that aspect of dramatic art, more than any other, that makes people think they want to be directors in the first place.

Ninety per cent of the job is simply knowing how to handle people, being sensitive to their needs, and knowing how to persuade them to express themselves so as to express your wishes as well as their own. Psychiatrists are beginners in human relationships compared with theatre directors. All *they* have to do is to find out what motivates people, what's troubling them, and what might make them feel better. Directors have to find out all those things, and then encourage their patients to make art as well. Psychiatrists only spend part of their time with dreamers and fantasists. Directors hardly ever meet people who are not. Psychiatrists are sometimes bigger fantasists than their patients. Directors always are. They not only construct a complete dream world within their heads, they attempt to persuade a group of apparently sane people to share it, act it out, and make it real. Anyone apart from actors and directors doing that on a regular basis would be sectioned.

There is often a kind of lying involved and manipulation of people's personalities on a grand scale. A director must sometimes conceal the truth of what he thinks from the person he is working with so as to encourage that person to express what is in them, and he must sometimes tell brutal truths he would hardly dare tell people he cared for. He will know that for a good deal of the time the actor too is concealing what he really thinks or feels, and that a kind of game or evasive dance is being enacted as a way of approaching a new reality or insight. Sometimes, when a director wants to tell an actor something particularly important, he can only do it by asking questions, and sometimes when he wants a particular answer he knows that questioning is the one way he won't get it. If you are not interested in people, what motivates them, why they behave as they do and how they can be influenced to behave as you want them to, and if you don't have the patience to listen to someone talking himself out of a dilemma that you could solve for him in two words, there's no point in becoming a director at all.

No two directors approach the task of directing actors in exactly the same way, and some directors direct in a way that would be quite incomprehensible to others. When so much depends upon the interplay of close personal-artistic relationships, there can be no standard pattern, any more than there is a standard pattern of a human being. The cliché says that all directors fall in love with their actresses, but the reality is that they fall in love with all their actors for a finite period, the length of the rehearsal period and the first week of the production. During that time, if the work is going well, no non-sexual relationship could be closer, and there is no doubt that a good many sexual relationships are more distant. A good director will feel and experience everything an actor is feeling, will cosset and encourage him or her, be sad or angry when sadness or anger are required, and try to understand every fleeting emotion that is qualifying the actor's behaviour, just as a husband, wife, or long time partner will. Some directors, I am told, even sleep with their actors or actresses, but this is not a necessary part of the process, though it may well be an extremely pleasant one. The gratification you seek and share is artistic, and a great deal more difficult to achieve than the physical kind. Simultaneous artistic orgasm for director and actors may occur only a few times in a lifetime, and when it does, you will probably write a book about it.

Nevertheless, there is a rehearsal pattern and a method of work that is followed by a good many directors which is worth outlining, if only so that other directors can disagree with it. The English theatre works on very limited time schedules compared with some European theatres, and this manner of work, though it can, in unimaginative heads, lead to dull and unquestioning productions, is a way of producing good work in a short time, in a profession which is very unforgiving of disorganisation, and gives no second chances. You can rehearse a play efficiently this way. The skill and insight with which you do it, as always, is up to you.

Most rehearsal periods in the English theatre cover four weeks before actually moving onto the stage for final technical and dress rehearsals. The big subsidised theatres will sometimes schedule five or six weeks or even more for a large-scale production, and there are West End commercial companies that insist you make do with three, but the one month outside rehearsal is the standard period for most plays.

More often than not it won't take place in the theatre where the play is to be performed. If it does, you are lucky, because from day one you

will be measuring yourself against the actual performance area – minus
the audience, of course, and that is a big minus – learning to wear the
theatre space like a new suit, pushing your arms in, feeling the stretch,
getting comfortable. Most times you will be in a rehearsal room, which
can be anything from a custom-built building, with full stage space,
clean lavatories, coffee facilities and a green room with a phone, to a
basement room in a pub, or an unheated dilapidated church hall on an
estate where civil war is taking place, and the local kids yell *oy, actor
pouffs!* and break the windows. What you need in a rehearsal room is
an uncluttered space which is more or less the size of the stage, with
no pillars supporting the roof in unhelpful places, sufficient room to get
at least a few feet back from your actors, and the basic creature
comforts, like warmth, decent air, lavatories and coffee. What you get
will depend on who you are working for, where, and how much
money they have. Some actors will simply refuse to work in uncivilised
conditions, but in these days of deregulation, weak Unions, and the
breaking down of workers' rights in all areas of society, it is not
suprising what some will put up with.

Directors should fight as hard as they can so that their actors can be
comfortable and the work can proceed in a civilised way. If he is
working for a producer or a large organisation, the director should try
to be the actors' representative to his own bosses, in so far as he has
the power to do so – which may be hardly at all. If the actors are going
to rely on him in their artistic world, they should feel that he is on their
side in every other, and is not likely to sell out their interests at the
slightest opportunity.

It is in the director's own interest too. Happy, comfortable actors will
work better and dig deeper in their pursuit of the truth. You can't
expect your actors to make brilliant discoveries if they are cold,
wretched and annoyed. They will just want to get home as soon as possible, and will perform the play the easiest and most obvious way, so
as to get it done and get out. If rehearsal conditions are intolerable, the
director should be the first, not the last to say so, and to insist on a
change.

Until recent years, hours of rehearsal were controlled by union
agreements, and no one would expect to work more than from 10 or
10.30 a.m. till 5.30 or 6 p.m. during the rehearsal period. In some areas
of the theatre these rules, written or unwritten, still stand, but in some
they no longer do, and people ask their actors to work longer hours
with no thought of overtime payments.

Quite apart from moral considerations, it isn't very wise to treat
actors like workhorse drudges. A good director should be able to get
in all the work that is necessary in an eight hour day, and, mostly, a

five day week. An intense eight hours, where the work is focused and no time is wasted, ought to be enough for anybody, particularly the poor director. Except in a solo show or two-hander, the director is likely to be the only person who is working all day without a break, and if he has worked hard for his eight hours, he ought to be like a wet rag, capable of nothing more than a drink, a decent meal, some chat, and perhaps a little light preparation for next day. It's only if rehearsal time is wasted that the pressure to work longer hours arises.

I try to give actors the weekend off from rehearsal if I can, to give them time to learn their text, and to brood on the week's discoveries. Sometimes I do find myself working Saturday morning, just to finish off the week's schedule, but I try never to work Saturday afternoon or Sunday, unless the alternative is disaster. Actors are not machines, and time spent sitting in a chair at home, looking at a script, or walking in the garden or the park thinking, is often quite as valuable as time in the rehearsal room. A director who overworks his actors is probably a bad director. He is making the actors suffer because he can't get his own work done to time. Conversely, actors always appreciate the professionalism of a director who structures his work so that it finishes on the dot, or a few minutes after. You don't have to make a fetish of it, as Granville Barker apparently did in his later years. Joyce Carey and Stephen Murray, who worked with me in 1977 on Barker's *Waste*, told me that in the late 1930s, when Barker had married a rich American woman, and mostly retired from the theatre, the uniformed chauffeur would march into the rehearsal room on the dot of 5.30, and Barker, who dressed for rehearsal in a morning-coat, and some-times wore a top-hat, would leave, even if the actor was in mid-sentence. That, I feel, is taking detachment rather far. But it will create a good impression if your rehearsals begin on time and end as planned, with the work for the day adequately done. It helps to create an atmosphere of intense and concentrated work with people who know what they are doing, and that atmosphere is what you must strive to create by every means possible if you are to have a successful and productive rehearsal period.

The first day of rehearsal is an important one. I always spend the first fifteen minutes socialising with my actors, while we all drink coffee. That time isn't wasted. Some of the actors may be old colleagues you haven't seen for many years, and most of your actors in a cast of any size, will have met each other in some capacity before. Actors have a talent for picking up a working friendship, even after years, and the hugs and kisses and laughter will all contribute to the creation of the warm friendly atmosphere in which the best work is done. The first fifteen minutes will also allow time for any of your actors who do happen to be late, as is always possible with modern traffic conditions and an unreliable overground and underground train service. Nothing is more terrible for an actor than to be late on the first morning – and the quarter of an hour chat can have other uses too. There will probably be two or three young or less-experienced actors who will be feeling terrified, particularly if you have stars present, and the social atmosphere, and the warm welcome they are almost certain to receive from their fellow actors, will make them feel much more at ease than they would if you all sat down at once and plunged into a reading. Nine times out of ten the senior actors will make a point of welcoming inexperienced players, or those new to the game. The real masters of our profession are warm and generous people, eager to share what they have learned, and still learning themselves. The monsters and the bitches – and there are a few – are usually not quite as wonderful as they think they are.

I always have a reading of the play on the first morning, though I know some directors do not. I find the formal reading useful for several reasons. You will be well aware that, though some actors will give you a very powerful and intense reading of the script, others will mutter, make mistakes on every page, or read in such a flat and unin- teresting way you might wonder if they are actors at all. Even so, most actors will give you a pretty clear insight into where they are starting from, even the ones who refuse to participate fully. By careful listening, you will get a good idea of where you will need to begin with each actor. Some, you will feel, are wildly off the beam, and though you won't make any critical comments on the reading itself – most actors would be mildly insulted if you did – you will be ready to begin work straight away on things you know will have to be radi- cally changed. You might make some general remarks after the reading, about the overall direction you hope the acting will take, or about the movement of the play as a structure. But actors themselves feel that read-throughs are a wary approach to the play, a sniffing out of a text, and will not expect any detailed comment on what they have done – except praise, of course, which is always welcome, and, used well, one of the director's most useful weapons. There will be some actors you will already have decided you are going to praise a great deal, and you will tell them how much you enjoyed the reading, and how tremendous their performance is going to be. But they will be the exceptions rather than the rule.

The actors too will find the read-through useful, in much the same way as you will. They will learn important things about people with whom they are going to be acting their main scenes, a first indication of their timing, and their vocal timbre and range, all of which details, though not yet defined or pinned down, will help to indicate to them how they are going to begin their own work. They will also, of course, be making their first assessment of the director, as much as he will be assessing them.

Read-throughs also give you an indication, and usually a pretty accurate one, of how long the play is going to be. Of course, you will feel that some passages will be too slow, others too fast, and that in certain places staging effects will slow up the movement of the play compared with a mere reading. But these profits and losses do tend to even themselves out over the rehearsal and early performance period, and it is remarkable how often plays, when they have reached their optimum performance time, prove to be within about five minutes either way of their original read-through time.

Finally, you will all hear the whole play read, and you will all be sensible of it as an artistic whole, probably for the last time for several weeks. There won't be another complete hearing of the play till the first run-through of the fully directed performance, which will probably not be until about a week before opening. During the read-through, you will all become aware of the play as a dramatic structure, of how it moves from scene to scene, where the great climaxes are and where the periods of relaxation, and this is crucial information, both for actors and director as they begin to work on the play. For weeks all they will be doing is dismantling the play into smaller and smaller components, so it is a good thing to remember how the whole thing functioned, even in the restricted circumstances of a reading.

After the reading is over, I usually demonstrate the model box to the actors, and explain to them in broad gestures how the production is going to work. If there is anything of a general nature I want to say, any introduction to the world of the play or detailed explanation of the kind of production I want to do, I will usually fit it in between the read-through and the beginning of blocking work. If I have only a little to say, I will say it before the reading begins, after welcoming the actors and formally introducing them to each other. I will hardly ever get into any kind of shared discussion with the actors at this stage.

The longer I have been in the business, the shorter my introductory speeches to the play have tended to become. If I have some essential information to give, historical background perhaps, or a particular personal slant on the play's meaning, I might talk about it at this time, simply to avoid making the same speech to each individual actor later. But I learned early the dangers of talking too much. When I was twenty-six I did a production of *The Winter's Tale* on BBC television, with a very distinguished cast, which included Robert Shaw, Rosalie Crutchley, Brenda Bruce, Ron Moody, Norman Rossington, Geoffrey

Bayldon and Alan Rowe. I had done a great deal of work on the play
at Oxford, and had begun a close study of Shakespeare's use of
medieval rhetoric, which can clearly be traced in all his plays. The use
of the formal figures of rhetoric, whether of word-change, word-order,
sentence-structure, or over whole paragraphs, figures of repetition,
inversion and climax, was second nature to Shakespeare throughout his
writing life, as basic techniques we have been taught at school always
are. There is not the slightest doubt that the understanding of
Shakespeare's verse, *as poetry*, is completely transformed by a knowledge of the technical devices or poetic structures he customarily uses,
but I was convinced that the actors' approach would be transformed
too. So, wishing to make clear to my cast at the beginning my own
unconventional – as I imagined – approach to the play, and the information I had gleaned from my study of rhetoric, I proceeded to lecture
the actors for *two days*! I sat them round in a semi-circle, and talked at
them, about anti-romantic comedy, patterns of tragedy and redemption,
and all the rhetorical figures, with references to their usages in the play.
I still go hot with embarrassment at the recollection of all those experienced and immensely gifted actors politely listening to this earnest
young man regurgitating his reading, without even one of them
shouting out *do you think we could possibly get on with the play now?* I
began to feel the falsity of the situation myself during the second day,
and cut short what I originally intended to say, which might well have
lasted three days! Coming out of the rehearsal room at the end of the
second day I asked Geoffrey Bayldon, whom I had worked with twice
before, if he though the information about rhetoric was going to be of
any help in acting the play. *No, none whatever,* he replied briskly, *but
it was interesting.* Which was a typically kind actors' way of getting an
enthusiastic young director off a hook of his own making. Since that
still hot-making occasion, I tend to make my introductory talks brief and
to the point, and rarely go on beyond about half an hour. I feel now
that most of what you want to say to actors is best said to them as
though discovered while working, even if you have known it for years.
It may involve a certain amount of repetition, but it is much more useful
than standing up before a crowd of probably slightly bored actors,
pretending to be a university don.

Of course, I do not mean to suggest that the sort of literary-historical
information I was trying to convey is not useful, indeed crucial. I am
quite sure some understanding of rhetoric and Shakespeare's use of it
contributes to the successful acting of his plays, and there is no information, however scholarly, that isn't useful in some way or other. Not
being of the ignoramus school of directors – of whom there are a good
many – I am a great believer in the validity of historical and poetic

information. But the point at issue is how such information should be conveyed. Working with a standing company over a period of months or years on several Shakespeare plays, it would be very interesting to investigate patterns of formal rhetoric and see how they might modify truthful acting. But standing up before a whole cast and lecturing to them turns them into a class and you a teacher, whereas the real relationship should be one of fellow-explorers investigating unknown lands together. That is when such information will be really illuminating, when you can offer it as a way to solve a particular problem the actor is experiencing. Most actors couldn't care less about literary or poetic history. But if you offer them some information which helps them to say a particularly complex line or paragraph more effectively and more truthfully, they will bite your hand off for it.

A good many directors at this point conduct what they call reading rehearsals. When I went to Poland in 1976, to direct my play *The Exorcism* at the Teatr Bagatela, Krakow, the actors and the dramaturg expected me to conduct at least a week of reading rehearsals, sitting round a table discussing every aspect of the play. They were very shocked and considerably put out when I said I never did reading rehearsals, and we would begin blocking straight away, on the first afternoon of rehearsal. They had never experienced anything like that before.

Similarly, a good many English directors like to sit round with their actors, sometimes for several days, discussing the play and the characters in great detail. To each his own technique, and if it produces a well-performed play, by definition it works. For me, nothing serious can be learned about acting sitting with your bum on a chair looking down at a script. That is just intellectual discussion, which anyone can do, and which a good many actors are not particularly good at. Every word in the play will be said in some sort of action, and the way the words are said, even what they mean, must be modified by whatever that action is. If you say a line crawling flat on your belly, or running on the spot, you will obviously say it differently, and it is precisely in the presentation of that sort of truth through speech and movement that the real actor's talent lies. So it seems to me that anything discovered by sitting round discussing things is suspect, because you are discussing things out of their proper context, which is dramatic action.

So, on the first afternoon, I get my actors up on their feet, texts and pencils in hand, and we begin to stumble into moves at once. Immediately all kinds of discussion points will come up, about meaning or characterisation or anything else, but they will be considered in the context of the action that is to contain them, and that is much more likely to make them true to the play.

There was one other early rehearsal technique I saw demonstrated in Poland which was so extraordinary that it seems worth a mention, though I have never heard of its use in the English theatre, and it probably could not be used with English actors without special training.

In the first blocking rehearsal, the actors stood up without their scripts. I was startled, but I assumed they had perhaps learned their parts as a compliment to a foreign director, or because it was their usual method. But I was distinctly off-put by the oldish woman, hunched over her script at the edge of the rehearsal space, who seemed to be muttering sotto-voce while the actors were speaking. My actors were working in Polish, of course, which I do not speak. I was directing them through the dramaturg, who spoke excellent English, and acted as my interpreter.

It soon became clear that the sotto-voce lady was a kind of repetiteur, quietly speaking the lines just before the actors were due to deliver them. The actors did not know the script at all, but this technique enabled them to begin rehearsing without having to carry scripts and pencils in their hands, so that some form of motivated movement and eye-contact was established from the beginning. Thinking through the part was not possible, obviously, but then neither is it when English actors are feeling their way into rehearsal, scripts in hand. To the Polish actors it was second nature, a technique they had grown up with, and, I must admit, a very efficient one. They returned to their scripts between sections of rehearsal, to make notes and study their texts, but they were trying experiments with their acting from the beginning, at a time when most English actors are mumbling with their noses in scripts, falling over the furniture and generally acting like grizzly-bears in a tap-dancing class.

Blocking

The word *blocking* is so generalised as to be almost useless – except for the fact that it is in universal use in the theatre and everybody knows what it means. But the range of movements it covers from, say, the absolute naturalism of a play set in a clothing factory to the abstract choreography of a Greek tragedy, is as wide as the dramatic repertoire itself.

Different kinds of movements demand a different kind of skill from the director. An ultra-naturalistic play, particularly a play that dramatises work, will require the most precise attention to detail from both director and actors, and may involve the learning of a specific technique, how to work a sewing machine so as to look as though you do it every day of your life, how to operate scientific equipment convincingly, or, memorably, in David Storey's play, *The Contractor*, how to put up a marquee on stage, and then take it down again. Here, both actors and director initially rely on the playwright and your first question is *has he got it right?* Do the actions he has described actually work? Can a tent be put up that way? Is there going to be time to do what the script requires, and does the dialogue he has written fit the actions, or are there too many words, or too few? Most often, if a playwright has written a play about some sort of work environment it will be because he has himself worked in it and knows what he is talking about, and then the director's task will be comparatively simple. He must, as far as possible, make himself familiar with the operations required, if necessary by going to watch them in the real world of factory or office, before rehearsal begins, so he can demonstrate them to his actors as though he has been doing them for years. The thing *not* to do is to grin at your actors and say *well now, how the hell do we work this!* You are paid your wages to find out that sort of thing, and even if you are not expert yourself, as it is hardly likely that you will be, you ought to be able to give your actor clear indications of how to start, and directorial advice about how to *appear* proficient. Actors do not have to be technical experts, they merely have to act as though they are, just as when you twist an actor's arm behind his back or punch him in the stomach, you don't actually hurt him, you *act* hurting him, just as he acts being hurt. Attention to detail is the beginning and end of the process. The more details of the technical operation you can incorporate, the more convincing the performance will be.

Too often, the director will be picking up the pieces for a playwright who has not worked out his play carefully enough. It is surprising how often a playwright has a character say *let's put the kettle on* and then three lines later *do you like it with milk and sugar?* In such cases the director will simply have to persuade the playwright either to cut the tea-making, or write sufficient dialogue to give the kettle time to boil and the actors time to make it. Any decent playwright, if he is red-faced enough to have been caught out in such a *pons asinorum* of technical incompetence, will usually go and sit in a corner, and bring back the required dialogue in about half an hour. Strictly speaking, the director should have spotted the fault long before rehearsal and had it put right then.

A more common playwriting problem is when the director finds himself confronted, in what purports to be a naturalistic play, with long speeches, or conflicts between the characters which go on for pages with no apparent reference to movement at all. The director and actor need to find creative ways of sustaining the long speeches or dialogues, which may be complex in their ideas or passions, by imagining natural moves which will not distort or distract from the words, but keep the characters as living presences on the stage, and not just talking machines. It is surprising how the most mundane movement or piece of business, the wiping of reading glasses before putting them back on the nose, the pouring of a drink, even an apparently aimless move to a window to look out, can give real theatrical life to what appears to be a long literary speech. Very many plays, from the summit of Ibsen, Chekhov and Shaw downwards, are written in this manner, and it is a test of the really good director how convincingly he brings such scenes to physical life. Sometimes it is very effective simply to let your characters sit and talk. But a well placed movement can be quite as effective as the speech itself, can even transform the speech and its meaning, if it is conceived by an actor and director who know what they are doing.

I link the two together purposely. A director should have a complete plot of such a scene in his head to fall back on if everyone's imagination simply seizes up, but working out a pattern of moves is so crucial for the actor's sense of his own reality, that most will want to participate in their creation, and indeed to suggest to the director moves that will help to express what they feel about the scene. An actor like the marvellous Alec McCowen who, as we began blocking my play *When the Actors Come*, said to me *oh, put me where you like, dear boy, I can act anywhere,* is still probably the exception rather than the rule.

In such scenes you will discover a pattern of moves with your actor, by trial and error, each of you suggesting ideas, which may or may not work, and gradually, perhaps over a period of weeks, coming to a happy agreement. There is no point forcing on an actor a move that feels wrong to him. He is never likely to make it convincing, and you will have to change it later, if not sooner.

At the other extreme, performing a Greek play or a Shakespearean text, when the setting and the style of your performance does not impose naturalistic detail on your actors, the blocking is much more the director's business. All good actors will suggest moves that feel comfortable to them, even in the most abstract theatrical contexts, and a good director will always listen and very often adopt the actor's suggestions. But there is not much point in an actor suggesting a move for himself, if he is one of a Greek chorus with fourteen others. There, the movements, if not actually choreographic, are likely to be stylised into some kind of formal pattern, and fifteen actors moving in absolute unison will certainly be performing the director's wishes rather than their own. At that level, movement on stage approaches dance, and you may well want to get in a choreographer or movement director to assist you in your staging. The theatre is becoming more, not less, collaborative and directors who forty years ago would always have directed all aspects of movement and designed their own lighting plot, are now happy to call in full-time specialists in those particular fields. The director as theatrical Renaissance man is a rare bird these days, and even if he is skilled in many fields he might well bring in a movement director or fight specialist because he wishes to add another imagination to his own. The director, like a spider at the centre of a web, reacts to the least touch on the silk, and has ultimate control of what all his collaborators do, so the overall vision is still his.

Moves should never be set into concrete until the play has reached its final form in your production, and not even necessarily then. There is no compulsion to get it right first time, and just because a move seems to be working for a particular speech doesn't mean that it wouldn't work better another way. The way the actors are moving on the stage, whatever the style of play, should be continually questioned in the director's mind, until he is absolutely sure that he has selected the best solution of the many that may have been tried. After leaving Oxford, I worked for six months as student director, general tea-boy and script-carrier to the excellent director Frank Hauser at the Oxford Playhouse, and of the many things he said to me during that time I remember one in particular – *If you can't get a scene to work in the way you want it,* he said, *it's probably the move that's wrong* – and my own experience over thirty-seven years since that time has confirmed his wisdom. Sometimes you can try a dozen different ways of doing a speech or orchestrating a conflict without any improvement, and then finally you realise that the slightest adjustment to the moves, a turn on a different line, or a cross in a different direction, unlocks the problem, and all the impassable barriers in the text simply disappear as if they had never been there.

There are no rules about *when* you do your blocking. My own temperament as a director leads me to throw a play onto the stage, almost to hurl a pattern of moves at the actors as quickly as I can, so as to get the whole play onto the stage within the first week. I have a horror of endless discussion of motivations in the first weeks so that nothing concrete gets done (I once found myself directing a particularly argumentative actor whom I indulged too much, till I realised there were only a few days before dress rehearsal and half the play wasn't properly blocked). Discussing motivations is immensely important of course, but I like to have something concrete in the way of dramatic action to work with, so I work very intensely with my actors during the first week, hoping to get every scene staged, even if only in a very rough form, knowing that we will return to every scene in great detail during the breaking-down process that follows, and that the best form of the blocking will be discovered then. It also gives both actors and director a warm feeling to go home with on the Saturday afternoon, knowing that a kind of rough-and-ready version of the play has been completed, and we can do it as we have blocked it if we have to.

But once again, there are no rules beyond the overall rule, *work till you get it right.* The young director Richard Osborne, directing the stage première of my translation of Euripides' *The Women of Troy,* in a smallish studio theatre, left the moves purposely imprecise through-out the rehearsal period, letting the actor and four actresses move more or less where they liked. During intense and detailed discus-sions of the play during the next three weeks, most of the moves emerged naturally and they were finally pinned down a few days before the final run throughs. Two completely opposed ways of working, both of which can, and do, yield excellent results, well-acted and beautifully blocked plays. Every director has his own method of finding a way to the scenario of moves that for him most completely expresses the play. All that matters is that he gets there, not what particular route he follows.

The DSM functions as the director's right hand during the rehearsal period, and never more so than in the business of blocking. When creative possibilities are being explored between a director and actors things may move very quickly, moves may be invented, or changed, and then changed back again, in a very short time. The top-rate DSM will keep a record of *all* these variations, not just keep rubbing the old moves out and scribbling in the new. Very often actors will decide, after the ninth version, that they were actually happier with the version they started with. Very often, too, the director will smile secretly, it having been his intention throughout the nine versions to lead the actor to a rediscovery of the first. But if no one can remember what the first was then the point of the tactic is lost. The best kind of DSM will be able to dictate exactly what happened during the first version from the prompt book, and in every other version too, should it be necessary. That way a great deal of anguish can be saved, and the director will be reminded once again, if he needs reminding, what a crucial person the DSM is.

Break down and synthesis

When the play has been roughly blocked, the breaking down process with the actors begins. By this time they will be becoming familiar with the text, and a good many will have loose-learned it, so that they can work off the script, even if they need regular prompting. During the breaking down process the first attempts at real acting will begin, even if only for the odd paragraph, and a script in hand at this stage becomes an impediment to both actor and director. Looking down to check the lines breaks eye-contact with fellow-actors, and carrying a script means that the actor cannot rehearse handling props with any accuracy. Most actors, in my experience, except when they are playing huge parts like *Oedipus* or *King Lear,* try to divest themselves of the script by the end of the first week, and most directors need them to do so at the earliest opportunity after that. Late-learners are the bane of everyone's life, fellow-actors as well as the director. They scare their colleagues too. All actors know that a script needs to have been learned at least two weeks before a show opens if it is to be safe. During that time it will become second nature, and short of some extraordinary occurrence, or one of those moments of blankness that sometimes happens to all actors, memory will not let them down. But if the text has been learned too late, the varying stimuli of live performance are such that the brain may be distracted and lose its concentration momentarily, and because they are not yet firm-set, the words will go. There is nothing actors loathe more than a colleague they cannot rely on. If an actor is having real trouble with words, on account of failing memory or stage-fright, fellow-actors will always help him out. If he has simply been lazy with his learning they will be very much less sympathetic.

During the breaking down process every minute detail of the emerging performance must be examined by the director and actor working together. There are two criteria that define the work that will be done at this time: truth to nature, Hamlet's injunction, that we should observe our fellow-men and women and try to reproduce their behaviour; and truth to art, so that what we act is relevant to the world the performance is creating. Each kind of truth depends crucially upon the other, and neither can exist independently without modification by the other's existence. The theatre is not real life. We do not simply imitate exactly what we see on the streets. There is a winnowing process, a selection. We imitate only what the art of the play we are presenting requires us to imitate. Unnecessary naturalism is boring on stage, but if you turn the idea round and look at it from the other side, so is unnecessary art. Art is a formal construct engendered in the human imagination, the art of acting no less than any other, but imaginative creativity has to be at work on something we recognise as true. The most supreme acting stylist, the most superb master of vocal nuance and movement becomes as boring as the most brainless naturalist if his style has no relation to the truth of the world around us. It is an equation that must be held in constant balance, and depending upon the style of the play, the balance will tilt one way or the other. But the balancing act is always at work, reconciling art and nature so as to produce the illusion of truth. Keats said it in the most memorable way when he said *Beauty is truth, truth beauty*. Art must always be rooted in the soil of reality, and reality must always be shaped into artistic form, or there is no work of art created. Those are the necessary conditions for the creation of a Grecian urn, and they apply as surely to the actor's art as they do to the potter's or the poet's.

In most plays, you begin with the text. If it is the purest street naturalism, there will be little enough meaning to consider, most streetwise talk skating over the surface of life into verbal effects and evasions, and the burden of the work will be matching the naturalism of the acting, in delivery and movement, to the banality of the speech. Subtext, what the character means when he says the words, will occupy most of the rehearsal time. Normal daily speech between people is as often a way of concealing the truth as communicating it, and may represent a person trying to understand what he or she thinks or feels, rather than a statement of that person's views or feelings. Silences, facial expressions, movements of the eyes, what is going on behind the eyes, all become extremely important in this manner of acting, and the actual delivery of the words, which at times may degenerate into a mumble, far less so. There is still nature, and there is still art, but in this kind of work the balance will be heavily tilted towards nature. The director's task will be to sort out a coherent development of subtext within the character, or maybe even an incoherent development, if the character is incapable of coherent thought, and to make sure the words, facial expressions and movements are all concentrated on making that sub-text quite clear. It is a fascinating process, in which detail is everything. The ambition is to act all the way down, right into the centre of the brain, to think as the character would think, so that even a deep gazing into the actor's eyes will reveal nothing of the actor and everything of the character. The director studies his actor as though through a magnifying-glass, looking for the least suggestion of naturalistic untruth and pouncing upon it.

But the fact is that there are very few plays as naturalistic as that. The theatre, with its two to three hour span of live performance, is a form inimical to total naturalism, not least because the performances have to be projected, even if only to fifty or sixty people in a fringe venue. Almost all plays have a considerable element of art in the balance, and some that appear to be the most streetwise in their dialogue will be revealed to have constructed a theatrical speech which *seems* to convey the language of the streets, but in fact conveys it in a vivid and compressed form which is far more exciting and expressive than common speech ever is. All plays, even plays in rhyming verse, make some compromise with natural speech, and pretend that they are imitating discourse between recognisable human beings. In the rhyming couplets of Restoration tragedy, or the highly compressed metaphorical speech of mature Shakespeare, the art is at a premium, but if the poetic feet aren't rooted in the common earth of observed experience we soon lose interest. As the language of a play becomes more a matter of art and less a matter of the tape recorder listening, the director's task develops and becomes more interesting, but it does not change its fundamental nature, which is always a relentless search for the truth within the words and the art which expresses that truth.

So the first thing the actor and director must do together is to break down the text of the play to the individual words and phrases which comprise it, and to examine them from every possible angle. Is it quite clear what the words mean? Language is a notoriously slippery form of communication, and poets in particular are crafty fellows, loading words with all kinds of borrowed baggage, associations from common life, or their own lives, unstated cross-references to current or fashionable ideas, so that each word can often mean far more than will be revealed by looking it up in the Oxford English Dictionary. Each word, what is more, exists in a relationship with all the other words in the sentence that contains it, and beyond the sentence, in the paragraph and the page. Every aspect of every speech must be examined in this kind of detail. What did the author mean by the use of this word or that, by this or that construction of a particular sentence? Would the meaning be changed significantly by the removal of one word and its replacement with a synonym? With all good writers the answer to that question will be yes, but the question is still worth asking, because finding the answer will tell you something more about the author's meaning.

Then the sub-text, the meaning beneath the words, must be investigated. Does the character mean more than he is conveying in words, and if he does, what is it? Or do the words actually mean what they say they mean? What emotion is the character expressing or concealing as he speaks them? Sometimes the sub-textual meaning might be revealed to be quite the opposite of what the words say, as when a character greets his mortal enemy, with steel in his eyes, and says *how very good to see you!* What overall traits of character do these various sub-texts and their tensions with the actual text reveal to us about the person we are trying to play, and how will these revelations help us make the character seem true across the length of the whole drama? This process of exploration of language, motivation and character is bottomless, and with good actors on a good play, it can go on for ever, so it is part of the director's task to see that it does not, that the work is shaped and comes, in reasonable time, to some sort of conclusion.

Gradually the process of stripping down language and motivation will reveal some sort of movement within a scene. In a sense, acting is finding out how to get on to the stage, and then how to get off it, and developing this process for the whole play: how to play your first entrance, and how to progress in a coherent manner through your scenes to your last exit. When director and actor can honestly say that they have understood that journey from curtain to curtain, they have produced the play

The purpose of this relentless breaking down, of reducing the play to its component words and actions, is to be able, eventually, to build it up again in a coherent and fully understood form. Finally, the actor must understand why he is saying and doing whatever he says and does, and how each cell of action and thought leads on to the next. The director's principal job during the breaking down stage is to ensure that the actor goes through this process with relentless honesty, and explores every corner and cranny of the part, leaving no dusty alcoves or secret cupboards unvisited. Only when every aspect of the play's nature and art has been disassembled, and is, as it were, strewn about the rehearsal room floor, so that the working of every cog or hinge of action and feeling is understood, can the process of re-assembly which will lead to a smoothly-running play begin.

There are many ways of conducting this process of disassembly, this pursuit of understanding through every level of the text and action, and for me the most useful is the *why* question. A director will often feel that his preparation has given him a clear understanding of a scene or a section, and that his actor is not yet anywhere near it. The least effective way of directing the actor is simply to tell him *this is what the scene is about, let me explain it to you.* Then, once again, the director becomes teacher, the actor pupil. If a director is quite clear where he wants the actor to be, it is far better for him to lead the actor step by step towards that goal, or indeed, to give the actor the impression that *he* is doing the leading. This is where the *why* question is so useful. If, to every question the text raises, the director, like a child, simply asks the actor *why?* the actor's answers will lead him step by step towards the desired destination. *Why does the character say that sentence, why does he use the word 'disingenuous' rather than 'innocent,' why do you move there in that way, why do you pause and look at your fellow actor with exactly that expression, what does that particular gesture of the hand mean?* By using this technique and carefully structuring his *why* questions, the director can lead the actor by a Socratic method of question and answer, to the interpretation of the scene he wants. The great advantage will be that the actor will feel that he has achieved the answer by his own creative efforts – as indeed in one sense he has. But you, as director, will have carefully eased him towards the desired destination. Something you have discovered for yourself always means more than something you have been told. If you lead your actors towards moments of self-discovery, their work will be much more convincing, to themselves, to you, and to the audience than if, like so many theatrical parrots, they are just acting what you have told them to act.

The *why* question itself can take many forms, the *you're not making yourself clear to me* form, the *I don't understand how you got from there to there, explain it to me,* and the *I'm just a stupid director who's not very bright, and you're going to have to make the story a lot clearer than that if you want me to understand it.* But they are all versions of the same questioning technique, and in the hands of a subtle practitioner they are very effective ways of getting from actors what the director wants.

The breaking down of a play is the most devastating and reliable form of literary criticism I know. With a good play, the more you tear it apart the truer it will seem, and every layer you wrench away will reveal another layer beneath, even truer. Like life, you will never find a final answer however deep you dig, so that your actors, night after night, will face their performances with excitement, not boredom, because they will know that there is always more to be discovered. Even when the play is scattered before you in all its disassembled component parts, each individual part will be glowing like a diamond, revealing within itself further facets of the truth the play is examining.

Bad plays, by contrast, fall apart in your hands. As soon as you take them to pieces you realise that they don't really fit together at all, or fit like a jigsaw, two dimensionally, not three dimensionally, like life. You are handling a limited construction, which will work as a clock-work motor works, when you wind it up, but which has nothing to do with the mystery of real life, which doesn't work with a key and a spring but through much deeper and more incomprehensible forces. With clockwork plays, or plays which fall apart in your hands and have to be hurriedly glued and strung together, the actors will ulti-mately get bored. There is limited enjoyment in making a clockwork toy work or in concealing a playwright's inadequacies, and it is not to be compared with the excitement of the nightly quest after truth the actor playing *King Lear* or *Oedipus* experiences.

But plays will not work if you leave them in pieces on the floor. After the breaking down process, when everything has been under-

stood as far as it can be with this particular play and these particular
actors, the play must be reassembled, and the building up process will
begin. If you and your actors have worked well on the process of
breaking down, and really understood each other and the play, then
the process of synthesis will begin of its own accord. The actors will
see all kinds of connections, and as they master the learning of the
words, whole sections will begin to cohere quite naturally into a
truthful statement of the play's meaning. It is just as well not to interfere with this process, if it is going well. It is a natural growth from
inside the actors' own personalities and talents, and if it continues into
performance, the most valuable part of your work will be done. What
the actor will be discovering by reassembling all his details will be the
unity of the play and the wholeness of his character within it. When
he comes onto the stage he will now understand the processes of
thought and feeling he must go through before he can get off, and
will enjoy trying them out. Eventually he will comprehend the whole
performance, and his part in the completed play, and you will be
ready to begin running through. The best advice to a director when
this creative process is happening is, *keep out of the way, don't interfere! The actor is going to do the acting, not you, and these processes
of inner growth are his own most precious contribution to the creation
of the play.* Only if you see the actor reassembling his components in
the wrong order, so that they don't make dramatic sense, should you
interfere. Then you must break the components down again, to see
where they were wrongly assembled, and start the process of
synthesis once more.

What you will have to do during this process of synthesis, however,
is to orchestrate the play. When a composer orchestrates a symphony,
all his themes and developments through different keys and melodies
to a final cadence are in place on his score, but he has not yet decided
what instruments he will use, or the details of speed and dynamics he
will write into the stave. A director's task in the last two weeks is anal-
ogous. He must make sure the play is going to sound right, that the
fast passages are slickly cued and really zip along, that the pauses in
the slow passages are not being clipped too short, that the climaxes
and relaxations occur where they should occur, and that the intensity
of emotion required during the dramatic high points of the play is
being sustained. Very often a good actor who really understands his
own part will be going too slowly for the scene. Everything he does
is truthful, but too measured, so that the play is dragging and
becoming dreary, and if two actors are playing a dialogue in this way,
the audience will soon go to sleep. What has usually gone wrong here
is that the actors are being too self-centred, they are concentrating on

their own truth, but not sharing their truth with each other, and they are ignoring the play's truth, its characteristic inner energy and speed of movement, so that the scene is two monologues rather than a dialogue. A play is always something of a tennis match, unless, like Harold Pinter, you sometimes require your actors purposely to miss a shot. Otherwise, most of the time, the more briskly you hit the ball back over the net, the more exciting the scene will become. There is nothing to compare with that Wimbledon-like interplay between a group of actors who are really on the ball. Each line adds another drive of energy to the scene, so that it can become as exciting as a rat-tat-tat of volleys in a doubles' final.

Good cueing is the simplest of disciplines the director should impose upon his cast at this stage. Of course, many lines will require to be delivered with a pause before them, particularly in naturalistic drama, where the fabric of the words is less important than the observed manner of speech and the thought-processes involved. But where any kind of style of language or literary formality, even to the slightest degree, is required, the cueing becomes crucial. The principle is quite simple. If something important is happening in a pause, a thought development is occurring, or an emotion is coming to the boil, the pause will be as long as it needs to be for that process to become clear, and must by no means be cut short. More often in such moments, the director will be challenging the actor to make it longer, not just by extending the silence, but by filling it with even more meaning. But most pauses in plays, particularly in sophisticated text-based plays, are not of this kind: they are little hiatuses while the actor focuses what is coming next, or gets his tongue round saying it, and they contribute nothing whatever to the play. These the director should remove with rigorous determination, like a sergeant major drilling his squad. After all, if there are fifteen speeches on a page, and the actor drops his cue by one second on each of them, and there are a hundred pages in the play, then that represents twenty-five minutes of performance time when nothing whatever is happening! Even a pause of half a second will waste twelve-and-a-half minutes, more than enough to define the difference between a lively performance and a dreary one.

Sharp cueing, on the occasions when it is needed, is not an easy technique to master, and has to be melded in to become part of the actors' thought-processes, not simply stuck on at the end of the previous line. Done well, it releases the play's own inner energy. Done badly, squirted on like hair-spray, it stiffens the texture of the dialogue into a completely artificial pace. The trick, handed down from generations of actors, is for the brain to instruct the mouth to begin speaking at the beginning of the last word of the previous actor's speech, not the end of it. Then, by the time the message reaches your tongue – unless the previous word is very long! – your first word will come out smartly on cue, not overlapping, but neatly butted up, like a good wood-join. It is startling how much energy this will release in a scene, especially if kept up over several pages. The play will be, in the actors' jargon, off the ground, and the audience will be vastly entertained. Of course, there is nothing more tiresome than this rattle of dialogue in a scene that doesn't require it, and which needs pauses to make its sub-text clear, or which simply needs to breathe a little. That leads to the worst kind of old-fashioned superficial acting, the upper middle class clatter of 1930s comedy style, when the plays mostly had no content and surface was all that mattered. But it is a technique that all actors should have at their fingertips, and if they don't, the director should train them till they do.

The older actors learned this technique during their apprenticeships, realising that the theatrical tennis match is not a competition, but an exhibition, and all four players are helping each other to keep the ball in play. The actors of that generation knew how to give the scene to their colleagues, with the slightest raising of an intonation at the end of the line, almost like lobbing the ball up to make it easy to hit. Then the actors or director would decide who had the important speech, who was going to score the point, and the others would work together to make sure he did so. Younger actors, most of whom, through no fault of their own, have not had a solid training of work in big theatres, very often do not know these tricks of orchestration and have to be taught them. If they have been badly trained, and think that acting is all nature and no art, they may even argue with the necessity, and say that such a raised intonation doesn't seem true to them, and their own truth requires that they drop the scene dead on the floor. But in most such cases the other actors will soon persuade their truth-obsessed colleague that acting is a team game – particularly the actor who is supposed to score the point!

These details of how one speech flows into another, where the climaxes are and where the relaxations, are the most important part of a director's work in the last weeks, if only because this kind of pacing is something actors cannot usually do for themselves, unless they are very experienced and have worked together in a company for several years. Left to themselves, actors will usually play a scene, however truthfully and powerfully, at a kind of steady jog-trot, not too fast, and not too slow. It is always easy to spot an undirected production of this kind, where there is no excitement in the pacing, and the whole evening is conducted at an even tempo, like watching medium-paced bowling all afternoon. This is the stage in the production where the actors really need the director, as a big orchestra playing a complicated score needs a conductor, and he must not be found wanting.

Orchestration, however, is not only a question of speed and pace, which are not the same thing at all: pace can be achieved while speaking quite slowly, and speed can be a very slow-paced business if it is being done without thought. It is also a question of vocal colouring. As a composer will decide whether to give his principal melody to a clarinet or a trombone, so an actor must decide how he will colour his own voice from moment to moment, and a director must be a part of that decision because it is the particular colour of the voice, as much as anything else, that creates emotion. If an actor wants to make us cry, he invariably does so by finding the right sound to convey what he is feeling, not simply by feeling harder!

A good, well-trained actor should have a whole orchestra in his voice, and be a master of every instrument within it. He must have trumpets and horns and trombones for his powerful heroic moments, when he wishes to shatter the glasses at the back of the stalls, and he must have ingratiating violins or melancholy cellos for his more passionate or tender moments. He should be able to touch a line with the delicacy of a harp, or sing it with the cold beauty of a clarinet or an oboe, or jangle like a xylophone if such a sound is required. In the greatest moments, in the supreme verse dramas of the repertoire, he must have the whole orchestra of his voice at his disposal, and thunder out a great *tutti* that will leave the audience awestruck. No one is going to come to terms with the storm scene in *King Lear* or Oedipus' vengeance in *Oedipus at Colonus,* without having the whole Vienna Philharmonic available in his voice, and actors who try without that sort of vocal equipment always fall short of the great roles. It is not a question of resorting to vocal tricks instead of the truth of the character, as some film-obsessed younger actors seem to think. It is a question of discovering truth by using the resources of the voice. A great deal of this vocal technique will have been created during the actor's training, and its usage is always the most personal part of the whole art of acting, never to be entirely predicted or pinned down. Some of the most exciting moments I have experienced in the theatre, in my own productions and in other people's, have been when an actor has suddenly discovered, in the very act of performance, a new sound which he hadn't achieved before. All actors, all directors, wait patiently for those moments of epiphany, knowing they are rare, and the true summits of our art. Nevertheless, during the later weeks of rehearsal, these questions of vocal colouring, in whatever type of play, should be a key element in the discussions between actor and director. The director will suggest, comment, criticise and praise, edging towards the sound that is in his own head, and hoping it will strike a chord in the actor's too. An experienced director knows that if he is lucky enough to be working with an actor who has the full orchestra in his voice, he can make suggestions and comments that may be helpful or not, but the actor, nine times out of ten, will deliver the goods in his own way when he is on stage.

Confidence

The final, and most important task in a director's detailed rehearsal process, is making it possible for the actor to act. Having been through both breaking down and synthesis with you, and sometimes, during that progression, having become on the most intimate terms, he will trust you as a kind of artistic father. Acting is such a terrifying art, with so much put at risk every time an actor goes on stage, that confidence in his own ability to deliver is what any actor, however eminent, needs in abundance in the last week before the play opens, and it becomes the director's most important function to help to create it. Sometimes even the greatest actors need it as much as any. I shall never forget Sir John Gielgud asking me worriedly in the last few days before he was to perform Tieresias in my *Antigone,* if it was really all right! I had been listening to him with the greatest possible pleasure, hearing my verses acted with such truth and verbal grace as I could hardly have dreamed of. *All right,* I wanted to say, *it's bloody marvellous!* That isn't what I actually said though. We discussed the matter a little, as I realised that even he, from his great eminence – he had just turned eighty – was sometimes unsure whether he was getting it right or not. Great actors sometimes find they get less direction than they would like, and perhaps I, in my respect for his unrivalled experience and unique verse-technique, had erred in that way. We spoke together for a few minutes, and some days later, he gave what I regard as a definitive performance. I wouldn't dare to say I *encouraged* him, but all actors do need encouragement, and it is a key part of a director's task to provide it as the performance approaches.

It is principally a question of stimulating your actors to take risks, and no one in any field will take risks unless they feel safe, they are quite sure what they are doing, and there is at least an even chance of success. If you have done your work well during the breaking down period, the actor will have learned to trust your judgement, not necessarily in opposition to his own, but certainly working alongside it. If you haven't succeeded in creating that trust with an actor, or within a group of actors, so that they feel at home with you, there is much less you can do. If your actors become a sullen and wary group, mainly concerned with their own survival, they will reject anything you suggest that might be at all difficult or out of the ordinary, and you will have become redundant. When that happens the director might just as well go home and leave the actors to get on with it. A director has no external authority, only the inbuilt authority that comes from respect, from the actors thinking, *this man knows what he is talking about, and my performance will be the better for listening to him*. Even if a director does have a degree of external authority, namely the right to hire-and-fire, it is not the sort of authority upon which you can base the production of a play. The actors must want to do what you suggest to them – not always, but more often than not – because your ideas are exciting and stimulating, because they are looking forward as much to working with you as you are with them, and for no other reason. Without that inbuilt respect from your actors, you can do nothing, and will be better off elsewhere.

If you have acquired that respect however, and have shown your actors in your working methods that you are technically competent and artistically stimulating, you will be able to nudge them towards performances they didn't know they had in them, and, if you are lucky, transform your production from a good into a great one. You will be able to encourage your actor not only to walk the high wire – all acting is that – but to do pirouettes and gymnastics on it too, or, to change the metaphor, to climb up to the highest board and stun the audience by the daring and precision of the dive. How you do this will vary from performance to performance and from actor to actor. Perhaps you will point to one little detail, that will open up vistas in the actor's understanding, or you will simply create an atmosphere of expectation, a metaphorical muttering in the ear which whispers *go for it, you can do it, nothing is beyond your reach*. It is the director's most subtle and profound task, and there are no rules for making it work. You must know your actor as an individual and an artist, you must judge what will excite him or her, and, crucially, you must pick exactly the right moment to make your pitch.

It has been my privilege in the last eleven years to work with two of the burgeoning great actresses of our age, Juliet Stevenson in 1984, when she was just beginning to emerge as a leading actress, and Fiona Shaw, who, when I worked with her in 1989, was already in her pomp. Both actresses were playing Greek tragedy for me on television, Juliet the incomparable heroine in my translation of *Antigone*, and Fiona, Clytemnestra, the mother of all vengeful mothers, in my *Iphigenia at Aulis*.

I had translated Antigone's great threnody, which she speaks with
the Chorus just before being buried alive in her mountain prison, into
rhyming verse. It is written in lyric metre in the Greek, and rhyming
stanzas seemed to me to be a feasible English equivalent. The threnody,
one of the great moments of Greek drama, was to be delivered accompanied by a live musical score, being piped in from another studio, so
that actress and musicians could feed off each other's intensity. Greek
drama, with its huge emotions and dark poetry, is hard to bring off on
television, where the audience has become accustomed to a relentless
diet of the most banal forms of naturalism. You won't succeed by
muttering the lines, pretending they're naturalistic really, and throwing
away the poetry. You can only do it by forgetting the filmic conventions
of the medium, and going for the mythic size and poetic splendour of
the epic stories.

This was the dimension of the problem Juliet was facing, the first
stanza of the threnody:

Antigone: In all my wandering, gentlemen, this place
Has been my home. I was born in this city.
And now I begin my last journey.
I look up at the sun in its familiar sky
And feel its warmth in my face
Only to say goodbye.
In the daytime of my life, in mid-breath
This security policeman, death,
Arrests me, as he arrests everyone, young and old,
At home, or in the street. To the cold
Waters of darkness we come, never
To return across that silent river.
No wedding for me,
No music, no guests in the room:
My wedding gift is eternity
In a stone tomb,
My dowry, for ever not-to-be,
Death my bridegroom.

There were three other stanzas, exactly similar in metre and rhyme-
scheme, separated by a series of rhymed interjections from the Chorus.

During the break down period, as we both faced this most difficult
but potentially most glorious section in the play, Juliet was justifiably
nervous, and her nerves increased when I said she needed to approach
it like an opera singer confronting a great aria, or singing the *Abschied*
from Mahler's *Das Lied von der Erde,* as a great outpouring of lofty,
stoical, grief about her approaching death. She had to use all the vocal

colours, I suggested, that a great singer would need, to express the pain locked up in those lines. In addition, it wasn't prose. The lines rhymed, and the rhymes meant something, part of the meaning was locked up in the way the words chimed with each other, and the way the metre delivered the words to the moment of rhyming. The RSC, where Juliet was rapidly becoming the leading young actress, were asking her to work in their own, at that time quite different tradition, emphasising meaning in verse at the expense of rhythm and sound, and what I was asking her to do, for a four week period only, as against a whole season at the RSC, went against all her instincts at that time. But I knew that if she played the part simply relying on the almost brutal quality of truth-telling of which she was already becoming a great mistress, she would miss the verse-music, where the profoundest levels of the poetry are located, and the play would be the poorer. There was no disagreement between us, no arguments about which way it should be done, just the usual mutual questioning and mental interplay between actress and director. Juliet saw what I wanted, but she was nervous about taking on that sort of grand style, in case it should destroy the truth she was seeking. Younger actors today do not normally consider the voice their greatest instrument, the most powerful truth-seeker they have. In the permanently shifting balance between nature and art, the pendulum has swung very much towards nature.

It was a good example of what I have been describing, the necessity for a director to encourage and inspire an actor to enter new and dangerous territory. With some actors you wouldn't attempt it in such exposed circumstances, but we had already seen enough of this young actress to know there was nothing she couldn't do, no mountain so high she wouldn't have an even chance of getting to the top. So my job was to use all my usual metaphors, *go out on the high wire, go off the high board, sing a great aria of grief and pain like nobody has ever done on television before,* and to say all those things in such a way as to make her quite confident that she could do it.

Of course, she delivered the goods magnificently, bringing new dimensions to the rhyming verse that were entirely her own. But you don't need to be working with an obviously remarkable actress to do this work. Any actor at any level can be pushed beyond his or her own personal frontier to discover things they never previously knew about their art and themselves, and it is one of a director's principal and most important jobs to do the pushing.

With Fiona Shaw, of course, it wasn't so much a question of encouraging her to go from the high board, more a question of discouraging her from hammering a hole in the roof and going from a passing helicopter. Faced with three or four enormously long, impassioned speeches, when Clytemnestra pleads with Agamemnon not to murder their daughter, there was never any doubt that she would go for it. Our discussions together were more about how the great moments were to be achieved from line to line, not whether she would take them on or not. On the last of three complete, uninterrupted recordings of the play – such things were still possible in BBC studios only seven years ago – I simply said, *this is the last opportunity with this production, so go for it, take all the chances, and if it doesn't work, we already have two good recordings in the can.* Such banalities were hardly necessary, but they seemed worth while, on the chance that something extraordinary would result. And it did.

A cameraman was making a short film of the production, and had been given permission to shoot unobtrusively during the recording. He happened to be focusing on Fiona for twenty seconds before she made her entrance for the confrontation with Agamemnon. Her concentration was almost terrifying, as she aimed a series of violent hammering punches at an imaginary punch-ball behind the set just before entering, to physicalise the passion of what she was about to attempt. The next ten minutes were quite extraordinary, as she gave a performance of an animal-like intensity. If ever the cliché of the lioness defending her cubs was justified, it was here. The physical violence with which she delivered some of the lines was quite terrifying, and none of us would have dared even to suggest it in rehearsal. It wasn't just a remarkable actress showing us what she could do. It was the essence of what Euripides asks for, the birth of the murderess who will later ensnare Agamemnon with a net and stab him in his bath in payment for her child's life. We saw the next stage in the curse of the House of Atreus being prepared, as the distraught mother turned into an implacable avenger. In films, when they do this kind of thing, when man turns into Werewolf, or Jeckyll into Hyde, they do it by trick photography. Fiona did it by sheer acting.

Two great ladies, and two high points in my own directing life, when they showed me what actors can do if you make the situation right for them; and it has happened other times too, at every level, from schoolchildren to great stars. It is one of the most satisfying, and certainly one of the most important of a director's functions to be able to inspire other people to excel themselves. In the best productions it is not by what you do, but by what you inspire other people to do, that you will be judged.

Run-throughs

The final stage of the rehearsal process begins when you start doing run-throughs of the play. If you have worked particularly well with your actors, and the process of synthesis is under way, you might get a run-through on the Saturday morning at the end of the third week. It will be what actors graphically call a stagger-through, but as long as the process of synthesis is beginning, it will be enormously useful, however many times it breaks down in laughter or disarray. It will be the first time the actors have experienced the play complete since the read-through, and if your break down has gone well, a good deal of the synthesising process will begin spontaneously during the act of running, as the actors pick up their hundreds of pieces and begin to see how they fit together. More often, you will get your first run-through early in the last week of rehearsal. If you have reached the Wednesday evening and still haven't run the play, the jagged landscape of panic will be beginning to dominate your vision. If you haven't done at least two decent run-throughs before you go into the technical rehearsals on the stage, you are dicing with death, and your fate is in the hands of the drunken God of the theatre, who may be in a kind and indulgent mood, or may not. It is suprising how many Friday disasters have turned into triumphs on Monday or Tuesday, with nobody quite understanding how. Perhaps the fruity old deity had had a few good drinks, and was feeling particularly mellow. But it is most unwise to rely on such immortal assistance, because there will be many times when it will certainly not be granted, and Friday's shambles will turn into Tuesday's disaster.

The run-throughs are principally for the actors, who must learn how to do the play as a complete performance, so the one thing the director must try to avoid doing is to interrupt them. If they degenerate into confusion and come to a stop it is a sign the break down work hasn't been properly done and the synthesis hasn't started. The director must intervene then, to ask the actors to begin again at a suitable point, with the ambition of continuing uninterrupted till the end. If the situation is too bad for that, he must return to detailed rehearsal, and give up the run-through for that day.

On a decently rehearsed play with well-trained actors that should not happen, so the director's task is to watch and listen with the greatest care, to identify the sections where more rehearsal is needed, or where the actors have taken a wrong interpretational turning, and to judge whether the overall meaning of the play which you intend to convey is actually emerging in performance. Do not trust your memory as you watch the play, but make detailed notes, so that you can remember in an efficient manner what further work you want to do on particular sections. Do remember, however, when you are making your notes, that the actors can see you, and will certainly be thinking *what is he writing notes for, what did I do wrong?* You must write your notes some time or other, but do it with consideration for the fiendishly difficult task the actors are performing for you. Acting requires intense and single-minded concentration. Make sure your rehearsal room is quiet, and that your actors are not likely to be interrupted by noisy outsiders or inconsiderate fellow-actors, and if you must make notes, do not write them during your leading lady's philosophically soul-searching speech, or your leading man's emotional breakdown. If you can write what you have to write without any of your actors seeing, so much the better.

I try to get as many complete runs of a play as I can in the last week, so that the actors give a series of performances without an audience, and I can judge them and give notes within a performance context: but that will depend on what stage you have reached with your work. It is fatal to do run-throughs if you are not ready for them. Sections of the play that are not working, because there is something basically misunderstood or not properly rehearsed, will not get any better however many times you run them through. You must rehearse them in detail, see what is preventing them from working, and put it right. If a scene isn't quite working because it is a little sluggish, or the actors are thinking too slowly, or don't know their words fluently, then running will certainly improve the situation without any further detailed intervention from you. As with every other aspect of direction, it is a matter of fine judgement, a consideration of how much rehearsal time you have left, and how it can best be used. If you get clear in your mind where the problems are, and can define them quickly during your notes session, you can then move swiftly into detailed rehearsal, and with luck you will soon find the solution. Your actors, too, will feel confidence in you, if you seem clear-eyed and know what you are doing. Even if you feel half-blind and all at sea, you should do your best to *act* as though you are completely in command. The actors at this stage depend crucially on what is coming from the director, and if he exudes efficiency and insight, their confidence will be bolstered. If they see him sitting in the corner in tears beating his head on the wall, they will not feel encouraged to go on stage at all, and some of the weaker spirits in the company might well be tempted to join him.

Of course, there will be deeper things to discuss with your actors, about the whole shape of the performance, the truth, or lack of it, in the overall portrayal, the relevance of what you are all doing, but it is wise not to squander rehearsal time by going into deep discussions of such things during the precious last few days. They can just as well be had over lunch, in the pub after rehearsal, driving an actor to the station, or having a meal in a local restaurant. Long phone calls in the evening or at weekends might be helpful too, for certain kinds of actor. Directors, like doctors on call, are never off-duty at any time during the production period. Always remember that all actors are different, and that among actors, as among any other cross-section of human beings, there will always be a fair proportion of distinctly odd people. You must find a way of talking to each actor which will be particularly useful to him or her. There are some actors who need to talk, and some who say nothing at all, some who love to be talked to, and some who hate it. There was one splendid character actress whom I had been looking forward to working with for a long time, who, after a few days of my usual sort of rehearsal, said *I can do it all right Don, so long as you don't talk to me!* Being a talking kind of director, the injunction was shattering. But I buttoned my lip, restrained myself, and of course, she knew perfectly well what I wanted her to do, though *how* she knew I still don't know to this day. There are other actors who need to talk hours of incomprehensible rubbish, which you must try to follow, and even if you can't follow it, you must act as though you can. Your job is to listen, so you nod a lot, and say *um, yes, I see,* and let the actor get it all out of his system, however confused it may be. For that sort of actor talking is an essential part of the working process, and should not be interrupted, because the actor will deliver the goods in his own way at the end of it. If he doesn't, then you have just picked a bad, garrulous actor, and you will have to live with the fact.

It is important to remember, as you watch your final run-throughs, that you are part of a two-way relationship. If you think a run-through has been particularly dire, slow and boring, you must question your own state of mind before laying into your actors. Were you tired? Did you have a row before rehearsal? Have you concentrated as much watching the run as the actors have acting it? It may be that they were doing their job well, and you weren't.

Being difficult

In the above pages, I have described a kind of idealised version of the rehearsal process, but of course in real life it will be complicated by the presence of real people, not just abstract 'actors', and a few of them will be difficult, even monstrous. It's one of the things about real people which we all have to learn to put up with it, in life as well as art, that sometimes they behave like angels, and sometimes like bastards. If you have sensitive antennae you will spot the bastards a mile off and run like the devil in the opposite direction. Or, to put it less dramatically, you won't cast them. One of the key elements in casting a play is to get together a group of people who are not only talented enough to play the parts, but whom you will enjoy working with, and who will contribute to the work of the group. But sometimes you will make a mistake, and realise you have cast a Gorgon, or a Medusa, who will turn you and the rest of the cast to stone. More often, you will have been handed some members of your cast as part of the package, you will have cast a brisk eye over one or two of them, sensed they were going to be a problem, and found out in due course how right you were. I have worked with three or four such monsters in my thirty-five years of working life, which is probably a rather smaller figure than a lot of directors might ruefully admit to. One of them I cast myself, the others came with the deal.

Difficult actors are nearly always difficult in the same way. They are entirely self-centred, see everything through their own needs and what they want to do, and very little in terms of the play, or the needs of their fellow actors. Some of them are simply a bit of a nuisance, who take up more rehearsal time than their share. Others are beasts of truly mythical proportions, the Hydras and Minotaurs of the profession, pretty well known to everyone, and universally recognised as a monumental pain in the arse. But because they behave badly, it doesn't by any means follow that they are bad actors. Many of them are not, and one or two are very fine indeed. Some good actors, without being truly monstrous, are self-centred and difficult, but most directors will put up with their tantrums and sulks, because, however tiresome they may be, they are genuinely devoted to trying to make the play and their own performance better. They won't put up with short cuts or easy solutions, and for the kind of directors who build their careers on short cuts and easy solutions – and, oh best beloved, there are a good many of them – their meticulous concern is intolerable. And, of course, self-centred actors who give wonderful performances, as long as they don't make life totally unbearable for their fellow actors, usually get away with it.

There is no easy way of dealing with the truly self-centred actors, the prima donnas of both sexes whose main concern is to keep themselves at the centre of the stage, only do things that will show them in the very best light, and who resent good work from any of their fellows, and do their best to sideline it. If you are stuck with such people, because they put bums on seats – and some of them do – you must use all your ingenuity and experience of dealing with people, do the best you can to keep them happy, and the rest of the actors happy enough to be able to perform on the same stage with them. With the worst of them you won't ever win, because whatever you do, they will behave like spoilt children. Most of them are neurotics of one kind or another, driven people who might wish to work another way but cannot, and some seem genuinely crazy. With two particular actors, one of each sex, and in different plays, with whom I was not getting on at all, I made a point of praising an aspect of their work I genuinely liked, in an effort to make some kind of working relationship with them. A fatal mistake. Next rehearsal they changed it, and I never saw it again. With such people you can really do nothing. They are concerned with point-scoring, power over other people, and constant buttering up of their own egos, and see acting in plays as a way of expressing their egomania, not a serious attempt to make theatrical art.

There are, of course, some pretty monstrous directors about too, and the actors' jungle telegraph soon beats out the warning who they are. The ones I have met, in my capacity as playwright, tend to be power-mad sadists. Fortunately, I have only worked with one, though I have seen others at a distance, as it were, and like everybody in our profession, heard some pretty grisly stories. Directors who like to make their actors cry or need all their actresses to get their clothes off, are to be treated with suspicion. It is a director's job to make actors feel confident, masters of their craft, not persecuted or covered in goose pimples.

There is also the kind of bad director who says silly or unfortunate things. Actors, like other creative people who lay their whole selves on the line every time they perform, are easily offended and upset, and a director must always be careful what he says in rehearsal. An ill-chosen word or phrase can destroy a whole week of patient work, or make the relationship between actor and director fatally compromised. The whole art of directing is finding the right words to say to each individual actor, the words that will help him or her to act better, and finding the wrong words is an uniquely disastrous thing to do, and may prove to be an irreparable error. It is not a good idea to say to your leading lady at the dress rehearsal *yes love, I think the dress was probably a mistake, but it'll have to do, and anyway you look lovely whatever you wear.* My favourite director's disaster story concerns a final note given by a BBC television director to a cast just about to record a Chekhov play: *it's all very nice dears, but can you all make it just a bit more Russian?* It would have served him right if they'd all spontaneously danced the gopak, sang mournful songs and shot each other.

Non-textual techniques

There are now a great many younger directors who will find the whole process of rehearsal outlined above very old-fashioned, and whose own work is done in quite different ways. What I have described is the traditional manner of rehearsal for a text-based play, and for many hundreds of directors and thousand of plays, it has worked very well for more years than anyone can measure, and is still working in theatres all over the world. But there are other methods, and though I cannot talk about them with the expertise of a practitioner, I shall mention some key discussion points for those who can. It cannot be said too often that the only criterion is the finished performance. If it works, if it is accomplished and genuinely mind-opening, no one will ever give a damn how it was rehearsed, or what particular rituals the actors and director constructed for themselves.

Many directors dispense with read-throughs, and may not initially have a script to read. Others who do have a script will approach it slowly, working through a series of theatre games or improvisation techniques before they confront the text. Theatre games range from group vocal exercises, through adult versions of party games, to more structured and complicated games/rituals designed to illuminate the psychology of the characters, or even the actors themselves. The justification seems most often to be to enable the actors to learn how to relate to each other as people and artists, and to unlock everyone's imagination and free up their passions so as to be ready to make startling discoveries. So objects are passed round the group, comments are made, scenes are played using a single word only, or sounds, there are sessions of group-chanting or noise-making, and different surrealist techniques are explored which involve actors personating inanimate objects, animals, plants, shouting at each other to the point of mania, or whatever the director will judge to be useful for the particular experiment in perception he is conducting.

None of these games are at all harmful, they may all be enormous fun, and some will certainly be useful, but I do rather question the time they take and whether it could be better spent. If the justification is to break down barriers between people, I can only reply that in my experience there are no barriers to be broken down between professional actors. Because they meet new people every few weeks, actors can plunge into complete intimacy with people they haven't seen for years, or have never met, within a few minutes. With the sort of actors I have worked with I have never felt the need to warm them up or to break the ice. They will be prepared to stage angry scenes or love duets at ten o'clock in the morning, if they are asked to, and probe deeply into their own or their character's psyche whenever the part requires it. Most of them will not want to get involved in mind-games unrelated to their parts, or for their own sake. But then, why should they? They are actors, not psychological toys.

My suspicion is that a good many of these techniques have been developed by university-trained directors – I'm not knocking them with a word, I'm one myself – who, working with raw students, have *needed* warm-ups and relational games to get a disparate group of untrained young people into the right mood to work, and have then carried their techniques with them into the profession.

Those who like to organise warm-up rituals at the beginning of every rehearsal should be warned that older actors, or even middle-aged ones, may be less than co-operative. *No old ducky, I don't chant, but I do like to fart a bit in the mornings. I'll join in with a few of those if you like!* Of course, all actors need to make themselves ready for work, but they can generally be trusted to do so in their own time, not yours. Warming up for a performance is another matter altogether. A cast performing a musical needs a good five or ten minutes of singing and dancing before the house comes in, and most actors have their own voice-warming and body-preparing techniques, which they work through in private on the empty stage an hour or so before curtain up.

Improvisation is another matter altogether, often a very useful rehearsal technique, though, in my view, very much less useful as a way of making a play. Many directors use improvisations as a way of getting close to the characters and understanding how they think or feel. They will ask an actor, or a group of actors, to place their characters in situations or social milieus that do not occur in the play, and to imagine spontaneously what the character might say or do. Particularly, if an actor has reached a knotty problem in a text that he cannot untie by the usual means, improvising around it may give him exactly the knife he needs to cut through it. In naturalistic drama, where the words are not at a premium and it is what is underneath the words that counts, improvisation can be invaluable in approaching an understanding of the most difficult moments in a character's development, or a relationship between two or more characters. In performances within that tradition, it is always likely to remain one of the most powerful rehearsal tools. In work where verbal style is more of a consideration, improvisation gets less and less useful, and it seems to me in the high stylists, like Shakespeare, Congreve or Wilde, it is quite pointless. It depends upon the idea that behaviour and the words that express behaviour are quite different things. In life, and in naturalistic drama, they often are, but in more literary work they are fused into a single verbal expression. The motivations and meanings in such work are contained in the words which express them, the two cannot be disjoined, and if different words are used, a different scene will be created. This scene may comment on the original textual scene, at a tangent as it were, but it cannot illuminate the problem of playing the scene in the actual words the text prescribes. To confront the problem of how to play *To be or not to be* by coming on stage and solemnly improvising *well, it's a question of staying alive, or not staying alive, isn't it! Whether I feel better in my head putting up with everything the world can sling at me, or whether I should say stuff it, get stuck in, and take on my troubles one by one till I beat the living daylights out of them!,* though it may get a few laughs, contributes nothing at all to the acting demands made by Shakespeare's famously compressed speech. Even to improvise the thought line rather than alternative words – *should I commit suicide, endure my troubles or attack them,* etc doesn't take us much further. Character, and truth, are indivisible from the words which express them. If the words are changed, the truth changes. So, though improvisation may be useful as an early rehearsal aid, as a route to the subtext, or to get at a complicated meaning by reflecting it in other words, once a sophisticated text has to be confronted and expressed in a specific and unchangeable language, it uses become more limited

Some directors, most notably, in England, Mike Leigh, have used actors' improvisations as a way of writing films and plays. The process is a careful one, of many improvised rehearsal sessions on a pre-discussed and researched plan, and a meticulous winnowing of the results, till a shape emerges, and the best improvisations cohere around it and form scenes, at which point the improvisations become fixed as a text. Great results can be and have been achieved by these methods. Mike Leigh's wickedly funny comedy *Nuts in May* is one of my all-time favourite television films, and there have been others, both funny and serious, though more often successful on television and in films than on the stage. The limitation, as you might expect, is that it is a method which only really works with naturalism. Actors are not writers, and they usually imitate what they remember people have said, so that nine times out of ten they improvise banalities. Mike Leigh's comedy was based upon the brilliant selection of a priceless catalogue of such banalities and the eccentric and slightly sad characters they illuminated. Writers too, when they are aiming at naturalistic targets, will write in carefully chosen clichés, knowing that much truth and pain can be concealed behind unimaginative language, thoughtless speech, and an impoverished vocabulary. The best kinds of writers though, from Harold Pinter and Arthur Miller to John Osborne,

Tom Stoppard and Alan Bennett, create a language that is entirely their own, as much a personal construct as the language of Wilde or Shakespeare. People in life do *not* speak as people do in such plays, which is what makes them memorable and worth their place in the repertoire. We enter a world of the writer's own creation, a particular balance between nature and art that is entirely his own, and no improvised dialogue can ever come anywhere near that.

The director must always be deeply suspicious of an actor in a text play who says *I was looking at the script last night, and do you mind terribly if I say this instead?* Nine times out of ten the actor's version will be quite terrible, and even if it isn't, if you are doing a play by a living writer he will probably have a fit and threaten to kill you both with a breadknife. Once you have agreed with the writer what the script is to be you must *never* allow actors to change it. If, as on rare occasions will happen, an actor comes up with a good line, you must ask the writer's permission – and you will very likely find out that it is an idea he had and rejected months ago. Actors can very often spot useful cuts, which the writer and director may bless them for, but they will hardly ever come up with usable lines of their own. As for ad-libbing – Shakespeare said it once and for all, and most writers since have agreed with him. Some actors are extremely good at it, and sometimes it can be very funny, but it is very rarely *right*.

In films, where scripts and scriptwriters are so little regarded, actors improvise their lines a lot of the time, and many directors encourage them to do so. But films are another matter entirely, with quite different parameters, both in acting and directing. A writer who writes for films writes with his eyes open, knowing very well the likely horrors and possible rewards.

Physical theatre techniques have emerged in answer to a long-felt need in the English theatre. It used to be asserted that English actors never acted from the waist down. They let their trousers take care of that. They put their hands in their pockets, showed off their creases, hitched up the waistbands, and generally paraded their lower limbs in tubular flannel or check. Sterner critics said the neck was the lower limit, and that English acting was entirely cerebral and verbal. That was never more than a fairly witless generalisation, and probably more to do with class and the class behaviour that dominated the theatre and films of the 1930s and 40s than physicality as such. When you have the greatest text-based drama in the history of the theatre, as the English and anglophone Irish have, it is not surprising that expression through the speaking actor should become your particular forte. Our great poetic actors, Gielgud, Scofield, Olivier, Edith Evans, Peggy Ashcroft, Vanessa Redgrave and the great ancestry before them, stretching back to Betterton and Burbage, have been and are complete masters of the English verse tradition, without competitors in their field. They had no need to turn somersaults or mime rainstorms to tear our hearts into shreds and project our minds to the far corners of the universe. Olivier was even known to swing on the odd chandelier if he needed to. We should be proud, not ashamed, of our poetic acting tradition. There is nothing else like it in the world.

Nevertheless the birth of the English actor who can do quite as much with his body and the way he moves it as he can with his voice, can only be a significant addition to the living tradition. There is no need for any sense of competition, it is not a question of speaking *or* moving. All young actors now hope to become as proficient and expressive at both, just as all directors realise that every single movement on a stage has a precision and meaning of its own.

In the new directors and young companies who put an emphasis on the physical, there is often less interest in what can be best expressed in poetry and speech, but that is a passing moment in a long parade, and entirely to be expected. No one wants theatre that is meaningless dumbshow and noise, all visual splendour and no content, and it is certain that the mainstream theatres will quickly assimilate all that is best from physical theatre, as they have already done from the avant garde theatres of the 1960s and 70s. The theatre, like the English nation, ravenously consumes new people and new influences, and assimilates them into its whole body of work, to everyone's benefit.

The theatre which begins with movement and asserts that the human body, singly and in groups, is fully as expressive as the human tongue and the human face, is not one that I have practised in any detail myself, but like all directors of my generation, I shall hope to learn from what is new, and what new generations of theatre workers are doing, just as I hope to learn as a playwright from younger writers. Those who wish to explore the detailed workings of physical theatre, should consult Simon MacBurney and his colleagues in Europe and America, and learn from their practice.

Rehearsing Shakespeare

Of course, he must have a section to himself. Like Homer and the Bible, Shakespeare has become the yardstick against which we measure all human activity, as well as the touchstone of poetry and theatre technique. As *The Odyssey* and *The Iliad* were judged by the Greeks to contain the essence of their civilisation, so most of what we think and believe about ourselves can be found somewhere in the Bible and Shakespeare. We recognise that fact by taking it for granted that a copy of each will be found, along with eight gramophone records, on Roy Plomley's mythical desert island.

Whatever we say about rehearsing Shakespeare can be said in varying degrees about any playwright who creates his own individual world of language. The Greeks, even in translation, inhabit the same dramatic planet, and the works of Congreve, Shaw, Oscar Wilde, Tennessee Williams, and Harold Pinter differ only in degree, not kind. These are dramatic artists whose essence is contained in the actual words they have written, and it is to the words as fountain and source of theatrical meaning that we must always return. Verbal analysis becomes a crucial part of the breakdown method, so that we can approach an understanding of the literary processes which create the text.

Everything I have written about every other aspect of preparing, staging and rehearsing a play, applies equally to working on Shakespeare. The key difference is that the majority of Shakespeare's text is written in the most sophisticated English Renaissance verse, and where he uses prose, as he does for a great deal of *Much Ado About Nothing,* most of Falstaff's speeches, and in many other places throughout the canon, his prose is so rhythmic and metaphorically conceived, it is more genuinely poetical than most other poets' verses. One of Shakespeare's greatest passages of poetry, Hamlet's *What a piece of work is a man,* is written in prose.

The situation is further complicated by the fact that he is by far and away the greatest poet in the English language, and probably any other. Other great English poets match him in certain aspects, Milton, Keats, Chaucer and Wordsworth on their good days, but Shakespeare is all good days. There is not one of his plays, not *Two Gentleman of Verona,* not *Henry VI,* not *Cymbeline* nor *The Comedy of Errors* that does not contain passages of remarkable poetry that no one else could have written. In his subject matter, his range of thought and sympathy, his relentless exploration of ethical dilemmas, his ability to empathise with all kinds of characters and every sort of experience, and his sheer gobsmacking mastery of the English language, which he uses as though he had invented it – quite a lot of it he did – he is incomparable, and this creates a whole host of problems for actors and directors that they don't quite confront with any other writer, even other poetic dramatists.

The simplest is that if you don't address his work as poetry first and last, you will miss half the play. Many directors are quite happy to miss half the play, or indeed all of it. They wish to use Shakespeare's plays to create scenarios essentially their own, so for them the problem doesn't arise. They cut the verses, interpret them in line with modern ideas to which they have no relation, rearrange and even rewrite them, so the subtleties of meaning and moral complexities locked up in the actual structure and movement of the verse will elude them, and never be missed. For such directors, ignorance is bliss.

The second problem concerns the audience. We live in a spectacularly unpoetic age, and serve a generation of theatregoers that, on the whole, has very little interest in poetry, and has almost forgotten how to understand metaphor. There is no doubt that earlier generations vastly enjoyed rhetorical and poetic speech delivered by a great actor for its own sake, rather as opera goers will enjoy a bravura aria by Handel or Rossini, but this is no longer really the case in the theatre. Impassioned and sensuous poetry used to move theatre audiences to tears, and though it still may with individuals, with the audience in general it does not. The magnificent cadences pass over our heads largely unheard. This is savagely ironic for a culture that can boast one of the world's greatest poetic literatures, and can also point to at least half a dozen living poets writing in English who, to our contemporary eyes at least, seem to stand a good chance of joining their distinguished predecessors in the pantheon. But it is a fact.

This isn't only a problem with plays from the past. Every contemporary writer knows that if you use metaphorical structures in a play, half your audience won't understand you. In the early 1970s I wrote a play called *Out on the Lawn*, about a group of English intellectuals and chatterers spending a whole long summer day in a garden, picnicking, dallying with sex and gossiping about politics, with an ominous and only partly defined threat hanging over them. In fact, with hindsight, the threat was the coming of the dreadful 80s, but I didn't know that then. What I did know was that I had given the audience all kinds of carefully placed clues, notably in the play's title, which referred to Auden's magnificent 1939 poem about the coming of the Second World War, and how a group of English intellectual friends might cope with it, which begins:

> Out on the lawn I lie in bed
> Vega conspicuous overhead
> In the windless nights of June.

The play was widely reviewed, and played to packed houses, but none of its many reviewers seemed to understand the title – none actually mentioned it – or how it illuminated, by comparison with Auden's poem, the dilemma of my characters. All playwrights who work in metaphor can quote similar examples, and I could quote another half-dozen from my own work alone. It is a fact of the present time. We are a very prosaic, plain-speaking generation. Speaking in parables and metaphors is not a manner of communication we naturally understand any longer. It is a grim realisation, and one every director of Shakespeare must take on board. If you want to convey to your audience the subtleties of meaning and feeling you find in Shakespeare's verses, you are going to have to work very hard.

Shakespeare is an extremely sophisticated creator of theatrical structures, but everything that matters about him is contained in the actual words he selects and the order in which he places them. Non-English productions of Shakespeare are always interesting, if only to see how completely Eastern European and Asian cultures take over his structures and make them a part of their own societies and dilemmas. They prove again and again how vital his myth-making is, and how effective his stage carpentry. His stories speak to all sorts and conditions of men, and the way he structures them is a lesson to all playwrights who follow him. But I never feel we are actually seeing Shakespeare when we see non-English versions, because, however accurate and full of integrity the translating poet may be, the words are changed, and it is in the words that the true mystery is contained. I feel the same with my own translations of Sophocles and Euripides. I do everything I can, within the limits of my knowledge and skill, to convey my understanding of what those great poets were trying to say, in roughly the way they were trying to say it. When they use narrative metre, I use it, when they use lyrics, so do I. When the Greek poetry is great, as in Hecuba's lament over the dead Astyanax, or in countless choruses, I try to write the best poetry I can. But I am well aware that what I am writing is Taylor, not Sophocles/Euripides. My hope is that behind my words their great shades can still be sensed, and whatever of their meaning my words can contain will be transmitted. With the Greeks, unfortunately, we have no choice. The language of the originals is dead as a public event, even the Greeks no longer speak it, so as theatre the great Athenians have no existence in their original form. They can be read by Greek scholars, but the theatre is a public art, and reading is no substitute. So the only way the Athenian masters can survive at all now, is through their dramatic structures, which do not need translating, and the various languages employed by their translators. It is not the real thing, but it is a long way better than nothing.

Every now and again it occurs to me, like a terror in a nightmare, that this process is likely to happen to the works of Shakespeare too. Language changes all the time, and Shakespeare's plays are now four hundred years old. If we go back two centuries further in English literature to Chaucer, we reach a great poet who is no longer immediately comprehensible to modern English people without study notes and a glossary. Will the same fate await Shakespeare in two hundred years' time? Will the language have changed so much that the people of that age will no longer understand him when spoken aloud, and the translators will have to get to work, to provide modern English versions? It is an appalling thought, but by the normal progressions of language, it might be expected that Shakespeare will be difficult to read in two hundred years time, and completely incomprehensible in six hundred, as the language of these islands in 1066, Anglo-Saxon, is incomprehensible to modern English people, so that its wonderful literature is only available to them in translation.

There are many influences in modern society that might slow up or to some degree freeze these normal linguistic processes. Our language is set in dictionaries and grammar-books now, and has been since the eighteenth century, and during that time there has been hardly any wall of incomprehension built up. But two hundred years is a very short time in the life of a language, and English is still changing. Film, audio recording and all the other retrieval systems, together with the fact that English has now become the principal language of the world, might slow up the process, or in some way preserve the language of past English writing, so that people have it as a kind of second language, no longer spoken, but fully understood. That has never happened in the past though. Demotics have always triumphed over literary languages in the long run. All the more important for us, then, to make sure that what Shakespeare wrote is fully understood, for this generation at least, in spite of all the barriers modern society and cheap consumer art put in the way.

For a director, who is not a literary critic nor a historian of poetry but a working supervisor and interpreter of play-production, what matters is knowing how to unlock the poetry so that it can reveal its treasures to actors, and they can transmit them to the audience. This will not be achieved by giving lectures on medieval rhetoric, as I believed at twenty-six, but by helping the actors to find ways of acting the words that will make all, or at least some, of their many meanings clear.

The thing to remember at the outset is that poetry is a way of compressing information and feeling into the smallest possible linguistic space, and presenting that information in a memorable form. So the director's task is to help the actor unpack this very tightly crammed baggage. In essence, it is the same process of breakdown and synthesis I have described taking place with all plays, but it is very much more complicated, because a single line of Shakespeare may well contain dozens of meanings and associations, whereas in most plays there will hardly be more than one or two. This degree of compression – which in the language of Shakespeare's maturity is extreme, and unlike anything any other writer has ever done with the language – has considerable implications, not only for the actual process of explication of meaning, but also in the way in which, when meaning is understood, it can be expressed. You may decide that five words of late Shakespeare will take three-quarters of a page of plain prose to comprehend all its meanings. But as an actor you don't have three-quarters of a page, you have five words. When you have unpacked the bag, and discovered everything that is in it – and like Dr Who's Tardis, it hardly seems possible so little could contain so much – then you have to pack it again, but in a such a way that its contents can be fully and instantaneously understood.

The work has three stages, the surface meaning, the metaphorical meanings, and the meanings that can be conveyed by verse movement, sound, and verbal and intellectual associations.

Let us examine a short passage, and explicate it, as I would if I were directing an actor in the scene. Almost any passage in mature Shakespeare would yield genuine treasure subjected to this kind of analysis. I pick these particular verses because they were brought to me by a couple of young actors when I was doing some student acting workshops in Cambridge, and I enjoyed working on them

In the first Act, Macbeth, while King Duncan dines, is considering the implications of murdering him.

> **Macbeth:** If it were done when 'tis done, then 'twere well
> It were done quickly. If th'assasination
> Could trammel up the consequence, and catch
> With his surcease, success; that but this blow
> Might be the be-all and the end-all here –
> But here upon this bank and shoal of time –
> We'd jump the life to come. But in these cases
> We still have judgement here, that we but teach
> Bloody instructions, which being taught return
> To plague th' inventor. This even-handed justice
> Commends th' ingredience of our poisoned chalice
> To our own lips. He's here in double trust:
> First, as I am his kinsman and his subject –
> Strong both against the deed; then, as his host
> Who should against his murderer shut the door
> Not bear the knife myself. Besides, this Duncan
> Hath borne his faculties so meek, hath been
> So clear in his great office, that his virtues

Will plead like angels, trumpet-tongued, against
The deep damnation of his taking off;
And pity, like a naked new-born babe,
Striding the blast, or heaven's cherubin, hors'd
Upon the sightless couriers of the air
Shall blow the horrid deed in every eye,
That tears shall drown the wind. I have no spur
To prick the sides of my intent, but only
Vaulting ambition, which o'erleaps itself,
And falls on th'other.

The process begins by simply following the surface meaning, and at the same time, unpicking the metaphors, showing what is being compared with what, what each comparison tells us, and considering any other arts of language that may be employed. In doing this work, as with any other kind of breakdown, it is always better to convey to the actor what you wish to convey by asking questions, rather than by merely telling. A lecture or simple poetic explication of a text as complex as this will more likely leave the actor bemused than excited, and quite at a loss how to act it. You must lead him with you into the many-chambered complex of the speech, get him to open as many doors as he can himself, so that he soon feels at home there.

Macbeth begins by expressing every politician's fear, his sense of the impossibility of controlling future events, and he expresses it through a grim pun, on the two meanings of the word *done,* 'finished' and 'committed'. The surface meaning is clear. If Macbeth could be sure that the act of murder would have no future unpleasant consequences, he would commit it at once. But the first thing director and actor would note would be the use of the word *done* three times in a line-and-a-half. What does that mean, in terms of what the actor will express? The word is short, monosyllabic, full of finality, as Macbeth hopes the deed might be. You might suggest to the actor that however he decides to colour the speech, *done* should be coloured in three different ways, to express the precise and changing shades of meaning contained in each of its three usages. The first expresses an act with no consequences, the second a brutal act being committed, the third an efficient action unencumbered with thought, and each of those three meanings would require a subtle colour of its own to be conveyed to the audience.

The second sentence is a complex one, and begins by extending the idea of escaping the future consequences of the present murder, by comparing the act of assassination and its likely results to a trammel, a large drag-net for fishing, the sort of net that catches every single fish it encompasses. If only the murderer could catch, like a trammel catching all the fish, all the consequences of his murder. No, I didn't know the exact meaning of the word trammel either. I had to look it up in the OED, the book that any Shakespeare director must always have at his elbow, or in his study, or, if he can afford the CD-ROM disc, on his computer. The modern actor will have a problem expressing the trammel image, because the word is not in common use, but the right kind of intonation and colouring of the voice, and perhaps a chaste gesture, ought to be able to convey to the audience the gist of what is being said. It is surprising how often the simple act of knowing what you are talking about can succeed in communicating an idea to an audience. If the actor can think, *a large fishing drag-net,* he is half way there.

The sentence continues with an extraordinary pun, on *surcease/success. Surcease,* with its intensive prefix *sur,* suggesting *on top of,* or *above,* is an unusual word, unique in Shakespeare in this usage as a noun, expressing the absolute finality of the King's death. By punning it in the very next word with *success,* which is the object of the murder, Shakespeare gives the actor a rich opportunity to say a great deal about his inner state in two short words. All actors will handle such a moment differently, and I would rarely tell the actor *how* to do it, merely explain what has to be done, and leave it to his talent to express the grim juxtaposition of the two words in the way that best suits him. Murder and success, jammed up against each other and sounding almost the same, as Macbeth, in his murderous mood, hopes one might become the other.

He continues the idea in an almost existential manner, with the coinages *be-all* and *end-all,* which have now become clichés, but must be delivered by the actor as if they were new-minted, to express the very modern idea of an action being purely itself, isolated from all other actions, and quite without consequences. For a moment we are in the world of Camus, and *L'Etranger,* where an act is simply itself, without motive or result.

By this time, Shakespeare, as he customarily does, is thinking in metaphors, not logical thoughts, and they come upon us in battalions. If only the act could end here, he muses, and reiterates it, *but here,* and then creates an extraordinary image of a man standing on a bank, which might be a river bank, but is more likely a sandbank or half-submerged shallow. The latter meaning is more likely because the line continues *and shoal of time,* suggesting that Macbeth is standing on a *bank and shoal,* the two words being alternate expressions of the same fact. But there is more to the image yet. The word *shoal* can mean a shallow place, or a school of fish, which connects with the earlier fishing image and has almost certainly provoked this train of thought. So the image seems to be of a man standing on a shallow place in the *sea* – where shoals of fish are usually located – which is the sea of time, the sea of eternity. The sea as an image of eternity is one of the oldest in human culture, but the idea of the river is there, in the double meaning in the use of the word *bank*, and the river too is an ancient *topos*, the river of life, the river of time, even the river Phlegethon, which encircles Hades, the place of eternal punishment. So Macbeth contemplates himself facing eternity like a man standing up to his knees in water, which may be a river, or the sea. If an act could have no consequences, then from this shoal in the sea, or this river bank, a murderer might jump across the river of eternal life, or eternal punishment, even right across the sea of eternity itself, and miss out on the consequences of his action by the leap. Significantly, the metaphor doesn't say where this jumper who is leaping over the life to come is going to land. Shakespeare is the most concrete of poets, and if he had wanted to suggest where the jumper would land, he could easily have done so. The hiatus is intentional. The metaphor has nowhere to go, because the murderer who tries to jump eternal punishment has nowhere to go either, because he knows very well that eternal life, be it punishment or not, cannot be jumped, as a man jumps across a stream. And if the murderer is standing in the sea, and tries to jump that, he knows where he will land: back in the sea. The fantasy of somehow committing an act that has no consequences comes to an end, significantly in mid-line. A stop is created, where the metre is pulling the actor on, creating a powerful pause. The dream fades in that pause, as Macbeth faces life in the real world, in which actions do have consequences.

He goes on to examine those consequences in that very *here* where he hoped he could limit their action. The repeated use of the word *here* is important, as with the word *done* earlier. *Here*, there are cases, and judgement – legal metaphors – and the act of murder is simply a set of bloody instructions given to others how to proceed against the murderer himself, so that the man who invented the idea of a murder without consequences is plagued by others who will hope to murder him without consequences too. The idea of judgement continues in the image of *even-handed justice* – had Shakespeare seen a statue or painting of Justice carrying balances, like the one on the Law Courts? – and then metamorphoses into a much more disturbing image of a glass of poisoned wine being offered to the poisoner himself to drink. The word *commends* is a brilliant touch, with its suggestion of politeness, a smiling host offering his best wine. But then the host emerges onto the surface of the verse, as Macbeth lists the obvious social reasons against the murder: kinship, the loyalty of a subject, and the ancient tradition of the host being responsible for his guest's safety and well-being. The idea is in the oldest of literatures, among the Greeks because a stranger might be a God in disguise – and Shakespeare is well aware of the emotional power of the ancient tradition he is evoking. The image that follows is almost filmic in its vividness. We can see the responsible host barring the door against the dangers of the night, then evilly drawing the knife out of his own coat.

In the final section of the speech, after pointing out Duncan's simple virtues, Macbeth rises to an extraordinary climax, in a cluster of related images which express multiple meanings in a few words, in a way only possible in the greatest poetry, or perhaps one should simply say, in Shakespeare. Duncan's virtues will plead against his death, like angels blowing trumpets. It seems certain that Shakespeare is remembering Renaissance painting here, in which trumpet-blowing angels are a common topic, and the whole of the passage that follows has a kind of nightmarish visual quality that suggests something by El Greco or William Blake. Pity, too, will plead for Duncan, personified as a naked newly-born baby – obviously enough, you might say. But this baby is *striding the blast,* riding the whirlwind in an image that is somehow full of terror. Babies don't stride, and they don't ride the wind, except in nightmares, which this is. Babies exhibiting adult characteristics are a very common nightmare image, and it is this kind of common experience Shakespeare is plugging into here. The cherubin are there too, also riding the storm wind, but the wind in their case is personified by a troop of blind horses, a quite extraordinary image of awesome power. Finally, the horrid deed itself, the murder, will be blown by these terrifying horsemen of retribution, like dust into the eyes of all the world, and make them water, so that a great flood of tears at Duncan's death will arise, and drown the very wind upon which these apocalyptic creatures are riding. So much for Macbeth's attempts to conceive of a deed without consequences. He is absolutely terrified of the consequences, not only *here,* where bloody instruction might very well teach a brisk lesson to his enemies, but in eternity, the sea he tried to jump, in which nightmarish horsemen, like the Furies, will never let him or the world, forget his deed.

Macbeth's powerful conscience, which he tries to overcome, and eventually does overcome in Act Five, when he is transformed from a human being to a savage bear being baited to death at a stake – a sight Shakespeare had seen many times – is well in evidence, even as he tries to suppress it.

After this terrifying climax, he sinks into a simple concrete image to express his lack of resolve to take the risk, both with the present and eternity. He is like a horseman with no spurs to goad his mount forwards. And then one horse suggests another, with almost comic banality. His ambition is like a gymnast, who in vaulting a wooden vaulting-horse, misjudges his jump, leaps too far, and crashes on the other side. Consequences again. A jump, and this time a landing: the disaster described at the end of the speech which can only be implied earlier. How can he commit the murder at all when he is so unsure, so scared what will happen in the future?

And that's just what the speech means, or what I, at this moment of writing can find in it. On another day, and with a living actor, we would no doubt find other suggestions and associations. But when that kind of analysis is made – and it must always be made with poetry because that is how good poetry works – the job is still barely begun. The components are in bits on the floor and must be put together. And how is the actor to act all that, with any hope of conveying more than a fragment of it? Not to mention the rest of the play which must be subjected to a similar detailed analysis.

There are many answers, but the first of them is to use the weapons of the poetic, not the naturalistic actor. The naturalistic actor, when he has understood all the ideas and patterns of thought in such a speech as this – not an easy task, because there is not a clear line of logical thought through it, rather a constantly shifting kaleidoscopic progression of images – will then try to motivate each change of thought as honestly and truthfully as he can. That is the touchstone of a good naturalistic actor. We can see each idea as it occurs to him, even if he says nothing or makes only a few incoherent sounds. We understand exactly what is going on in the character's brain and what he feels, because the actor has understood and felt each change of thought, and passionately expressed it.

Such an approach is disastrous in Shakespeare, and though actors and directors every now and again feel constrained to try it, they usually end up with the same half-cock shot, a production that goes on for hours, with half the text cut. There are so many thought changes, so many fine shades of meaning, even in a twenty-seven line speech, that to motivate all of them with naturalistic honesty would take all night, and the audience would be asleep, even before the actors were. The playwright has performed a gigantic act of compression in fusing so many varied thoughts into so few words, and the actor must do the same thing. He must give full value to all the thoughts, each passing facet of emotion or ratiocination must be registered, but he must do it at the speed the words require, which is a great deal faster than naturalistic speech could ever contemplate.

Fortunately the poet has given him the weapons to do the job, and the first is the metre. The metre, because it is a continuous pulse, like a heart beat or the rhythm of a song, wants to continue, so it is always pulling the words forwards with an energy of its own, and if an actor can get up onto that energy, he can ride it like beach boy on a surf board, harnessing all the energy of the sea. Words in any kind of speech have a relationship to each other, in their grammar and their word order, but in metrical writing they have another relationship too, that conferred by their position in the line, and their placing on either a strong or weak beat. Good poets realise that the real motive energy of verse lines comes from the syncopated relationship between the artificial line of verse – in Shakespeare's case, the five-foot iambic line, where each foot consists of one weak followed by one strong beat – and the emphasis of natural speech. The iambic line is the underlying pulse, like the time-signature in music, which gives the verses their formal shape. But natural speech, like melody, has another shape of its own, the shape of its melodic phrases, the inflections of spoken language, which might exist in any kind of relationship with the formal verse form.

In the case of incompetent poets, there is no relationship at all. The poet doesn't have sufficient skill to make what he wants to say fit the verse in any natural or individual way. Technically competent poets can make their meaning fit the five-footed alternate weak-and-strong beat form very snugly, and in narrative or lyric verse they often do. But strict verse, where the natural stresses of speech neatly fit the artificial stresses of the verse line, soon becomes boring in drama, as Marlowe was beginning to learn at the end of his short writing life, and Shakespeare had learned by 1593-4. Both poets started with strictly scanned iambic pentameters, often set out in rhyming couplets, but that verse-music soon becomes too regular for a form which intends to come to terms with natural dramatic speech. The metrical progress of Shakespeare's writing life was towards greater and greater freedom, till by the middle and last plays, he was using the pentameter form like a master, not a servant, making it do exactly what he wanted it to do, dominating it like a tyrant or cosseting it like a lover, so that he could make it express any shade of meaning or emotion his brain was capable of imagining. What he gradually learned was that if you set the normal rhythms of natural speech against the artificial rhythm of the pentameter, even if you syncopate the rhythm, just as modern jazz-influenced composers do, and Haydn and Bach were doing a hundred and fifty years before that, so that strongly emphasised words sometimes come on weak beats, and vice versa, great tension and energy is created, and the kind of compression we see in the Macbeth speech becomes possible. We hear something like it when we listen to Frank Sinatra or Ella Fitzgerald drag their melodic phrases right across the bar-lines that ought to contain them, creating great rhythmical excitement in the process. A simple example of this in poetry can be given by quoting, not Shakespeare, where examples are legion, but Donne, whose *Twickenham Garden* begins:

> Blasted with sighs and surrounded with tears

where a ten-syllable line, which technically scans as a five-beat iambic line, in natural speech scans as a four beat line with six weak beats, and as we speak the line aloud, we hear both scansions together, thus creating great poetic energy and forward movement.

It is this inner energy which a good poet imparts to his metre that enables an actor to take verse lines fast enough to keep them continuously moving, while still making their meaning clear. Instead of having to drag the lines along by sheer force of arm and shoulder, as the naturalistic actor does, there is an energetic little motor in the lines which carries the poetic actor along with it, so that the speech, not having to create its own momentum for every word, is all lightness and muscular energy. The verse does all the donkey-work, while the actor creates the stunning effects. What we listen to are the actor's elegant variations of the verse pulse, and it is those variations that create and contain the meaning. The actor must, as part of his training, be able to deliver the verse so that its underlying form is always audible, and develop a fine ear for these minute shifts in rhythm and emphasis, because they are the absolute foundations of Shakespearean playing, the building-blocks without which the house cannot be constructed.

Meaning, which in naturalistic playing is created by truth to human emotion and thought, facial expression, and speech patterns, is principally created in verse by sound, the exact timbre chosen by the actor with which to colour each word. It's like a kind of aural shorthand. Because the movement of the verse has created great energy which is carrying the lines forward, each change of the actor's tone or timbre of voice, like each variation of rhythm, becomes enormously significant and capable of carrying a great deal of truthful emotion, which is why the right vocal colour at the right moment can reduce us to tears. Of course, the actor's truthfulness of thought must always be present. He must think, but he must think as fast as the verse does, no easy task when you are dealing with a poet of Shakespeare's calibre. There is nothing worse than actors who are using all their rhythmic and vocal skills to cover emptiness, untruth, and lack of mental commitment, unless it is the actors who try to play verse without any attention to rhythmic movement or tone and timbre whatever, as though it were naturalistic speech. That is always a disaster, and we have seen it often enough in the last thirty years to be quite sure of the fact. A study of the last ten lines of the Macbeth excerpt on page 160, will reveal the great metrical excitement, the growing crescendo of the lines describing the nightmare storm, and in the actual juxtaposition of vowels and consonants an actor with a good ear can hear the storm blowing, and will colour his intonation accordingly.

The great advantage the mastery of this sort of verse technique confers upon the actor is that it enables him to speak the verse quickly, without any lack of truth, and with great benefit to the dramatic move-ment of the play. Shakespeare's plays, like all highly-verbalised drama, are meant to be played fast. Shaw, another high stylist, famously said *there are no pauses in my plays,* and when you direct Shaw, you soon find out that the old boy was right. If you play his plays with natural-istic pauses they drag appallingly, but if you play them fast and light, they coruscate, as the outrageous Irishman so often did himself when he wished to impress the company. Shakespeare tells us what he wants in *Romeo and Juliet* when he speaks of *the two hours' traffic of our stage.* He wouldn't have *allowed* an actor to stand up in front of an audience and say that if the play was going to take three hours, or, God help us, four, as it sometimes does these days, when directors insist on inserting all kinds of irrelevant naturalisms at the expense of the play's movement. Most Shakespeare plays, excluding *Hamlet* and *Lear,* can be played in about two-and-a-quarter to two-and-a-half hours, and if they start getting much longer than that, the director should begin to ask himself why. Many other things might be expressed in long and slow-moving productions of Shakespeare, but rarely the truth contained in the poetry. That requires a sense of the natural quick movement of the verses, if all the deepest treasures are to be mined and brought to the surface.

It is for this reason that in recent years, when I have been dealing with any kind of poetic or highly literate play, I have often found myself in final run-throughs closing my eyes and listening to the play rather than looking at it. Very often I go away to the corner of the rehearsal room and turn my back on the action. I know what the actors are doing. Their movements and facial expressions will always be much as rehearsed, intenser or less intense. But the *sound* of the play will tell me whether it is going well or not, the verbal music that so wonderfully focuses feeling and meaning. If an actor discovers something new and compelling, I will hear it first, and then I might turn round to have a look. Listen to your play, listen to the sounds your actors are making. If the sounds startle and amaze, you will know you have done your work well, and the actors are ready to startle and amaze the public. They will go out on the stage well-prepared, leap up onto the energy of the verse, and sing the most marvellous theatrical song. There is nothing at all like it in the theatre. To write such moments, which make it possible for the actors to create their own particular magic, is the summit of all playwrights' ambitions, and to direct them, is why directors enter the business in the first place.

Directing Shakespeare, and working with the details of verse-movement and language-colouring, is a bottomless subject, and many books could be written on it alone. But one other aspect of rehearsing Shakespeare might perhaps be mentioned, in the form of a question. Is there a sub-text?

The historical answer is probably no. The idea that there is a stratum of meaning and experience which exists below the words spoken, and moves in counterpoint with them, is essentially a twentieth century notion probably drawn from ideas which were in the air at the end of the nineteenth century, and which inspired Freud to posit similar concepts about the conscious and unconscious mind. Nowhere that I know in descriptions of the performances of great actors in the past, do you find anything like it. Voices are mentioned: Betterton and Mrs Jordan had remarkable vocal instruments, and Garrick was famous for the air of absolute reality he could create in his acting, on or offstage. Mrs Siddons had a grand tragic personality, and Janet Achurch, before she destroyed herself with morphine and brandy, had the kind of charisma that men fall in love with, as Nell Gwyn probably did, right at the beginning. Nowhere do you find critics and theatregoers remarking on the truth of the emotions being expressed *beneath* the words.

Shakespeare's actors probably thought mostly in terms of the rhetorical and vocal effects they could achieve with their speeches, and the formal gestures they should adopt, gesture being a quite separate and rich language in seventeenth century acting which is lost to us now, except perhaps in the conventional descriptive gestures of classical ballet. Shakespeare exhorts his actors to be true to nature, but he doesn't exhort them to study what the character is thinking in opposition to what he is saying. To a seventeenth century actor, what the character was thinking *was* what he was saying.

But we are not seventeenth century actors, and to us, the concept of the subtext is crucial to the way we act. We cannot any longer consider simply the surface of a text, and though, as I have made amply clear in the preceding paragraphs, we must give full value to the rhythm and colour of the words if we wish to find their unique meaning, we must be true to our own culture and act for the audiences and theatres of our own age. Nothing is worse than archaeological acting, experiments that try to revivify the dead art of formal gesture or pretend to know how seventeenth century actors pronounced their language. We are twentieth century people, we speak as our contemporaries do, and if our audiences do not understand the messages conveyed by formal seventeenth century gestures, and see an actor artificially waving his arms about, there is no point in employing them.

But the fact is, although the concept of sub-text is a modern one, all good playwrights, in trying to make their characters act in a lifelike way, have instinctively employed something like it, and good plays only benefit from its application as a rehearsal tool. You *can* analyse a character's unspoken motives in a Shakespeare play, you *can*, indeed you *must*, talk of what Hamlet is thinking while he says his words, and as long as you realise that eventually the profoundest meaning, and even a contrapuntal sub-textual meaning, must principally be expressed through the words themselves, doing so can only enrich and deepen your understanding of the character. *Act on the words, not in the pauses between them* is the simple motto, and for word-based and poetic drama of all periods, it works. I have directed four of my Greek tragedy translations using normal sub-textual methods of analysis, and found only that you cannot direct choruses that way! Choruses, being a twelve or fifteen-headed character rather than a group of individuals, have to be approached through group motivation and concensus, in which sub-textual investigations play no part at all and can be a positive hindrance. When an actor in a Greek chorus asks *what am I thinking at this point?* you have to point out, tactfully, that *he* or *she* isn't thinking anything, *they* are.

The only circumstances in which the idea of sub-text can get in the way in Shakespearean production, are if the actor insists on playing in the full naturalistic manner, and asserts that the principal truth of the character exists on a level below the words. Sub-textual investigations can help an actor to make his conception of a character more truthful, but all that truth must eventually be expressed within the formal patterns the movement of the verse dictates. Then the reality of the character, simply observed, as we observe people all around us, can begin to emerge. There the solid bed-rock of acting lies, as it always does. But that is where the synthesising process, in rehearsing Shakespeare, differs from the process in other, non-poetical plays. The rhythmical movement and vocal colouring of plays is always important, but in Shakespeare it is absolutely crucial, the king-post that support the whole building.

Modern theatrical culture has made the relationship between actors and directors far more complicated in this matter of playing

Shakespeare than it used to be. Up to thirty-five or forty years ago, all actors knew how to play Shakespeare, and if they had been trained to play him at all, they had all been trained in the same way. That training was a kind of watered down version of the great tradition of poetic acting I have been trying to describe. But for a great many actors, though not the best ones, this tradition had become an unquestioned technique that was not coming to terms with the new truths being discovered by film actors, and new forms of naturalism in the theatre. By the 1950s it was beginning to seem, particularly to young directors, of which I was one, like an excuse for not seeking the truth of the character. An empty verse-speaking technique, like the smooth and shallow technique of the West End comedy, seemed at odds with the kind of acting Kenneth Haigh was doing in *Look Back in Anger* or Albert Finney in *Saturday Night and Sunday Morning*. It was time for a new injection of nature into a style where art had become artificiality, and for most of the time since the 50s this process of a continuous search for greater realism has been under way, mostly with very beneficial results. Our most practised and subtle speakers, the likes of Ian McKellen, Ian Holm, David Suchet, Michael Pennington and Roger Allam, colour and rhythmically vary their lines with great skill, but quite as truthfully as the most scrupulous natu- ralist, and for me such actors point the way forward.

But there is no longer any sense of a shared tradition in Shakespearean acting. Every time an actor begins to rehearse a Shakespeare play he can have no idea of how the director will want him to act, whether in the great tradition, going back to Betterton, or in a totally filmic manner, that mutters lines, or shouts them with great emphasis and a complete disregard of metre. Similarly, the director can have no confidence in what his actors are going to bring him, with regard to verse technique. Many fine young actors have almost none, will throw away ends of lines so they trail almost into silence, or will never have been taught the basic mechanics of an iambic pentameter line, let alone the subtleties of metrical variation. This is not a situation where praise or blame is to be distributed, simply the fact of life at present in the profession. So each new Shakespearean production is something of a leap into the dark for the actors and the director alike, as each finds out what the other wants. When there is no longer a shared tradition, you must invent your own, and this is what the good Shakespearean productions always do.

The opening of the New Bankside Globe may prove to be a signif- icant moment for Shakespearean production and direction. It is very revealing to put Shakespeare's plays into the architectural space for which they were written, as I found out when I worked on some of the first productions at The St George's Theatre in north London during the 1970s. George Murcell's stage was by no means an exact imitation of the Globe, but architecturally the stage-relationships between actors and the movement of the play from scene to scene were the same. The actor, exposed on his open platform, was once again thrown back on the poetry and his voice, and this is going to be so to a far greater degree in the newly reconstructed Globe. The director's role will inevitably be much reduced, with no scenery or lighting for him to play with, and once again the actor's voice, his personality, and his poet, will come to the fore. Personally, being the kind of director who has always been much more concerned what Shakespeare sounds like than what he looks like, I can't wait.

6

Fit-up to opening

Production weekend is the time when the director will work hardest, and when his efficiency and talent will be most severely tested. It's called production weekend because in the old rep system the set would be changed on Saturday night, the technical rehearsal would take place on Sunday, and the dress-rehearsal on Monday, for a Monday evening opening. Nowadays the production is more likely to open in mid-week, and the technical rehearsal might take a great deal longer than Sunday afternoon and evening. A really good director will show his strength during the tech. A bad one might collapse into complete disorder.

Assuming a Monday/Tuesday/Wednesday opening, you should normally rehearse with your actors up to the Friday beforehand. If things have been going particularly well, and the play has been running through efficiently, with the kind of intensity of acting that makes it clear that you can do no more with your actors till they meet their audience, you will hope to have the final run-through on Friday morning, with a few notes and perhaps a little light rehearsal on Friday afternoon, before an early finish. It may sometimes be necessary to rehearse Saturday morning and afternoon, but in an ideal world you should try to give the actors some time to themselves before they go into the theatre. There is a great deal of mental preparation goes on in actors' heads in the days leading up to opening. Some of it is conscious, but a great deal of it is not. They may spend their weekend going shopping with the family, or playing with their children. The slow processes that will lead to a public performance, an unhurried opening of doors and windows in the mind, will already be under way, and if you ask actors to work too hard in the last hours before going through the stage door, you will interrupt them.

From the director's point of view, everything by now should be well prepared. Throughout the rehearsal period he will have kept a close eye on the development of the set, the progress of the costumes and the recording and editing of the sound tapes. He will have seen all his leading players have costume fittings, and made sure they were happy with what they were going to wear. Nothing should be left to chance. Even if you have worked with your colleagues for many years you must never trust them completely, nor would they expect you to. If something is not right, it is *always* the director's fault, not anybody else's. If the set or costumes are wrong, and you haven't found that out before dress rehearsal, that is not your designers' fault, it is yours. It was up to you to cast an eye over their work, and if you felt it was going wrong to say so while there was still time to put it right.

The director must enter production weekend with a very clear idea of how every aspect of the production is going to fit together. Acting, design, light, music, sound effects, stage furniture and properties should all have become a satisfying theatrical whole in his head before he begins the technical rehearsal. There is no time during that, at best hard-worked and at worst frantic, period to sit around having creative ideas for half an hour. Not that there isn't the opportunity to have new inspirations, sudden insights that will take your production into whole new areas of truth. Every director hopes that will happen, though perhaps not too often on technical days. But if it does happen, it should happen swiftly and efficiently, because the harmonic framework of your production is so clear that the brilliant new variation is immediately playable.

All the practical preparations should have been made too, and committed to paper. You should have talked the whole scenic flow of the production through many times with your stage director, and you, or your production secretary, if you have one, should have given him all the cue-sheets and flying or scenery schedules he and his crew will need. Your DSM will have prepared the prompt book, with all the cues and standbys and dressing room calls noted down, and be ready to go into action, and you should also have provided your lighting director with all the cue sheets he needs to begin rehearsal, well aware that a lot of the detail is likely to be changed or emended during the rehearsal process. The more detail and clarity your cue sheets contain, the simpler and more efficient a rehearsal you will have. And to get that clarity down onto paper, you must be quite clear in your own mind what you intend to happen, and when. There is no time for fuzziness. Action is about to begin, and like a good general your battle-plan must be clear, in overall strategy and tactical detail.

The fit-up

The fit-up will usually take place on Saturday night, or during Sunday. Organising it is entirely your stage director's and designer's business, and will enter areas of skill and experience about which you know nothing, so it is wise to leave them to it and keep out of the way. Here you must trust other people's expertise and experience, and not interfere unless your advice is specifically asked.

The fit-up itself is one of the most exciting moments in the whole theatrical production, whether it's an all-night job or starts early on Sunday morning. Last week's play is cleared away, and your own play begins slowly to take shape upon the bare stage. However romantic a moment you find it, you should keep out of the way, and preferably go home and get a good night's sleep, or work through the lighting cues in your mind. Don't ever go up on the stage and start asking damn-fool questions, or try to join in. To begin with, the stage does not belong to you. It is entirely the stage director's domain, and you should never go on stage during the fit-up period, or, strictly speaking, at any other time, without asking his permission, just as you should never barge into the lighting box unless invited. These questions of etiquette may seem old-fashioned, and for ninety per cent of the time they will be ignored, as a group of colleagues works together, but a director who appreciates, and can make it clear that he understands who's in charge where, will go up in his colleagues' estimation. The conventions are based on simple rules of safety. Only the stage director, during a fit-up, knows what is going on, what's done and what is not, and when something heavy and dangerous might come plunging down from the flies. Stage hands know the dangers of their job – which can be considerable. Directors do not, and there is nothing more annoying than to see an amateur wandering around the stage, getting in everyone's way while they are trying to work, and perhaps endangering himself and his crew.

The one thing you must *never* do during a fit-up is to poke your nose in everywhere saying *this doesn't look right to me, are you sure it shouldn't be over there?* Stage crew, who may be the most sophisticated of men and women during daily life, philosophy students and minor poets – or they may not – will usually look like something between Cro-Magnon man and a Manchester United supporter during a fit-up, and are likely to be as communicative. They will mutter at you with a mouth full of nails, and gesture vaguely towards the stage director, who, if he has any sense will tell you to get out of the way. Scenery in an unfinished state often looks horribly wrong. But stage crew know when it is unfinished, and do not expect you to make unhelpful comments until the job is done.

If you do appear during a fit-up, beam at everyone in a fatherly fashion, say how wonderful it is all going to be, and put several six-packs, packets of crisps and/or portions of chips on a nearby but not inconvenient table. Don't bring bottles of wine. Your crew may knock back Cloudy Bay by the case in social life, but lager and lemonade are the thing for fit-ups. Then smile, give a cheery wave, say *see you all tomorrow, I hope it goes well,* and go. Probably no one will answer you, and when you have gone they will grin at each other and say *who was he?*

When you next appear, early Sunday morning if it has been an all-nighter or late Sunday afternoon or Monday morning if it has not, the first thing you should do is to sit down with your stage director or designer and get a progress report, so that you know what has been done and what has not. An efficient stage director will tell you what still needs doing and when he hopes to have it done, so there will be no point in complaining. The only reason for putting pressure on your stage director at this time is if something has been left unfinished that will make it impossible for you to conduct any kind of rehearsal, like basic rostra not set up, or doors or entrances not in place. Even if there are basic failings of this kind, it is as well to remember that every job takes the time it takes, and there is no use you making a fuss when people are working as hard and fast as they can. Patience is always a key virtue for a director, and never more than during a fit-up and technical.

When the stage has been finally set and the lights have been rigged and focused, always a long and precise process which it is extremely unwise to rush, you will finally be ready to begin, and it is important to begin in the calmest and most efficient manner. Don't hector people, and make sure that not even half a minute is wasted because of some inefficiency on your part. If the director, without being frantic or bullying, hits the ground running, the whole crew, most of whom he won't yet know at all well, will be, if not impressed – they are never impressed with anything, as an article of professional pride – at least reasonably pleased. They will think *this guy knows what he is doing* and the whole pattern of work over the next few days will be the better for it.

Before you start anything, make sure your communication system is in place. You will be seated in the middle of the darkened auditorium, and in any decent theatre and most fringe venues, you will be set up with a portable desk which sits on the seat backs, a shaded light or a torch and an intercom system, and you will have your script, some pencils, something to drink and all your cue sheets with you. For most of the time, you will hope your designer will be with you, though very often he will still be supervising work being done and still to be done. In an ideal world he should be at your side from now on. How the play looks is his principal responsibility, and you and he should be in permanent discussion throughout the technical and dress rehearsal period, assessing how far the marvellous ideas you saw in your mind and on the model are being realised on the stage.

You should also be provided with an intercom system through which you can talk to the DSM in the prompt corner, the lighting designer, whether he is in the box with his operators, or on the stage, and the stage director. You should always insist on this if you can, not only because it is wearing on your own energy and temper and everyone else's to have to shout instructions to people, but also because shouting is imprecise, and will bring the wrong person on stage as many times as the one you shouted for. We are living in the twentieth century, and there should be no theatre so small or so shoestring-funded that it cannot afford a decent intercom system.

Throughout the whole technical rehearsal, trust your fellow workers to do their jobs, and give them time to do them. Remember that someone may be working as fast as a human being can back-stage, while you are sitting for ten minutes staring moodily at a stalled rehearsal. With good planning such a thing should not happen, or not too often, but it will happen now and again, and when it does you must wait patiently and not expect the impossible of people. The last thing to do is to climb onto the stage shouting *Oh for Christ's sake, I can do the job better myself!* It will almost certainly be untrue, and even if it isn't, it will be a public relations disaster towards the rest of your team, who will very soon begin to wish you elsewhere.

The technical

Your technical should normally begin with a rehearsal of basic lighting states. For this the actors should not be called, and you should work quietly in the theatre, with as few people as possible. Normally, you will need only your lighting people and enough of the crew to move the scenery between states if required. You will also need someone to move about the empty stage, to see that it is evenly lit, and actors will not be passing from bright to dark areas or find themselves with lines of shadow across their faces. By tradition, such a person is an ASM, or a young actor from the company you have called for the purpose, or a trainee director – they have to do something! The DSM, on cans in the prompt corner, is the crucial link in the communication chain, hearing from you whatever instructions you give over the intercom, and, if you don't have a separate connection to the other key people, transmitting them either electronically on the system or by sending messages backstage via the stage manager.

Don't call the actors before the technical-proper is scheduled to begin, because there is nothing for them to do. Some of them will be in early anyway, getting to know their dressing room, sorting out costumes, wigs and make up, talking to dressers, if there are any. You don't need them till you start tech-ing Act One Scene One, but there is no reason why they shouldn't come in to get the feel of the place as long as they don't wander about poetically on the stage while technical work is going on, or come on asking ill-timed questions about their dressing rooms or costumes. This whole process, after all, is being undertaken for their benefit, so that they will be able to perform with all the theatrical aids, scenery, light and sound, safely in place.

Rehearsing basic lighting states ought to be a fairly simple business, if you and the lighting designer have talked the play through and planned it carefully. The designer will have made his initial decisions with regard to lamps, gel colours and how the lights should blend for each scene, and will now show you the result of his labours. With luck, when you have watched your actor walk through the various areas, always facing front so the light can be seen on the face, you will be able to agree the state and move on to the next one. If you don't like it, you will say why, and the lighting designer will ask his team to make the changes. Sometimes, if the changes are minor, you will wait till they are done before moving on to the next state, but do not insist on that. If the lighting designer says he will have to re-hang or re-gel half a dozen lamps to get what you want, but it will be OK, you can take his word for it. He will hang his lamps when he isn't holding anybody up, and you will see the effect next time, whereas if you insist on seeing what you want straight away, you may find your-self sitting for half an hour or more, doing nothing, watching people in dirty jeans, and tee-shirts bearing obliterated or incomprehensible messages, climbing up ladders or being wheeled about on talloscopes (platforms on wheels, with guard rails for safety, and high enough to work on the lighting grid in comfort).

Lighting states are not cues, but overall lighting set ups for whole scenes. If a play is set in a midnight ravine, a brilliantly-lit castle, where all the candles are blown out in the middle of the scene, and on a lightning-blasted heath (ah, those were the days!) you will have four states to see, the ravine, the castle, with and without candles, and the heath, with lightning effects. You should not rehearse cues at this time. If the overall stage looks right, all the details will be sorted out during the technical-proper.

Sometimes you may not have time to have a separate lighting states rehearsal, and will be forced to set up and agree the lighting of each scene as you tech it, but this should be avoided if at all possible. It never takes less than about half an hour to light a scene, even if you are lucky, and if you go through the process in the middle of a tech, everyone else on the play, which might be a very large number of people on a big production, will be sitting around doing nothing. There is enough necessary sitting around doing nothing in any tech, and adding to the sum should be avoided. With long delays people get tired, scratchy and nervous, and tempers begin to fray. It is much better to keep everybody as busy as you can. Then they will work till they drop, and you will get a great deal done. As always, it depends on careful forward planning: in this case, making sure you have scheduled at least a couple of hours, and on a big show, perhaps a whole day, on lighting states alone.

Technicals can vary in length from a brisk afternoon and evening to a week, or even longer. A short and straightforward play might be got through in not much more than a few hours, whereas a big musical, or a play full of electronic scenery, lasers, holograms and flying and trapdoor effects, might take a week. The key thing to remember, however long a period is scheduled, is that the rehearsal is finite. It will end when it is scheduled to end, there will be some kind of dress rehearsal, and the play will open on schedule. We are working in perhaps the only British industry left that never lets down the customer or delays delivery. When we say we will open, that's when we open. I have known plays that have opened with their technicals uncompleted and with only one often interrupted dress rehearsal, but they have opened, the deal with the public has been honoured, as, with very rare, and usually very public, exceptions, it always is. It's no use telling the audience as they come in, that the parts were delivered late, you've lost the invoice, or the computer's out of order. Leave that to the world of business. In the theatre there is only one deadline, and we always meet it.

During the technical you are more aware of that deadline than at any other time. You have an enormous amount to do and a strictly limited time to do it in, so you must always be working out the equation in your mind, and recalculating to make sure it comes out right.

In the technical you must rehearse everything except the acting. You must never do any acting at all, unless it is needed for the purpose of technical rehearsal, and if that is the case, then you must rehearse every relevant word. One obvious example will demonstrate the point. Half a dozen of your actors are playing a light comedy scene together, while laying a full-scale dinner for five. Most of the jokes are verbal, and have been getting good laughs in the rehearsal room, where you will have rehearsed the scene in detail with rehearsal props. By the time it is finished the scene takes nearly a quarter of an hour. In the technical you will have to re-rehearse every aspect of the table laying with the real props, which not only means where the objects are placed, the table, the plates, the cutlery and glasses, but where the actors get them from, and in what order they approach the table. Having sorted out workable answers to the many questions that will arise from your actors and property master or stage manager, you will then have to run the whole fifteen-minute scene and see it is working effectively technically before you can afford to move on. Word mistakes and rotten acting won't matter, unless they influence something technical, but all the physical details will have to be got right, because if the problems are not solved in the technical they will never be solved at all, short of desperate extra rehearsal squeezed into a schedule already full. At the opposite extreme, an actor may be making an emotional speech about his wife, in the middle of which he removes her uncompleted manuscript from a drawer. The action of the drawer and the removal of the manuscript will need to be carefully rehearsed by the actor. No two drawers are ever the same, a big bundle of typesheets is a notorious hazard, and neither action must interfere with the emotion of the speech, indeed, they must add to it. Then you will have to allow the actor to play the speech through, including the completed actions, before you can be satisfied.

These two examples are a good illustration of a key fact about technicals, namely that the word doesn't only apply to the obvious technical aspects of the production, light, sound and scenery. During the technical, you must carefully rehearse everything that you haven't been able to rehearse fully before coming to the theatre. You will have rehearsed your table laying in outside rehearsal with a couple of plastic tables jammed together, and some cardboard plates and mugs, but that is not the same thing.

So you must carefully rehearse all lighting cues and music cues, in relation to each other and with the actors who are on stage at the time, and all sound cues too, whether recorded or generated live backstage. You must rehearse all scene changes and furniture and prop changes, together with the music and light cues that go with them, and you must rehearse all the props, even the minutest. Every prop has to be waiting somewhere, onstage or backstage, must be used, and must be put somewhere afterwards. The actors will not know where to find it and are likely to put it back absolutely anywhere unless they have been told otherwise. If these small details are not carefully rehearsed, chaos will soon ensue.

Do not be tempted to cut corners. Rehearse everything, and do not move on to the next cue until you are quite convinced the one you are working on is right. That doesn't mean it has to be up to speed, or as slick as it will eventually be, particularly in the case of scene changes. As long as you have the mechanics of a scene change right, you do not have to get it up to speed at once. Over the next few days to the opening, it will get faster of its own accord, as the stage crew begin to assimilate what they have to do, and find ways of cutting corners. You can rely on them to do that themselves, so that if your scene change initially takes a little longer than the sound cue prepared for it, do not despair. If you have planned carefully enough, the chances are that within a day or so the problem will have sorted itself, the change will be up to speed, and the music will fit so neatly people will think it is specially composed to fit the gap.

The simple rule for a technical is to start at the beginning, work cue to cue, getting everything right as you go, and then stop. Bear in mind that, to your stage crew and light and sound operators, the show is a completely unknown quantity. Your actors will know the whole play inside out, but your technicians will be like people at a first day rehearsal, blundering around with their eyes in the script and falling over the furniture, and you must be patient with them. The cues may seem blindingly obvious to you, but take care to explain carefully what you want, and then give your technicians time to write their own notes on what they are required to do. If you don't give them time to write their notes, or to programme the computer properly, you will pay for it in the dress rehearsals when things go wrong. Three qualities are required of the director during a technical. The first and most important is patience. It is no use getting irritable if people cannot do things as briskly as you can say them. That is a fact about human beings and you had better get used to it. The second is efficiency, having prepared yourself so that there are no avoidable delays, and the third is speed, the ability to think fast. Problems will arise during technicals, some things will not work as you have planned, and a decision will be required. There is no time to brood for three-quarters of an hour weighing up the pros and cons. Your mind must do that in an instant, and you must decide, to plough on determined to achieve your original effect, or to cut your losses and compromise. Nine times out of ten in a technical, the latter is the wiser choice.

Some actors affect to find technicals boring, but good ones never do, and some relish them. Wise actors know they can spend those one or two days really getting to know the stage, walking about on the set to feel its contours, opening and shutting doors and windows, getting to know all the furniture and props they will have to work with, and really living in their costumes, judging the weight and feel of them, and how they modify their performances, as all costumes do to some degree. Running the odd passages of dialogue too, even when only for technical purposes, will reacquaint them with their text, from which they will feel worryingly distant for a day or two till they get the opportunity to do the first dress rehearsal. Inevitably, there will be long hours spent in the dressing rooms waiting for a call, and nervous or self-centred actors might get irritated and behave badly. You should always stamp on such behaviour as soon as you can. The tech, though it is valuable for the actors, is principally the technicians' time. It is their turn to get their work sorted out, and only a really selfish actor will attempt to deny it to them. Don't let the actors come on stage to rehearse little bits of their own when they are not wanted, and never get involved in any acting rehearsals, runs of sections, or worst of all, discussions of motivations and meanings. The stage crew will stand round in meaningful groups if you indulge yourselves in this way, and look more prehistoric than ever, as they will have every right to do.

Some actors will not make up till the dress rehearsal, but you will want to see them in full costume, at least some of the time, to check that everything looks as it should under lights, particularly if your actors are wearing long skirts or wigs which might affect their movement or knock things off tables. You must see all the make up under lights eventually, but the dress rehearsal is soon enough.

If you have costume changes that are scheduled to take five minutes or less, you must rehearse them in detail, and at accurate playing speed. This can be particularly tiresome if a scene change is involved – or if you have only a page and a half of fast moving dialogue to cover a complete change, right down to corsets – and very time consuming, but it is time very well spent, and a great deal better than waiting for an entrance that doesn't happen on cue because a desperate actress is still half-dressed. If a big scene change is involved which takes perhaps two minutes, you must rehearse it till it is right, however many times you ask your stage crew to go through routines with which they are thoroughly familiar. If you rehearse such a change two or three times and the actress is still not ready, you probably have a problem on your hands, and will either have to find some legitimate way of making the scene change slower, or the costume change faster. Once again, good forward planning ought to have avoided the problem in the first place.

Finally, make sure your DSM has worked out an efficient calling system, and that none of your actors wanders off to get a pint or a pie at exactly the wrong time. There is nothing more infuriating for a director and a group of technicians than to work hard at a series of effects for hours, call the actors, and find they don't arrive on stage for fifteen minutes. There is no need to keep actors sitting in their dressing rooms for hours on end when you don't need them, but you must make sure they are called back well before they are wanted, and that they stay within range, so that they can be found at a few minutes notice. Normally you can leave this to your stage manager and DSM. They will sort things out much better than you can, and you will have, or should have, other things on your mind.

The first dress rehearsal, which may occur very quickly after the end of the tech, is the next big hurdle, and will be the first proof of how well your planning works and how meticulously you have rehearsed the technicians. I have seen well-rehearsed shows blossom into immediate and compelling performances on the first DR, and I have seen disasters too, where things have gone wrong again and again, and the show has continually had to be stopped and restarted so that it has taken hours longer than it should. Such disasters are a trial and a battlefield for everyone, actors and technicians alike. The actors will begin to get very nervous, knowing that their performances can easily be spoiled by technical cock-ups, and so will the technicians, if they know they have not been properly prepared and there is an element of hit or miss. If things go badly wrong, and the play grinds to a halt, it is better to stop and get them right, but if the play keeps going, in however rocky a fashion, you should let it. People will get a buzz from having got through the thing, however shakily, and the various errors can be put right, one by one, before the second DR. Really good first dress rehearsals, where nothing goes wrong and the actors are good, are slightly unnerving, and lead to a lot of superstitious muttering that things are going to be much worse in performance. There's no reason at all why that should be anything but one of those honoured theatrical superstitions, like whistling in the theatre, using real flowers, or quoting the Scottish piece. There will be plenty of adrenalin flowing when the audience is in, to screw the performances up a notch or two higher, and a good, efficient rehearsal is much to be preferred to a bad, shambolic one.

A word about those superstitions. They are all based on good historical precedent, going back into theatre history. You don't whistle in a theatre because in the eighteenth century, sailors often worked as stage hands when they were ashore, and they would communicate with each other by way of whistled codes, based on seagoing practice. So if you whistled in the theatre, you might accidentally whistle a call that would bring half a castle down on your head from the flies, or cause a trap to open and swallow you up. Real flowers were similarly forbidden, particularly by dancers, because if they fall on the floor, they can be dangerously slippery underfoot, and the prejudice against lines from the Scottish play is usually considered to be because it was always reckoned a winner with audiences, and to hear someone quoting it meant that they were rehearsing it, and you would be off in a few days.

Whatever their origin, you should respect these old prohibitions. Young actors who know no better, sometimes delight in marching into theatres and flouting them, just to show how modern they are, but they should try to resist such shows of personality. Many old actors become genuinely disturbed and unable to work properly, if the taboos are flouted and they become particularly nervous where the Scottish piece is concerned. And it *is* surprising how often people get hurt or ill if the forbidden words are spoken within the theatre building...

The dress rehearsal

By the time the first dress rehearsal approaches the director will be in a strange dual, almost schizophrenic, state. On the one hand, he will know that his work is nearly done and that at this stage there is nothing he can do to change the production in any radical manner. It is in the actors' and the technicians' hands, and if they perform up to scratch everything ought to be OK. So there is a kind of relaxation in his mind, a relief that his own hard work is over and now it is up to other people. On the other hand, the imminence of public performance, probably only thirty-six hours away, and the realisation that triumph or disaster may depend upon one or two last minute instructions he may give or changes he may make, can't help concentrating the mind wonderfully. He sits in the stalls, probably exhausted, in a state of relaxed high excitement, knowing there is nothing more he can do except the crucial thing that might make all the difference.

What he can do is to look and listen hard. In most first dress rehearsals there will be a good number of technical errors. Lights will come on at the wrong time, or not at all, the leading actor will give his great speech in complete darkness while a focused spot illuminates an irrelevant vase; all sound cues will be two seconds late, so that the actors are left with egg on their face waiting for something to happen, or too early, so that the French military band will blare in before the love scene is finished, or the gunfire will start two scenes before war has been declared. Furniture will be wrongly set, or not at all, a hat-stand will mysteriously remain in a forest glade, and the roller blinds which the leading actress raises so poetically so that the morning sun expresses the radiant joy on her transfigured face, will not work. None of these things need be too serious. The technicians are still learning what it is like to run the play, and how the sections they have rehearsed fit together. The director, ideally with the designer and costume designer at his side, watches with great attention, and all three make copious notes. That is what the first dress rehearsal is for. If you are lucky, and it goes well technically, you may be able to give your actors some notes too, but it doesn't matter too much if you can't. Their minds will be principally concerned with how they get on and off stage, where their props are, why their costume is so uncomfortable, and why the backstage lights that stop them tripping over stage braces can't be a bit brighter.

The important thing with a first dress rehearsal is to note everything that went wrong, in meticulous detail. If the list seems far too long, and there is clearly not enough time to make all the changes required, don't panic, organise. Write down everything that needs doing in a neat list on your notes, and get to work solving the problems in the most convenient way possible, not necessarily doing the most important first. Do the one easiest to do, and tick it off immediately. If you work that way, and don't sit around despairing that you can ever get everything done, it will be surprising how quickly the list will shrink, and how often you will find you have done an impossible number of jobs in an improbably short time.

It's a good idea to call all your cast and technicians on stage together at the end of the first DR, to read them the notes that apply to them, and to invite both cast and technicians to contribute their own notes and questions. Listen carefully to what they say. Having just experienced the practical results of all your planning, they will know better than anyone what the real problems are, and you will probably find that more than half your notes will solve themselves and can be crossed off your list after a few moments' discussion with the actor or technician concerned. There will be a reason why a light cue was late, a sound cue garbled, an actor's entrance muffed or missed, and the actor and technician will know what it is. Vary rarely will the mistakes be mere omissions or forgetfulness, if you are working with decent actors and professional crews. They will have occurred because your colleagues were unable to perform as they wanted to, and they will want to sort out the reasons for that as much as you will.

When the group session is over, after thanking everyone for their hard work – it is always good to be polite to your fellow workers and appreciative of their efforts – that bread always comes back cake in the end – you and your designer and costume designer can set about sorting out the more structural defects, the re-light required in a certain scene, the changes to one or two costumes, the removal of a piece of furniture or unnecessary scenic effect. Give your instructions, and then go to the pub or the café, and let people get on with their work in their own time. Don't hang around fussing, or making sure people do what you have told them to do. Trust your fellow workers. If they turn out not to merit your trust, you won't work with them again. They know that as well as you do, so quite apart from their sense of professionalism and desire to see the job well done, which is almost universal in the theatrical profession, they are likely to deliver the goods.

How you structure the last two days before opening is always important. It will depend upon several parameters which will be different with every production: the length and difficulty of the play, how well rehearsed it is, how tired everybody is after outside rehearsal and the technical, and not least, the personalities and stamina of your leading players. If your play runs for four-and-three-quarter hours, or needs more rehearsal, and your leading player is seventy, or an appalling pain in the arse, all your decisions will be qualified by those crucial facts. You will have to consult both distinguished elder and anal pain and ask how they would like the last two days to go. You don't necessarily have to do what they tell you: you will probably do what you intended to do all along: but it will be wise to canvass their opinions, and at least *appear* to be acting upon them.

In most average length productions with reasonable people you will probably plan to finish your technical on the afternoon before opening night, and to do your first DR that evening, more or less at the time the play will normally be performing. Short of disaster, that will get everyone to bed at a reasonable hour, with the good feeling that, even if there were some pretty catastrophic mistakes, they got through the play and can now perform it in front of the public.

In that situation, I would not call the actors at all on the morning of the first night, unless there were some sections where the acting had to be rehearsed, and even so I would be very chary of working more than half an hour or so. As a production and an artistic idea the play should be ready by now, short only of its performance polish. If there are still basic things that need rehearsing, you are in trouble.

I would normally give the morning of the first night to the designer and lighting designer. There will probably be dozens of small jobs that need doing on the stage, little bits of painting here and there, the leg of a chair that needs strengthening, lighting that needs sharpening up with a couple of different gels or a slight re-angling. The technicians are sure to have dozens of small things they want to do, and particularly they will wish to organise themselves, so that they have a neat and efficient way of doing everything. Leave them to it, let them get on with their work in their own time. Personally, I always come in at the beginning of the morning, even if there is nothing crucial for me to do, merely to show solidarity with the crew, to be a part of the working team, not skulking in bed while they are all slaving. Having shown my face, I keep out of their way. It is always just as well to be on the premises, because if something does come up, you are there to be consulted. A director is never short of things to think about on the opening night, even if there isn't anything he must immediately do.

What time you call the final dress rehearsal will be a matter you must certainly discuss with your actors, and their opinion, when a consensus has emerged, must be the one you will follow, unless you can come up with a very good reason not to. Actors vary in the length of time they like to spend between the end of the final dress rehearsal and opening before the public for the first time. Some like the gap to be as short as possible, not much more than an hour or so. If that is the case, you will arrange for your final DR to end no later than 6 p.m. if you are opening at 7.30. Whatever happens, and whatever the actors think, the techies will want a rest, a drink and some food, and you ought to make sure they have a full hour to get them.

Other actors will prefer a longer gap. Acting is always a terrifying business, first nights most terrifying of all, and all actors have their own rituals of preparation. Some sit alone on the top of the steps by the grid, and fast speak their way through the whole part. Others go for walks, running through their lines in their heads – as I myself did in the autumn of 1994, when, not having acted for thirty-six years, I was obliged to go on at two days' notice and play a largish part on the press night of my play *When the Barbarians Came*. Some actors divorce themselves from their lines, and just prepare themselves in silence in their rooms. Others will chat with complete insouciance on anything under the sun, up to the last second before they walk out into the light. Most two and a half hour plays opening at 7.30 should call their actors to the theatre at 1 p.m. and hope to begin the DR at 2 or 2.30, and finish by 5 or 5.30. At this stage the actors' opinions matter far more than the director's, and their foibles, in this matter, should be indulged.

The main thing you require of the final dress rehearsal is that it should be efficient, that everything, both with the acting of the play and its presentation, should be in place and functioning. If the performances are not there, it doesn't necessarily matter. Most actors will coast to some degree, and they will all know that it will be how they act from 7.30 onwards that counts, not how they act all afternoon. A good many actors are very suspicious of a well-acted and gripping final DR. They feel, I suppose, that they are spent for the day, and have given too much of themselves when it wasn't necessary, so that they will have less left when it is. But if the play does flop in the evening in front of the public, it is likely that the reasons are more serious than simply having expended too much energy in the dress rehearsal. After all, week after week actors prove that they can do a stunning matinee, followed by an equally stunning evening performance. No two performances are ever the same, because no two audiences are, but the passion and excitement of that first audience will usually be enough to encourage most actors to do their very best.

What the director does between the end of the final dress rehearsal and the opening will depend on specific circumstances, but even if everything is right and the play is ready for the public, there are two other crucial tasks he must perform before the premiere begins.

There will be some sort of notes session after the final DR, though if the time is short, it may have to be very brief. If there are important points that need making, the director will try to make them, but he will soon be made aware that his actors want to get away from the stage as soon as possible, so as to prepare themselves to perform, whether that involves a cup of tea and a sandwich, warm up routines, or lying flat in the dressing room with their eyes closed. There will be some fine judgements to be made. If there is something quite seriously wrong that needs putting right, the director will have to weigh whether it is serious enough, for the play to be put at risk if it is not done, or whether it is simply an enrichment or improvement he wants to make, in which case he may well decide it's wiser to leave it till the first night is over. A crucial element in that decision will be whether the actors are aware that something needs doing or not. If they are, and it is clearly worrying them, then he will have to try to work on it and improve the scene, however close he comes to the actual opening. There have been occasions when work has been going on onstage till just before the audience were let in: but the situation does need to be pretty serious to warrant such extreme measures.

Most times you should hope to get your notes over in five or ten minutes, and let the actors get away to their dressing-rooms. You should remember, too, that so close to such a test of all his qualities, there are some notes an actor can take and some he cannot. Of course, it will depend upon the individual. There are some actors who can take quite detailed and complex notes shortly before performance, and incorporate them into their performances with such flowing dexterity you would think they had been rehearsing them for weeks. But the majority of actors cannot do that, and some will be positively flustered or thrown by anything beyond the very simplest note before curtain up. As a general rule, most actors can take simple, two-dimensional notes, whereas notes that involve anything subtle or thinking in a new way are dangerous. The actor's thought-line is what is going to lead him through the performance, and asking him to modify it without time for his brain to assimilate the modification can be very dangerous. More times than one I have seen an actor's concentration go on stage, and a dry – actors' jargon for forgetting the words – result, and realised that it has been my note, unwelcomely sitting in his mind, that has been the culprit. If an actor, in mid-performance, finds himself thinking *now what was it he said he wanted me to do here?* he is probably lost. But a simple idea, a twist to an intonation, a slightly modified action, can lodge in the actor's brain without disturbing the thought-line. Not being an actor myself, I can comment from my own recent hair-raising experience in *When the Barbarians Came*. In the notes session before my first performance of the part the director merely asked me to remember to keep my head up in my first scene, where I was sitting on a bar-stool talking and drinking gin. I had been playing it too much into the glass, so that only the top of my head was visible to the raked seats at the back. During my terror in the first few moments on stage, the simple injunction to keep my head up managed to survive, without interfering with everything else I had to remember. All actors are far more practised than I was on that startling night, but the general point remains. A simple note can be taken safely on a first night. Complex ones are a way of courting trouble.

The second crucial task is wishing your actors good luck. I always try to make my rounds of the dressing rooms at about twenty minutes before curtain up, and certainly no later than fifteen. For most people it is no more than a kiss, a hug or squeeze of the hand, depending on your relationship with the actor. With some actors in some situations, the right brief sentence said at this time can be crucial. If you find the right imaginative thing to say, that will lodge in the actor's brain and explode into his imagination, you can turn a good performance into a great one, or indeed a bad performance into adequacy. But it is a question of the finest shades of judgement, knowing your artist very well, and knowing what will inspire and what might destroy. Because, of course, if you say the wrong thing, disaster could result. It will brood in the poor actor's mind all night, and ruin his performance. There is no way of knowing what the right thing is, or what the wrong. Like George Orwell's ultimate horror, it is different for every individual. But then, that is the most subtle and most crucial part of a director's job: knowing what to say, who to say it to, and when to say it. There is no training for it and it can't be learned. Your instinct for people and for art will tell you, and if it tells you wrongly, tough. You can become a teacher or a critic, and leave the directing to those whose instinct is more reliable.

Never go round to see your actors and wish them well just before curtain up, and if you do, don't be surprised if you get kicked out. A director grinning broadly in the dressing room and saying jolly things is the last thing an actor wants to see as he is just about to make his way down to the stage. As for actually going into the wings to speak to your actors, when the magic lighted space is already within focusing distance, such an action is the province of the theatrical idiot. By the time an actor is standing in the wings, he is beaming in his concentration on the task of acting, and his performance has effectively begun. You wouldn't dream of barging on in the middle of the first scene to wish everyone good luck, and you should think of the preparation period in the same way. Twenty minutes is close enough. Then it's all in the actors' hands till the curtain comes down.

Similarly, I never go backstage during the interval, though some directors do. It seems to me that there is nothing useful you can say to an actor while his performance is in mid-flow. If you come round and start making criticisms or trying to give notes, you will very likely ruin the actor's concentration for the second half, and if you come in and say *that's wonderful, keep it up* the actor will be well justified in thinking *who is that idiot, get him out of here!* Acting is actors' business, and while it is going on, directors are redundant. When the play is over, or next morning in rehearsal, you can move into action again. But during the performance you are an unperson, and your presence backstage, where the actors and technicians are putting on a show, is not required.

Which is not to say that you are not working extremely hard for your living. Watching the first performance is one of the most important things a director does, the one moment during the whole production where he learns a great deal about the play and his own work very quickly.

The opening

On the first night the director will see demonstrated in the plainest possible way whether his mental production, which was the foundation of the physical production, was well imagined or not. The audience's attention is the crucial touchstone. There is no mistaking the rapt silence that denotes an audience totally involved in the play's story and characters, just as there is no mistaking the shuffling and coughing when the audience is bored. The first is the greatest glory of the theatre, the second its biggest nightmare. Generally, you will know within about fifteen minutes if the audience sounds right, though some plays reveal themselves more slowly than that. There have been occasions when a play that has seemed to be going badly in the first act has picked up so much in the second that it has been a tremendous success, but they are not common. A dull first act will usually mean a struggle in the second, and may presage total disaster. Whatever the verdict, pro or anti, the audience's opinion will be quite clear, if you listen to the sound they are making. The most obvious sound is laughter, and I suppose there is no more joyful occasion in the theatre than the first night of a comedy when the laughs come thick and fast, the play takes off, and the audience comes out red-faced and weeping, having laughed and clapped themselves into exhaustion. It really is one of the greatest rewards the profession can offer, and truly unforgettable for actors, director and playwright when it happens. In a serious play there is a wonderful paralysed silence when the curtain comes down, and a long pause before people start clapping, which tells you you have succeeded. That, and muffled sobbing, which always makes the actors feel good. Then as you watch the audience coming out of the theatre, red-eyed, and trying to hide their handkerchiefs, you can feel almost as exhilarated as by tidal waves of laughter. One of the best things that ever happened to me, as a playwright, was at a performance of my play *Retreat from Moscow*, which was partly about the anguish of daily life under Communism, in a world of informers who are as trapped by the system as their victims. A group of émigré Russians came up to me in the foyer, their eyes red-raw, twisting their handkerchiefs, and said *how did you know?* Those are the real rewards. Sometimes we make money, more often we do not, but these moments, when we know we have communicated our bit of truth, matter far more to us. As artists, they are the centre of our lives.

It will take more than one performance to be sure, but during the first four or five, the director will know exactly where his production has succeeded and where it has failed. There is no point in making excuses, saying the audience was very slow, or the weather was bad, or there were some idiots in who insisted on laughing in the wrong places. The theatre is a public art form, we cannot choose who our audiences are, and their verdict is instantaneous. A play may reveal more and more on later readings and performances, but if it doesn't reveal enough of itself to an audience at a single sitting to create their interest, it is dead. That is why modernism has had less influence in the theatre than in all the other arts. Poets can assert their poem is a masterpiece even if their readers don't understand it, visual artists and avant-garde musicians can say they are ahead of their time, and the audience will eventually catch up with them, but the theatre will not put up with pretensions of that kind. As artists, we *have* to communicate with our contemporary audience, at least enough to make them want to come again. There have been some plays that have been damned on first viewing that have proved to be masterpieces, but they are few in number. In general, we still say, with Dr Johnson:

> The drama's laws the drama's patrons give
> And we who live to please must please to live.

It's true that popular plays may well not last either, if they are merely popular, and have no literary quality. But plays that are not popular enough to be performed twice don't make it into the repertoire.

The actors will be just as aware of the audience's reaction as the director is, and will soon make their feelings known. If the play has gone badly, with mistakes that need putting right, you may very well have to call rehearsal the next day, as everyone will expect you to. Otherwise, you will perhaps call your actors in at about four or five, to discuss the first night, to hear their views and offer your own. Don't leave your technicians out of the process, give them what notes you have and listen to what they have to say. As with the actors, having performed the play to the public they will have worthwhile experience behind them and will probably have some good suggestions. You don't have to agree with them, but it's always wise to listen. Don't call the technicians at 4 or 5 though, or you will be unpopular. Unless you have major relights or resets to do, don't call them much before 6 p.m. for a 7.30 curtain, and do what you have to do with them quickly and practically, without any abstruse discussion.

If, as a director, you deceive yourself, pretend that some effect or pacing in your production is working, when in reality you know it isn't, you won't be doing yourself or the actors any favours. There is nothing worse for an actor than having to play a scene night after night that he knows is wrong, and which he knows can easily be put right, particularly if he realises that it is only the director's arrogance or stubbornness that is preventing the improvement. If it is a question of pacing, the actors will quietly put it right themselves, slowing up or going faster as their instinct directs them. If the mistake is something more structural, a fundamental misconception about how the play works, the actors alone won't be able to solve it. The play will never improve, and will limp lamely till the end of its run, when the actors will probably wish it good riddance.

A good director always recognises his mistakes as soon as possible, and puts them right. In the world of the arts, when there are so many variables, we all make wrong choices again and again, and it is no humiliation to breeze into rehearsal and say *well, I made a real cock-up of that scene didn't I!* and put it right. That way you will earn your actors' respect, especially if you make good use of their experience of playing the scene in your reworking. If the scene is too long, cut it, if the pace is too slow, speed it up, if the scene change stops the play dead in its tracks, change it or cut it out.

The theatre is the most brutal of mediums of communication, the one that has the least mercy. However much we try to deceive ourselves, it will keep on telling us its simple truth – *it's great,* or *it doesn't work,* and it is merely a comment on our own natures whether we choose to believe it or not.

Some directors avoid this essential step of self-examination by never putting in an appearance after the first night, leaving the whole production to sink or swim. It surprises me how often this seems to happen, because as far as I can see it is the crassest kind of unprofessionalism. A play without an audience is unfinished, and a director who has not seen and reacted to the way his work faces that ultimate test has only done half his job. You must face the music with your actors, join in the triumphs and share the disasters. It is no excuse to say you have to move on to another job. You should not have contracted yourself to another job without making sure the conditions existed where you could finish this one.

Most plays will change a great deal during the first week of performances, whether they are previews or public. That is what previews are for, so there is sufficient time to incorporate what everyone will learn into the production before the Press sees the result. The play will pull together without any help from you, like a voluminous garment shrinking to a nice tight fit, so that you will probably notice a marked shortening in playing time. When that running-in period has taken place, you will usually be able to tell how well or badly the play has been going, even if you haven't seen it, by consulting the DSM's chart of nightly timings. If the play suddenly gets twenty minutes longer, you can be sure something has gone wrong. If it plays every night within two or three minutes of the same length, you can be pretty sure you have presented a good, well thought-out and well rehearsed production which is going well.

In the first week you must see the play every night and give the actors what notes you have gathered, realising that the production won't have found its final form for four or five days at least. After that time you should ration your visits, and not be tempted to watch the play too often. You will soon get bored, however much you like observing the productions of your own genius, and your reactions will consequently become dulled and useless. If the play is to run for a long time, a visit every two or three weeks, or popping in for an odd act will keep your critical faculties fresh, so that if you feel the need to say anything other than well done to your actors it will be worth saying. On the whole, once they have the performance set as they want it, the actors won't want to hear too much from you, and will be deeply resentful if you call extra rehearsals, so you should not do so unless you regard it as absolutely essential. If your production was any good in the first place, it is unlikely you will need to do anything to it. The actors, as they learn more and more about the play, will deepen their performances, and the way the play develops in that sense is really more their business than yours. You should never interfere with the free play of their creativity. Your job was to put the play on. It is their job to play it.

The one thing you may have to keep an eye on is variation of pace. All actors are prone to drift towards a steady medium pace, because it is easier, and safer. So passages you intend to be dramatically slow, will get faster, faster ones slower, and the dramatic graph of your production will be flattened out as a result. This is the most important thing the director should do in keeping an eye on his production, particularly if it runs for some time. Make sure the actors keep on taking risks: don't let the production become routine, something the actors come in to do every night because it is their job, and which they can do with their eyes closed. Good actors won't trouble you in that way, and the best of them will take greater and greater chances the better they know the play. But it is something that needs watching, and if you feel the production needs gingering up, then do not flinch from calling a few days of re-rehearsal. Always let the play grow as it wants to grow, but like a good gardener, be prepared to prune if required, and train the new shoots in the right direction, otherwise you will end up with a luxuriant but ragged bush, and no fruit.

And then go on to the next play, and start the whole process all over again.

7

Conclusions

This book has been difficult to write. As a working director and play-wright, I can no longer feel – as I might have done forty or fifty years ago – that I am writing, for all my contemporaries and colleagues, a handbook that we would all recognise and assent to. On the contrary, with almost every sentence I have written, I have been aware that there are directors whose work I respect who would probably disagree with me profoundly. It is the purpose of the opening two chapters of this book to make something of the background of these disagreements clear, so that my readers, whether professional or not, will understand the parameters of any arguments they might have with what I have written.

All coins have two faces, and the other side of this particular diffi-culty, is that, in spite of the funding crisis created by a philistine Government, it seems that we are living through a remarkably exciting and vivid period of theatre, a time of great achievement in established forms, and relentless and widely varied experiment. There were those who once said that the coming of film and television would sound the death-knell of live drama, but though the film, both in its cinema and television form, has become a world-wide medium of commerce, propaganda, and occasionally, art, the theatre has flourished as never before. Perhaps people know what contemporary theatre is for now, in a way they didn't quite before the alternative examples of film and television helped to define it for them. The living experience, the participation in an event where you know that your presence as an audience has a clear and profound effect on the performance, the element of ritual, of the attendance at a kind of temple to enact a kind of rite, is quite unlike anything that happens in a cinema or in front of a TV screen, and people are much more aware of the particular rewards that going to a theatre to take part in the performance of a play can offer. It is taking part, even if you stay seated in the stalls, and are not required to be a Roman crowd. In essence theatre is still what it was in fifth century Athens, a mixture of religious ceremony, philosophical exploration, public entertainment, political demonstration and holiday treat, and I see no reason why it shouldn't continue in that way, and grow as the world's literate populations grow in every continent of the globe.

I have also made it clear where I stand in these debates about the nature of theatre and the best way forward, and I make no apology for that. I am a playwright-director, and for me there is no substitute for a great actor with poetry on his lips, animating a space with his presence, opening doors and windows in our minds and revealing thoughts and emotions we didn't know were there. But I love seeing good work by directors and writers who don't share my own particular verbal preconceptions and values, and I delight in the argument I hope they will have with some of my more personal statements. The theatre is a large baggy blanket, with room for all of us underneath, and if we kick and fight a bit and try to pull ourselves a bit more of the blanket than our share, so much the better. There is no point in being bland, saying, *this is how we do plays,* as though we all agreed – which we don't – and without the mental fire that normally attends our working processes. We make the plays we do because we love the idea of theatre, as the one art that contains all the others, and want passionately to express ourselves in our own way within it. The Chinese said *let a hundred flowers bloom,* but they didn't mean it. In the theatre, we do.

Index